Mesa Verde National Park

DEVELOPMENT OF WESTERN RESOURCES

The Development of Western Resources is an interdisciplinary series focusing on the use and misuse of resources in the American West. Written for a broad readership of humanists, social scientists, and resource specialists, the books in this series emphasize both historical and contemporary perspectives as they explore the interplay between resource exploitation and economic, social, and political experiences.

John G. Clark, University of Kansas, General Editor

DUANE A. SMITH

Mesa Verde National Park
Shadows of the Centuries

University Press of Kansas

© 1988 by the University Press of Kansas

Published by the University Press of Kansas
(Lawrence, Kansas 66045), which was
organized by the Kansas Board of Regents
and is operated and funded by Emporia State
University, Fort Hays State University, Kansas
State University, Pittsburg State University, the
University of Kansas, and Wichita State
University

Library of Congress Cataloging-in-Publication
Data
Smith, Duane A.
    Mesa Verde National Park : shadows of the
centuries / Duane A. Smith
        p. cm.
    Bibliography: p.
    Includes index.
    ISBN 0-7006-0371-9 (alk. paper)
    ISBN 0-7006-0372-7 (pbk. : alk. paper)
    1. Mesa Verde National Park (Colo.)—
History. I. Title
    F782.M52S55 1988   88-14773
    978.8'27—dc 19   CIP
Printed in the United States of America

10 9 8 7 6 5 4 3 2 1

The paper used in this publication meets the
minimum requirements of the American
National Standard for Permanence of Paper for
Printed Library Materials Z39.48-1984.

For Jan and Glen

≡ CONTENTS ≡

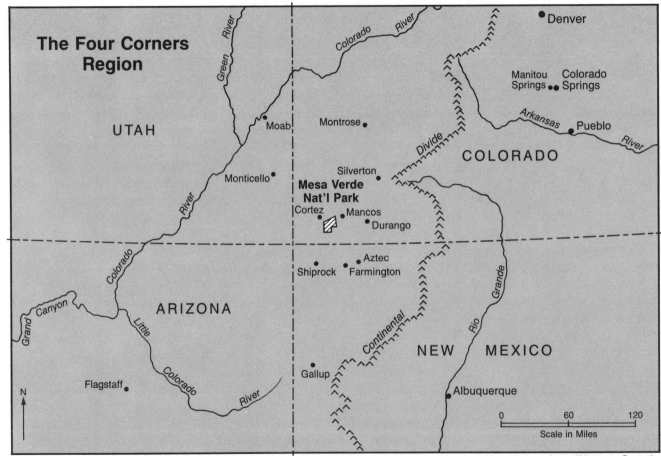

Laura Kriegstrom Poracsky

Located in southwestern Colorado and part of the Four Corners region—the only spot in the United States where four states come together—Mesa Verde National Park is America's first cultural park. Unlike its predecessors, it is not filled with the rugged topography and environmental wonders that made Yellowstone and Yosemite famous. Encompassing 80 square miles (52,074 acres), it celebrates a culture that slipped silently into history centuries earlier, and it is separated from today by an abyss of time. The first and only national park in the world to preserve solely the works of prehistoric people, Mesa Verde sits on the fringe of the American Southwest, among more natural and man-made attractions than any comparable part of North America —perhaps of the whole New World.

The eminent archaeologist and historian Robert Lister considers it likely that more people have examined firsthand the remains of prehistoric American Indian settlement at Mesa Verde than anywhere else in the United States. But the question lingers: How much does the visitor really understand?

Al Wetherill, one of the brothers who brought these ruins to public attention in the 1890s, commented several generations ago: "It is strange how unobserving some people are, or what little impression the Mesa Verde leaves upon them." Its vastness, he believed, contributed to the visitors' failure to grasp the significance of the park. Mesa Verde has not yielded its rich treasures to a quick glance here and there in the rush to reach yet another vacation attraction. The park

must be savored and pondered to be understood and enjoyed.

It is difficult for us today to understand that the prehistoric world was very different indeed from ours. Failure to appreciate Mesa Verde comes from our inability to imagine what took place so long ago in these canyons and mesas. Visitors need to renew their curiosity so that they can learn from what they see. Perhaps all of us need to look at it with the wondering, expectant, exploring mind of a child.

Too often the public, burdened with twentieth-century parochialisms, arrives and departs in haste. In the summer of 1986, I overheard the telephone conversation of a California visitor telling someone back home about where she thought she had landed: "We're here at this Indian National

Forest. You've heard of the Costa Mesa Cliff Dwellings—I'm calling from the parking lot." Mesa Verde deserves a better fate than to be a victim of ignorance. This book, however, does not tell the story of the people who called Mesa Verde home. Instead it traces the history of the area from the discovery of the abandoned cliff dwellings and the mesa sites to the struggle to save them, describes the creation of a national park in 1906, and assesses the impact of the years since then on Mesa Verde National Park. Although the superintendent of Mesa Verde National Park has been in charge of several other areas over the years, including Colorado, Aztec Ruins, and Hovenweep national monuments, these are not included; the focus of this book is solely on the national park.

Mesa Verde is timeless. When visitors today peer across the canyon to catch their first glimpse of Spruce Tree House, they probably feel some of the same excitement that came a hundred years earlier with its discovery. The past wields its influence on them in prosaic, as well as profound, ways: a mistake in the early days resulted in the misnaming of Spruce Tree House. It was a Douglas-fir, not a spruce, which once grew there. But somehow Douglas-fir House does not slip off the tongue quite so smoothly—or maybe, like an old hat, Spruce Tree just fits better. In the following pages, the story of Mesa Verde—on multiple levels—unfolds as Americans and their government grew to appreciate the heritage preserved in the canyons and mesas.

Winston Churchill once said that writing a book is like "having a friend and companion at your side . . . whose society becomes more attractive as a new and widening field of interest is lighted in the mind." That certainly has been my experience with Mesa Verde, an evolution that would not have occurred without the assistance of many friends and colleagues.

No author could expect more helpful, cooperative support than I received from the personnel at Mesa Verde National Park. Special thanks go to Superintendent Robert Heyder, who gave me the "keys to the kingdom"; ever-helpful librarian Beverly Cunningham; cheerful Bill Creutz and his photographic work; insightful Jack Smith; and Allen Bohnert, Doug Caldwell, and Don Fiero.

The staffs of the Colorado Historical Society, the Western History Department of the Denver Public Library, the Western Historical Collection at the University of Colorado, the National Archives, and the Smithsonian Institution provided a variety of help. I am grateful also to the Pioneers' Museum at Colorado Springs and to Becky Smoldt for assistance with the McClurg material. The cheerfulness of the Durango Public Library personnel will always be appreciated, as will their allowing me to pester them continually for the key to the locked collections—even after the key once traveled home with me! Brenda Bailey, who enthusiastically ferreted out interlibrary loans, and Danny LaVarta, a long-time friend in charge of the Fort Lewis College periodicals and microfilm, came up with some valuable gems. Tom Noel offered his usual sage advice.

My thanks to all those people who allowed me to interview them or who spent time corresponding about Mesa Verde matters. Bill and Merrie Winkler were especially helpful in sharing information, photographs, and memories of their era in the park. David Lavender went far beyond professional courtesy when he shared his research and writing on the park, as did Art Gomez, who allowed me to read chapters of his dissertation. Marty Brace spent hours searching for information at the University of Arizona, and Clay and Jean Bader and Kathy and Dale Anderson kindly shared interviews, photographs, and enthusiasm. Fellow southwestern enthusiast Jackson Clark supported my efforts in so many ways that he deserves more than the traditional three cheers.

To all of these people, and to the many others who helped in so many ways, I extend my warmest thanks. Again, my wife Gay's sharp editorial pen and skillful computer work carried me through to the end. The staff of the University Press of Kansas cheered and assisted with all their accustomed professionalism. I hope that they all feel that the final effort was worthy of their contributions and support.

This volume is dedicated to two dear friends, Jan and Glen Crandall, who have shared many an adventure in the San Juans, at Mesa Verde, and along the trails of the mining frontier.

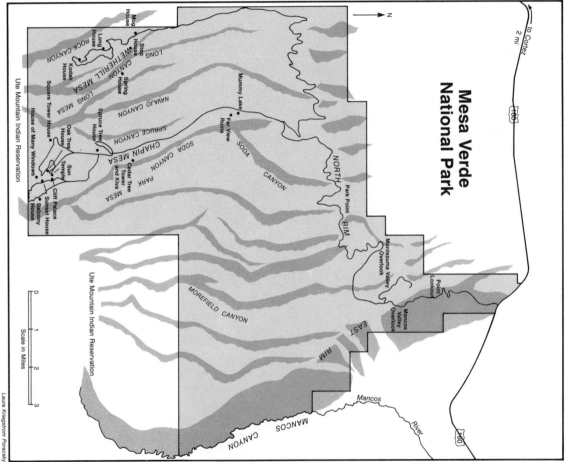

Mesa Verde
National Park

to Cortez

2 mi

N

Mug House
Long House
ROCK CANYON
Step House
WETHERILL MESA
Spring House
Kodak House
LONG MESA
NAVAJO CANYON
Spruce Tree House
SPRUCE CANYON
Square Tower House
Oak Tree House
House of Many Windows
Sun Temple
CHAPIN MESA
Cliff Palace
Sunset House
Balcony House
Cedar Tree Tower and Kiva
PARK MESA
SODA CANYON
Mummy Lake
Far View Ruins
SODA CANYON
NORTH
Park Point
RIM
Montezuma Valley Overlook
Point Lookout
Mancos Valley Overlook
EAST RIM
MOREFIELD CANYON
Mancos
MANCOS CANYON
River

Ute Mountain Indian Reservation

Ute Mountain Indian Reservation

0
1
2
3
Scale in Miles

Laura Kriegstrom Poracsky

It dominates the skyline and dwarfs mere mortals as they lift their eyes from the valley floor to its two-thousand-foot cliffs and steeply ridged slopes. What they see is Mesa Verde, named by lost generations of Spaniards when they first perceived it as a "green tableland." For travelers coming from the east, a rock promontory intrudes into the view of the valley. The aptly named Point Lookout would have made a superb castle site for a feudal knight from which to survey his fiefdom and repel challengers to his temporal power. But when armored barons were lording it over Europe, a much gentler people were roaming the green mesas in the New World to hunt and eventually settle. They grew crops and built communities, all without the trappings made possible for their European contemporaries by the use of iron.

From the north, Mesa Verde appears to forbid entry, but here first impressions deceive. From the rugged northern escarpment the mesa slopes gently southward toward the Mancos River, which carved the mesa's canyon eons ago. In fact, Mesa Verde has been described as an almost classic cuesta (another word of Spanish origin), a land elevation with a gentle slope on one side and a cliff on the other. The Mancos River flows out of the La Plata Mountains and meanders across the broad Mancos Valley, from there to be clutched by mesa and mountain and then released into a deep trench that circles Mesa Verde to the south. From this curving main canyon, numerous finger canyons slash into Mesa Verde's southern rim, giving birth to small mesas that, taken together, form the larger unit. Some canyons climb slowly almost all the way to the northern crest; others rise more steeply to dissolve into the mesa's heartland. Erosion has carved shallow caves into canyon walls and never stops shifting and shaping. Mesa Verde, after all these millennia, is still changing.

It was at least two thousand years ago, long before the Spanish came, that the Indians first appeared and disturbed nature's busy stillness. They must have been intrigued by the unusual rocks and soil that they found; centuries later geologists would classify the basal rock as Mancos shale, a deep marine deposit from the time when all this land was under water. The overlying sandstone gives the mesa its colors, which range from gray to yellow-orange, complemented by a deep layer of rich, red aeolian soil that covers the mesa ridges. All that the virgin land needed to make farming possible was water and someone to till it.

The climate and vegetation varied considerably then as now, because elevations on the mesa range from 6,000 to 8,500 feet. For anyone who ventures into these canyons unprepared, water is more precious than gold, although Mesa Verde is neither as dry as its neighboring valleys and plateaus nor as dry as much of the larger semiarid area in which it sits, a borderline component of the American Southwest. Adequate winter moisture is critical to survival of vegetation, animals, and humans. Except for the Mancos River, the streams that carved these canyons dry up in the summer heat, and pre-cious few springs come to the rescue. The hot summer days drive the animals to the shade, and the cold winters lure them down into the warmer, sheltered canyons. Thus does nature observe the changing seasons.

The variations in vegetation at Mesa Verde are noticeable even to the most casual observer. The lower, or south-ern, portion of the mesa supports piñon pine–Utah juniper forests, whose dark green color probably gave rise to the mesa's name. They cover about half of the park lands and, at the right season, perfume the canyons and mesas with their fragrance, as do some of the less dominant wildflowers. The delicate blue lupines, vivid cactus blos-soms, and spindly cliff roses of Mesa Verde provide a connoisseur's delight, although some visitors proclaim the mariposa lilies the loveliest of all. At higher elevations Gambel oak, service-berry, sagebrush, and other mountain shrubs vie to cover what the piñon and juniper do not. A few Douglas-fir, ponderosa pine, and aspen have taken hold where the moisture and climate suit their individual needs.

Through them all scurry sundry desert and mountain creatures and overhead soar a wide variety of their winged counterparts. Long after all this land became a national park, observers counted approximately 175 species of birds flying over and nesting in Mesa Verde.

Each season at Mesa Verde has its own beauty, as visitors have discovered —and all who come here are visitors. No one has permanently conquered this boldly deployed outpost between mountains and deserts, valley and river. Spring is shortchanged; winter turns into early summer almost overnight. But when the snows melt and the rains come, when the grasses grow and the flowers bloom, most people agree that it is a beautiful country. That lushness lasts all too briefly; the hot sun and warm winds soon parch mesa and canyon as summer settles in. The early, colorful fall days, with their crisp nights, end that season and herald winter's coming. Winter holds the most surprises for even the experienced visitor; its temperatures and weather can encompass all four seasons.

Time had no meaning, no beginning, no ending, and no name at Mesa Verde—until human beings arrived. A thousand years could have been only a moment in yesterday's time, as the pattern of seasons succeeded in endless cycles. At some point several millennia ago, historic time suddenly jarred nature's serenity, providing a point of departure for a new story; human beings walked and climbed into Mesa Verde. What they called themselves we do not know. They apparently had no written language; certainly none survives. To give them a name and reference, we have called them hunters and gatherers, basketmakers,

cliff dwellers, and Anasazi (Navajo for "ancient ones"). The exact time of their arrival has eluded scholars, who have established it as roughly two thousand years ago. Modern researchers remain determined to establish a firm date, and the search continues.

Hunters and gatherers drifted in first, depending on wild animals and nature's bounty for food; they lived in caves or on the canyon floors. Eventually some of them changed their nomadic life and evolved into an agricultural people. When the hunt was abandoned and a reliance on crops superseded hunting and gathering, settlement came to the Mesa Verde region.

In time, these prehistoric people evolved into what we know as the basketmakers, a reflection of their impressive skills. Before their era ended, about A.D. 750, settlement had extended into Mesa Verde proper. By then, they had abandoned caves and

were living in pithouses that were clustered into small villages, usually built on the mesa top. They had also mastered the techniques of making crude pottery and the bow and arrow. Farming methods had improved, harvests had increased, and their life in general had become better. The population increased correspondingly, and life assumed a rhythmic seasonal pattern.

Slow changes modified that life pattern, and in the Pueblo period, forsaking their pithouses, they experimented with building houses above ground. These eventually became so-called apartment houses several stories high. By about A.D. 1000, the Anasazi had advanced from using rather crude pole-and-adobe construction to the skillful stone masonry for which they are justly famous. The pithouse moved underground and became the *kiva*, a Hopi word used by archaeologists to describe the room that resembles the modern-day Pueblo ceremonial chamber. An adjunct to the kiva was the *sipapu*, or small opening into the ground, symbolizing the entrance to the underworld, or Mother Earth. All signs indicate the kiva's primary purpose was for religious ceremonies, but it was probably also used for recreation.

In this period pottery making steadily improved, as did farming; corn, beans, and squash dominated, as much of the mesa-top land was cleared for cultivation. There is evidence that agricultural water-management techniques—check dams and storage reservoirs—helped to compensate for the semiarid environment. The Anasazi traded extensively for such items as seashells, turquoise, cotton, and salt, none of which were found near Mesa Verde.

Their wide-ranging commerce indicates the advancements of these ancient people. At the same time, however, many things about them remain inscrutable. Their accomplishments were achieved without a system of writing, horses, or other livestock (they domesticated only the turkey). Nor did the Anasazi ever develop the wheel or the use of metals. Yet, from their simple hunter-gatherer beginnings, they built a complex culture that reached its zenith in the years from A.D. 1100 to 1300, known as Mesa Verde's classic period, the golden age of the Anasazi. During this period the pueblo dwellings became larger and more concentrated, forming compact villages of many rooms. The several thousand people who may have lived on the mesa represented only a small part of a much larger population that inhabited villages scattered for many, many miles in all directions in the surrounding region and south to the intriguing development centered in Chaco Canyon.

Throughout these golden years, the level of craftsmanship in masonry, pottery, weaving, and jewelry rose markedly. Towers appeared for the first time. The massive stone walls of the large pueblos represent the finest workmanship at Mesa Verde; each stone was carefully laid in a neat, even course.

Then, in the midst of this progressive era, a most startling reversal occurred. There began a major shift of the population back to the caves that had been abandoned centuries before for the more open, healthful, and accessible mesa-top sites. The reason for this change continues to be one of the great mysteries of Mesa Verde. Paradoxically, here within these confined caves, facing building problems more challenging than those on the mesa top, the Anasazi builders produced their architectural masterpieces. The hundreds of cliff dwellings that remain attest to the magnitude of the migration from the mesa-top pueblos. Cliff Palace, with over two hundred rooms, was the largest; others were tiny, one-room structures. Against the back walls of the caves stood the largest apartment houses, rising three and four stories. Structures of this scale and complexity would not be seen again in the United States until the 1870s, hundreds of years later. The quality of the masonry construction and the interior plastering and painting of the walls in red and white demonstrate techniques refined far beyond anything known before. Architecturally, no standard ground plan emerged—the builders simply adjusted to the available space.

The urban concentration that resulted was to be unequaled for centuries. Not only were the inhabitants crowded together in limited space—they devoted what seems to be a disproportionately large share of the space to their kivas. There are twenty-three of them in Cliff Palace. Life could not have been easy—climbing up to the fields each day or clambering down to reach water sources must have taxed young and old alike. One wonders how young children were kept from tottering over the edge of the precipitous cliffs and whether the overcrowding in the caves proved vexing after the spaciousness of the mesa top.

The possible causes for this migration have perplexed archaeologists and historians for decades. One obvious explanation lies in the defensibility of the sites; the cliff dwellings provided an uncommon measure of security for their inhabitants. The weather might also explain the move. The mesa tops, with their higher elevations, were colder in winter; the caves, lower and with southern or southwestern exposures, would have been warmer and sheltered from the wind. Perhaps some religious or psychological reasons motivated the movement. With or without a reason, however, these ancient people gave Mesa Verde the cliff dwellings for which it is now famous.

Strangely, after all the work required for relocating and rebuilding, the Anasazi lived in their new homes for only a few generations. By A.D. 1300, the cliff dwellings had been abandoned, and the people had disappeared. They may have traveled south into what would be New Mexico and Arizona and become the ancestors of some of the modern Pueblo Indians.

Their exodus created another great Mesa Verde mystery: What impelled them to leave? Perhaps it was an extended drought that settled over the area in the years from 1272 to 1299, a devastatingly long time for farming Indians to experience repeated crop failures. The inevitable stresses and social unrest of congested urban living may have constituted a psychological reason for leaving. The population growth had put intense pressure on the land and its resources. The Anasazi may simply have overexploited their environment and exhausted the soil, the forests, and the animal supply, leaving themselves facing bleak prospects even without the drought. The deforestation of the mesa, in all likelihood, led to serious silting and soil erosion. Long-range concern for the environment seems not to have played a role in these people's lives; pressing daily needs undoubtedly overwhelmed any thought of the future. Today we realize that they failed to be stewards of their resources; seven centuries ago that concept had not yet arisen.

Another plausible explanation for both the migration and the abandonment is the possibility that an outside enemy pressured them to move first into the caves and then, when the threat became unbearable, ultimately to flee altogether. No evidence, however, has been uncovered to support the theory that conflict was associated with the abandonment. Without a doubt, overcrowding could have rendered the Anasazi susceptible to all kinds of pressures, including disease. In the face of all these misfortunes, the Anasazi may have thought their gods had deserted them; a change of location could have been a desperate gamble to reverse their fortunes. Most likely, a combination of both natural and man-made conditions motivated them to wander away. Their culture, which had promised so much and advanced them so far, suddenly fell apart. Such severe trauma could not have occurred without terrible individual and group wrenchings. The number of things they left inside their homes makes it appear likely that they seriously expected to return when times improved.

For whatever reasons, the people departed. By the end of the thirteenth century, the cliff dwellings had become ghost towns. When the last Anasazi walked out, silent shadows settled over Mesa Verde. It was to be many centuries before another party would return, discovering the rich heritage that the Anasazi left behind.

CHAPTER ONE

Terra Incognita

Across the canyon, the startled cowboys saw a never-to-be-forgotten sight. Years later, that first impression remained vivid in Charlie Mason's memory:

> From the rim of the canon we had our first view of Cliff Palace. . . . To me this is the grandest view of all among the ancient ruins of the Southwest. We rode around the head of the canon and found a way down over the cliffs to the level of the building. We spent several hours going from room to room and picked up several articles of interest, among them a stone axe with the handle still on it.[1]

Mason and his brother-in-law, Richard Wetherill, made history that December day in 1888. The ruin they eventually named Cliff Palace was only one of many that they and their friends would explore in the weeks ahead. They carried the news of their find far beyond Alamo, their home ranch.

Those men rode into history that December and rode out with controversy—the first of many that would figure in the Mesa Verde story. Two discovery dates were claimed, two reasons for the trip were asserted, and even the credit for the first sighting of Cliff Palace was debated.[2] In the excitement, no one had the foresight to jot down the salient facts soon after the events occurred.

Far more important in the long run was the fact that the discoverers explored the region, gathered artifacts, and successfully promoted what they had seen and collected. The once-silent canyons of Mesa Verde would never be the same again; the present had caught up with the past. Yet although Wetherill and Mason forever changed the solemn stillness, they were not the first to have explored the ancient ruins in the Mesa Verde or in neighboring Mancos Canyon.

More than a century earlier, Spaniards had journeyed into the region. Twice in 1765, Juan Maria Antonio Rivera led expeditions out of the Rio Grande Valley northwestward in search of precious metals and trade. His men saw ancient ruins but made no identifiable reference to Mesa Verde in their journal. Nothing proves that the Spaniards were the first Europeans to travel into present-day southwestern Colorado, but they did leave the first written record.[3] Eleven years later, the more famous Dominguez-Escalante expedition followed Rivera's footsteps, though with a different purpose—to find a route to the recently founded California missions. Profit was not the primary motive of the expedition. This group passed north of Mesa Verde but again made no mention of it that can be identified as such. After an August

10–11 camp on the Mancos River to allow Fray Francisco Atanasio to recover from a cold and fever, these explorers reached the Dolores River Valley to the northwest. Here Escalante recorded in his journal on August 13, 1776, that they had discovered a small settlement of ancient times, the same type as those of the Indians of New Mexico.[4]

These two probes into this unknown land provide the earliest recorded glimpses of the region around Mesa Verde. But the hush of lost centuries would only slowly be broken. Spanish traders and explorers must have come north in the generation that followed, but they left no written evidence. The American trader William Becknell— "the Father of the Santa Fe Trail"— who had opened the Santa Fe Trail, turned to trapping in the winter of 1824–25. His winter quarters probably lay within the boundaries of the present park and, as trapping was poor, he had plenty of time to look around. Becknell

found an "abundance of broken pottery . . . well baked and neatly painted" and many small stone houses, "some one story beneath the surface of the earth."[5] His letter to the *Missouri Intelligencer* gave Americans their first description of the ruins in that part of the Southwest, then a part of recently independent Mexico.

The Dominguez-Escalante expedition had faded to a memory by the time the route to California was finally opened in 1829–30. On November 7, 1829, Antonio Armijo led about sixty men out of the isolated village of Abiquiu in what is now New Mexico. After many tribulations, he reached California's San Gabriel Mission in late January, 1830. En route to California, Armijo marched to the La Plata River and a day later reached the San Lazaro (Mancos) River. Tantalizing questions arise: Did the party descend the canyon to the San Juan River, or did it skirt Mesa Verde to the south and then reach the Mancos River below the future park? Armijo's sketchy diary gives no details of how he reached camping points or of what he found.[6] Yet although Armijo did not describe the ruins he and his party must have seen, the expedition was responsible for calling further attention to the area.

The Spanish Trail did not follow Armijo to the San Juan; instead, it returned to Escalante's route. The Old Spanish Trail, the "longest, crookedest, most arduous pack mule route in the history of America," would become a minor commercial route during this period. Both the north and south sides of Mesa Verde had now been explored. Each year the area became a little better known, but no one had as yet been motivated to attempt a climb of the region's prominent mesa. Since most of those passing by saw only the rugged, cliff-lined north side of the mesa, their reluctance was understandable.

Orville Pratt, a young lawyer on his way to California in September, 1848, described the land that ranged between the Animas and Mancos rivers as one of the "most attractive countries" he had yet seen in New Mexico.[7] Moving on to the Dolores River Valley, he drastically changed his tune, calling the country by "no means very desirable." This reaction, typical of many early visitors, did little to promote an attractive image to lure future settlers.

Pratt made no mention of Mesa Verde, which by now was being identified by that name. Who gave it the name and when remains a mystery. Most likely, it was Spanish or Mexican sheepherders, although they viewed the mesa from a considerable distance because of the presence of the Ute Indians, who claimed the land that included Mesa Verde.[8]

On August 8, 1859, an adventuresome soul finally dared to climb the mesa. Geologist Dr. John S. Newberry came as a member of the 1859 San Juan Exploring Expedition. (The party itself actually skirted Mesa Verde to the north but in the process gained the distinction of being first to use the name in an official capacity.) The breathtaking view from the mesa top prompted this comment from Newberry: "To us, however, as well as to all the civilized world, it was a *terra incognita*." Finding nothing to interest him further, Newberry came down and the group moved on. The expedition failed to receive recognition when attention was diverted from it by the Civil War. And as its leader, Major John N. Macomb, complained, Newberry never finished his part of the report.[9] The journal was not published until 1876, and by then Mesa Verde had found new fame.

As an element of added interest, the Macomb party had encountered some "lost Mexicans," who provided evidence that official parties were not the only ones in the region during these years. More proof comes from a weathered name and date found in Bone Awl House in Soda Canyon: "T. Stangl, 1861." [10] By the time of the unknown Stangl's visit, the mining frontier had extended temporarily to the Animas Valley, only a day's ride from Mesa Verde. However, the Civil War, the mountainous isolation, and the Utes, who still claimed the land that included Mesa Verde, collectively deterred settlement. No profitable mining discoveries had yet been made in the San Juan Mountains, but legends of mining and lost gold mines, which dated back to the Spanish period, would lure miners back in 1869–70—and with them, eventual permanent settlement.

The end of Mesa Verde's tranquility came with the appearance of a party of California miners, led by the fascinating, enigmatic John Moss, who claimed the title of captain. Their mining and their ranching on the Mancos River brought permanent settlement in 1873. Moss, a slender New Englander, had been led by his roving spirit to an acquaintance with the Utes and their language. He was able to negotiate a private treaty for the land in La Plata Canyon (northeast of Mesa Verde), and at its mouth, he established Parrott City, named for his benefactors, the Parrotts of San Francisco banking fame. They earned little more from their investment than a few geographic names, although Moss and his men explored, ranched, and mined for several years. Parrott City, with fewer than one hundred residents, had no rivals in southern La Plata County, which at that time stretched throughout southwestern Colorado.

Neither the mining efforts nor the camp amounted to much, but a chance meeting on August 27, 1874, between Tom Cooper, one of the party, and his old friend from Omaha, William Henry Jackson, set in motion the chain of events that increased interest in the area and in Mesa Verde and that eventually led the Wetherills to Cliff Palace. Pioneer photographer Jackson, an adventuresome member of the Hayden Survey, was photographing in the San Juan Mountains to the northeast of Mesa Verde, where miners were once again caught up in an excitement that was also the primary reason for that season's survey. Jackson's striking photographs made during Hayden's 1871 Yellowstone expedition helped to publicize that region and to persuade Congress to create the nation's first national park. Now this native New Yorker, a born-again westerner since his 1866 arrival on the frontier, turned his unquestioned photographic talents and catholic interests farther south. Cooper whetted Jackson's interest in something besides mining with his stories of the wonderful ruins the Moss party had found. Cooper promised to show his friend some of the more important ones, if the survey party would come to the camp on the La Plata River. Jackson and New York reporter Ernest Ingersoll could not resist that temptation and journeyed southward.

There at Parrott City, which Jackson described as a "few small tents and some brush 'wickiups,'" they met Moss and fell under the spell of his undeniable charm. So persuasive was his "entertaining company" that the Hayden group stayed to vote on election day, Jackson explaining that there were no residency requirements. When Moss offered to guide them to the site of the ruins, they moved off to the southwest to his ranch on the Mancos and into the canyon beyond.

As they started down the rough trail on September 9, 1874, the survey crew saw evidence of ruins and other signs of habitation and stopped to visit three or four rather unimpressive sites. By late afternoon, Jackson had begun "to feel a little doubtful & discouraged," because he had found nothing that

"really came up to my idea of grand or picturesque for photos." After a supper of sowbelly and bread, he discussed his doubts with Moss, who pointed to the nearby cliff.

Jackson peered through the gathering darkness: "I see it. I beheld something that appeared very much like a house." With great excitement, they left at once to investigate the phenomenon. Only Jackson and Ingersoll persevered; the others turned back because of the late hour. By dint of much "pushing and hauling," according to Ingersoll, they reached the ledge, explored briefly, and "got down easily" to camp, guided by the glow of the "glimmering camp fire." [11]

The next morning Jackson returned to photograph what became known as Two Story House, a nine-room ruin on the extreme east end of Moccasin Mesa (directly east of Chapin Mesa). With Moss leading the way, Jackson took the first photographs of a cliff

dwelling in the Mesa Verde region. The men then trekked down the Mancos Canyon, going about forty miles west to McElmo Canyon and the Hovenweep area, each one rich with its own unique ruins. Their return to Parrott City completed the circle of Mesa Verde. In light of their excitement and interest, why did they not probe farther into Mesa Verde? Jackson referred to his sojourn as a "hasty trip." Perhaps a better explanation is his description of the Mancos and its side canyons that went northward into the mesa: "[a] thick-matted jungle of undergrowth, tall, reedy grass, willows, and thorny bushes, all interlaced and entwined by tough and wiry grape-vines bordering its banks upon either one side or the other." [12]

Jackson gave Moss credit for his "accurate knowledge of the locality of the ruins and the best way to reach them," which makes it evident that Moss's party had indeed prospected the

William H. Jackson photographed Two Story House in September, 1874. Jackson's photographs helped to call attention to the region.

Courtesy: Mesa Verde National Park

region. No gold or silver ever rewarded their efforts there, although Ingersoll did report a coal outcropping. Their disappointment sent them back to the La Plata Mountains, ignorant that what they had found might be worth far more than the minerals that eluded them.

News of the ruins traveled surprisingly fast, especially considering the mountainous isolation of Parrott City. At the time of Jackson and Ingersoll's arrival in Denver in July, before the start of the survey, "strange stories" were already being circulated in the city by prospectors who told of "marvelous cities of the cliffs" in southwestern Colorado.[13]

On Jackson's heels came William Holmes, the geologist of Hayden's San Juan division, who enthusiastically wrote that he had been "assigned the very agreeable task" of examining the ancient remains. He came to Man-cos Canyon in August, 1875, where he found inscribed upon the ruins photographed by Jackson the names of three men who had accompanied the photographer. He also discovered, about a mile from Two Story House, a much more imposing cliff dwelling that Jackson had overlooked. Moss gave Holmes the only two-handled mugs that he obtained during his trip. Holmes collected pottery and would subsequently write an article on it, in which he quoted Moss several times. Appreciating what he had seen, Holmes forecast an exciting future: "It seems to me probably that a rich reward awaits the fortunate archaeologist who shall be able to thoroughly investigate the historical records that lie buried in the masses of ruins, the unexplored caves, and the still mysterious burial-places of the Southwest."[14] Jackson, Ingersoll, and now Holmes—writers all—left accounts of their ad-ventures and discoveries in documents that ranged from newspaper articles to government reports.

And they did more. Before the nation's one-hundredth birthday party, celebrated with the Philadelphia Centennial Exposition, Jackson and Holmes spent six months shaping clay, forming molds, and casting in plaster exact scale models of southwestern archaeological sites. According to the *Rocky Mountain News*, Jackson compiled a model, in its natural colors, of "one of the curious and interesting villages of the ancient Aztecs of southern Colorado." (Jackson's generation—logically enough in their view—connected these ruins with the better-known and seemingly more advanced Aztec culture.) For their efforts the two men were rewarded by a bronze medal; their display "drew almost as many visitors as Dr. Alexander Graham Bell's improbable telephone."[15] Jackson wearied of the same questions asked of him over and over again and was glad to leave Philadelphia behind and return to the Southwest for a third visit in 1877.

Jackson and Holmes, through their articles, photographs, and exhibits, called the public's attention to the wonders of southwestern Colorado, which had become a state in 1876. Their efforts sparked the beginning of a national archaeological interest in Colorado's prehistoric ruins. One of Moss's men even had a letter published in a Detroit newspaper, which told what he had found.[16]

Evidence that the publicity also attracted international attention comes from a lecture by Alfred Morgan on "Cliff-Houses and Antiquities," delivered to the Literary and Philosophical Society of Liverpool less than a year after the closing of the Exposition.[17] The published article in the Society's *Journal* displayed Morgan's complete reliance on Jackson, Holmes, and the Hayden Survey. The map, drawing, and ground plan of the ruin, all of which were included in the article and avidly perused, came from the 1876 survey report.

Soon people were enticed by the publicity to come to visit and dig around the Mesa Verde area; local residents made a hobby of collecting artifacts they found. One John Howe wrote to the *Rocky Mountain News* to tell of his 1877 visit; William Morgan went into Mancos Canyon the next year, guided by local rancher John Gregor. Morgan recounted his finds for the American Association for the Advancement of Science. Visitors appeared in numbers sufficient to justify an 1880 advertisement by an Animas City business, Myers and West's Livery, Feed and Sale Stables: "We furnish complete outfits, including tents, camp equipage, etc.," for persons desiring to visit the "far famed Aztec ruins on the lower Animas" or the Cliff Dwellings on the Rio Mancos.[18]

Despite its growing fame, Mesa Verde was plagued by isolation, the hardships of travel, and even the potential danger posed by the Utes (everyone trespassed on their land when visiting Mesa Verde). Colorado's Western Slope, the area west of the Continental Divide, trailed the eastern slope by a decade in settlement and general development. Frank Fossett, in his 1876 edition of *Colorado*, expressed a still prevalent reaction to the "region of the dead cities of the ancient Aztecs. . . . [It] remained a *terra incognita*."[19]

Even so, enough collecting was under way that in Denver the state's first governor, John Routt, a Civil War veteran and mine owner, had shown concern for the ruins and expressed dismay over losing the collections to private individuals. In his annual message in 1879, this conservative, reform-minded governor encouraged the state legislature to take measures to preserve "as far as possible the ancient ruins of Southwestern Colorado from total obliteration." Routt recommended retaining all so-called school land (the Ordinance of 1785 reserved one square mile of each township as a bounty for public schools) upon which ruins were found for the benefit of archaeology and establishing a state museum to provide suitable care for collections.[20] The legislature failed to act, the moment passed, and the ruins remained at the mercy of sightseers. The problem of depredation did indeed cry for a solution before more damage could be done. The rapid settlement now coming to the region surrounding Mesa Verde benefited the visitor but threatened the ruins.

Ranchers and farmers began settling in the Animas Valley in the 1870s, responding to the needs of the miners in the San Juans. The little village of Animas City, where Myers and West were domiciled, grew along the banks of the Animas River and reached a population of 286 by 1880. As the crow flies, the town sat slightly less than thirty miles east of Mesa Verde; by horseback, the distance was much greater. Somewhat closer to Mesa Verde lay Mancos, which took root in 1879–80 where Moss's miners had pastured their stock. To the west, in the Montezuma Valley (these early settlers were determined to tie the Anasazi into the Aztecs, if by no means other than geographical names), settlement came a little later, but by 1886 the hamlet of Cortez had a name and some businesses. Thus, small communities struggled for existence on the northeast and northwest corners of Mesa Verde, while ranchers and farmers settled along its northern boundary. The army established Fort Lewis about twenty miles southwest of Animas City to protect all these pioneers.[21] Modern America was coming to this *terra incognita*.

Meanwhile, the railroad—that wonder of this age of America—penetrated these hinterlands. The city fathers of Animas City made a fatal mistake when they refused to accept the terms of the Denver & Rio Grande Railroad as it moved toward the mining heart of the San Juans. As retribution, the railroad company created Durango in 1880, two miles down river. Within six tumultuous months, Durango's population soared to over two thousand, making it the largest community on Colorado's Western Slope. The town's precipitous growth encouraged the parent Rio Grande Railroad to promote the region as never before. When the track was laid in July, 1881, the comforts of train travel ended the tourist isolation of Mesa Verde forever. Now it sat only thirty-plus miles beyond the Durango depot, and some of those miles could be traveled by a stage owned by Horace Tabor, Colorado's famous silver millionaire. Where Tabor went, other investors followed, and Durango grew and prospered.

It is not surprising that travel to the area's ruins picked up noticeably in the 1880s. Durango newspapers were filled with accounts of visitors and locals who rode down the Animas to the Aztec site or west to the Mancos and beyond. Relic collecting caught on as a popular pastime; "pothunting" has frustrated archaeologists ever since. The collectors came from everywhere, despite the deterrent of rattlesnakes. Among the officers from Fort Lewis who visited some of the Mancos ruins was Dr. Bernard Byrne, who very cautiously climbed through them, praying all the while not to encounter one of the rattlesnakes. He found no rattlesnakes but was rewarded with pots and the "mummy" of a child.[22] At least as early as 1887, an array of relics was exhibited in Durango. As the pothunters collected, they speculated wildly about the origins of the people who once resided in southwestern Colorado.

No one had yet penetrated the canyons of Mesa Verde to find any more prehistoric structures, however. That hiatus ended in the winter of 1883–84, when S. E. Osborn spent months among the cliff dwellings. As he later told readers of Denver's *Weekly Tribune-Republican*, December 23, 1886, he passed "many pleasant days . . . among those ruins." He and a companion, Walter Hayes, carved their names on the wall of a cliff dwelling in lower Soda Canyon on March 20, 1884, thereby perpetuating a tradition that unfortunately has lasted even into the present.

Osborn, a native of Iowa, was prospecting at the time and discovered coal beds, of little economic value, in the Mancos Canyon. Readers of his accounts were intrigued by what he found, which may have included Balcony House and Cliff Palace, a "building" 250 feet in length and six stories "in height in front." Osborn gathered "dozens, yes hundreds of relics . . . that would have made the heart of an antiquarian glad, but did not carry one away with me when I left." He mentioned that other prospectors had named some of the canyons. The Wetherills later learned about ruins in those canyons from trappers, prospectors, and freighters, so it was clear that Osborn was not the only one to enter them. His fame came from writing about the experience.[23]

Another who ventured to this part of the West was Virginia Donaghe, a *New York Graphic* correspondent. This pleasantly attractive, fashionably plump young woman came to Mancos in 1882 "in a freighter's wagon, seated on a vinegar barrel." "Wet, weary and uncomfortable," but determined to see the ruins despite some Ute troubles, Donaghe managed to secure a small cavalry escort from Fort Lewis and

S. E. Osborn spent at least part of the winter of 1883–84 in Mesa Verde. He was in southwestern Colorado as early as 1882.

Courtesy: Mesa Verde National Park

to explore a couple of small ruins. Undaunted by her misadventures, she vowed to come back; for the moment, she returned to Colorado Springs to her teaching and poetry. In 1886, she did go back to Mesa Verde, intensifying what became her life-long passion with it and with the cliff dwellers.[24] Married in 1889 to Gilbert McClurg, who encouraged and supported his wife's interest, Virginia McClurg had found her cause.

So popular had the region become by 1885 that George Crofutt added a chapter about it to his *Grip-Sack Guide of Colorado*. He included drawings and a good description of tourist attractions to be found in La Plata County, now reduced in size after being divided into several more counties.

All this attention bothered the *Tribune-Republican* editor, who renewed the plea in December, 1886, to "preserve the remains from destruction." He called for Congress to set aside part of the Mancos Canyon as a park and to make appropriations for preserving the ruins and constructing roads and trails to make them accessible to tourists. The "vandals of modern civilization" threatened to destroy these ruins, the editor cried; "It is for this reason that Congress should provide for their preservation, or else turn them over to the State in order that it may preserve them."

State pride also had a stake in Mesa Verde's future, and at least one Denver newspaper was determined to uphold Colorado's honor: "Colorado is looked upon as crude and new. But in the Canon of the Rio Mancos there are ruins which are so old that in comparison with them the oldest buildings of the East seem but as the work of yesterday."[25] That was a slap at easterners, who tended to look down their noses at Colorado. State chauvinism or not, the clarion for preservation had been sounded, but again it went unheeded.

The philosophical musings of newspaper editors and other writers attracted little attention in the Mancos Valley, where the struggle just to make a living on the isolated Colorado frontier dominated everything else. Visitors to the ruins certainly eased the hardships by bringing money into the valley, but tourism seemed somewhat exotic to these pioneers. More typical were the efforts of Benjamin (B. K.) Wetherill and his family to establish a cattle ranch against the usual long odds. A restless Ben Wetherill had brought his family to Mancos in 1880. Married twenty-four years before, he and his wife Marion had lived in Iowa, Kansas, and Missouri before they moved to Colorado in 1879; by then, the family consisted of five sons and a daughter, all reared in a Quaker household. Twenty-two-year-old Richard, the quiet and gentle, yet firm, eldest son, emerged quite naturally as the leader of his brothers, who all worked as a team to make the Alamo Ranch and farm successful. In his fifties and not in the best of health, Benjamin did more supervising than toiling in the fields.

The family lived to the south and west of tiny Mancos; only rarely did the Wetherill name appear in newspapers of nearby Durango. At a meeting in October, 1881, the Wetherills joined with neighbors to petition Governor Frederick Pitkin about Indian depredations. When sister Anna married Charles Mason (who so endeared himself to the family that he literally became one of the brothers at the ranch and a partner in their Mesa Verde adventures), a short notice appeared in *The Idea*, as did one praising B. K. Wetherill's "fine wheat" exhibit at the fair in 1887. B. K. received more praise six weeks later in November, when the "result of industry and hard labor" could be seen in his farm, described as enclosed with a substantial board fence and divided up into fields ranging from four to ten acres.[26] All in all, though, nothing remarkable distinguished the Wetherill family from their friends in the Mancos Valley in these closing years of the American frontier.

For the Wetherill boys, cattle ranching held more interest than the more mundane farming. It gave them the freedom to ride and explore the valley. Richard, like his father, loved to roam, though he was confined at the moment to the Mancos Valley and its environs by family responsibilities. His next two younger brothers, Al and John, were the most involved with Richard's activities during these years. Both were experienced at a variety of jobs, took easily to ranching, and had reputations as good cooks. Hardworking Al, the horse breaker of the family, was the closest in age and companionship to Richard. Unlike some of their contemporaries, the Wetherill family befriended the Utes and treated them fairly. The Utes, in turn, allowed the Wetherills to graze their cattle on Ute land without intimidation. The family quite naturally moved down the Mancos Canyon to winter their stock in its more sheltered, warmer depths. Each winter they set up a camp to keep track of the cattle, and with time on their hands, they explored the side canyons.

The Wetherill brothers came across numerous sites on their own and learned of others from various people, including a Ute named Acowitz. Acowitz confided to his friend Richard that many houses of "the old People— the ancient ones" could be found deep in what later came to be called Cliff Canyon. The Utes, though, never went there, believing that when the spirits of the dead are disturbed, "then you die too."[27] The Wetherills, unfettered by such cultural beliefs, had no fears. In their leisure hours, sometimes trailing cattle, they began to search out the secrets of Mesa Verde.

Their searches led to cliff ruins in

The Wether-ills: Al, Win, Richard, Clayton, and John. They opened, publi-cized, and along with Nordenski-old, named many of Mesa Verde's ruins.

Courtesy: Mesa Verde National Park

the canyon walls and pottery and other relics buried under the debris of the ages. They realized that others had been there before them to dig and damage. Mason visited Balcony House in 1887 and signed his name in charcoal on the cave roof; Al was the most inquisitive and enlisted Richard and Charlie in support of his interest.

Al was given credit by Mason and the others for the first actual sighting of Cliff Palace one wintry afternoon near dusk in 1887–88. After a long day of scouting up and down canyons, Al had neither the energy nor the time to follow up on his discovery. He told Richard about it later, but the cattle business had to come first, and they proceeded to drive the herd back to the ranch.[28]

They did manage to gather at least one small collection of pottery and stone implements, which Benjamin sent to Denver to Mrs. J. A. Chain, wife of a Denver bookseller and stationer. As a visitor to the Wetherill Ranch, Mrs. Chain had taken a short trip down the canyon, exploring some cliff dwellings in the process. Much interested in what she had seen and done, she may have asked Benjamin for the collection. Or perhaps he believed her absorption in the subject sufficient to warrant sending the collection to Denver.

By now, the Wetherills realized that their hobby could pay financial dividends. Tourists arriving at the ranch in the summer and fall supplied welcome income, even while somewhat disrupting life. Frederick Chapin, who stayed with the Wetherills in September, 1889, left perhaps the first recorded impression of their place. Cordially welcomed, he immediately felt at home. Everything about the ranch, with its large and well-filled barns and a strong and compact log house, gave "evidence of thrift and comfort." A later guest was amused by that "queer, pleasant house," with its added rooms that poked out in all directions and gave proof of a growing family and prosperity. The Wetherill boys, the Alamo Ranch's prime resource, were hailed as "hardy young fellows of uncommon versatility and energy."[29]

That December day in 1888 when Richard and Charlie spotted and climbed into Cliff Palace changed their lives and put the Alamo Ranch on the map of Colorado. They did not sense it, but from that moment on, neither their lives nor the towns of Mancos, Cortez, and Durango would ever be the same. A new era had dawned for American archaeology in southwestern Colorado, as one hundred years of exploration and a decade of delving into Mesa Verde had reached a culmination. The Wetherills did not know what else lay in those canyons, but they, Mason, and their friends determined to uncover and explore whatever the centuries had to hide.

CHAPTER TWO

"Like an Immense Ruined Castle"

After exploring Cliff Palace, Richard Wetherill and Charlie Mason found Spruce Tree House and Square Tower House within twenty-four hours. Then the two cowboys turned toward home with the news of their find. They did not arrive that day. When they reached the camp of several friends, they excitedly told of their discoveries in the canyons. Catching the fever, the whole group, joined by John Wetherill, set out on foot, with packs, to collect artifacts. Success rewarded their dig; John later wrote that they dug for about thirty days and took out a fine collection, which they carried back to the Alamo Ranch. In the spring, Mason and Clayton Wetherill went back to collect more; the "rush" had begun.

According to John's recollection, B. K. Wetherill grasped the significance of what his sons and friends were uncovering and wrote to the Smithsonian Institution to inquire about selling the collected relics. He contacted the Smithsonian because it administered the United States National Museum, the designated repository for artifacts found on federal land. Unfortunately, museum funds were not available, and the Smithsonian became the first, but not the last, to pass up a momentous opportunity.[1]

The institution's decision reflected the economics of the situation rather than a lack of interest. Americans in the 1890s were showing more concern for conservation and preservation. Yellowstone National Park had already been established, and a movement for creating national forests was gaining momentum. The Wetherills, in their own quiet way, were in the vanguard of the so far unsuccessful movement to establish some form of protection for the ruins; they looked beyond mere collecting to preservation.

It has been documented that Benjamin Wetherill wrote again to the Smithsonian Institution in December 1889 and several times in early 1890 to seek assistance and guidance for exploration. In so doing, he revealed much about his sons' activities and attitudes. "We keep a strict record of all our discoveries where found etc and all other items of interest," he proudly noted and included a copy of the notes for December 11, 1889. Considering the state of archaeology at that time and the Wetherills' lack of training, the six handwritten pages displayed an astonishing competence and sensitivity. Of the cliff houses, which he claimed the boys had been exploring for four years, he said: "We now have a number of photographs of some of them." Tragically, the Smithsonian did nothing to support the family's explorations, a not unexpected response from an institution that depended so extensively during these years on donations and volunteers to supplement its chronically underfunded budget. With incredible insight, the senior Wetherill wrote on February 11, 1890: "We are

particular to preserve the buildings, but fear, unless the Govt. sees proper to make a national park of the canons, including Mesa Verde that the tourists will destroy them."[2] Nothing happened, the moment passed, and Mesa Verde's treasures were left to chance.

Meanwhile the Wetherills took the first collection to Durango on March 2, 1889, where it was placed on exhibit the following week in the Fair Building. Several hundred Durangoans toured the exhibit in its first three days, to Mason's amazement: "We had not expected that other people would be as much interested in the collection as we had been." The excitement the show generated led the Wetherills to charge twenty-five cents admission in order to pay for their time in showing visitors around. Several citizens of Durango considered buying the collection, which the *Herald* rated as the "finest collection of relics in existence . . . a valuable one." They, too, failed

to come up with the necessary funds. In mid-April, when B. K. Wetherill appeared with some new artifacts, which included an "infant dried to bones," the curiosity seekers flocked in once more.[3]

Realizing the public's interest and hoping, no doubt, that a larger profit could be reaped on their previous winter's work, the Wetherill boys packed up the collection and sent it off to Pueblo, Colorado, under the watchful eye of Charles McLoyd. McLoyd had been among those in the stockmen's camp on that day, which now seemed a lifetime ago, when the first news of the discovery of Cliff Palace had been related by his spellbound cowboy friends.

Pueblo proved to be less than a rousing success, so it was on to Denver. The exhibition landed a prime site, opposite the famous Windsor Hotel on Larimer Street. Enthralled Denverites flocked to see the "best collection of

Cliff Dweller relics in the world." The *Weekly Republican*, May 30, 1889, urged the people of Denver to purchase the collection, saying editorially that "it will be an offense no less heinous than a crime" if it were to be removed from the state. The writer added that it would be of great benefit to the town and the state to have the collection permanently placed in the Historical Society.

At last, the Colorado Historical Society showed interest in purchasing the collection. Fearful that the relics might be taken from the state, the Society agreed to buy them for three thousand dollars, giving a handsome profit to the boys back in Mancos. The Society lacked sufficient ready cash, so it accepted personal notes from several of its members until appropriations the next year could provide funding. It was, crowed the Society's annual report for 1889–90, "the largest and most complete collection owned by any

institution," far outranking the one in the National Museum in Washington.[4]

Both groups involved in the transaction were pleased with the outcome of their negotiations. The fears of the Society that the relics would leave the state had been assuaged. Now it owned the fine collection, which was first exhibited in the Chamber of Commerce building and later, in June, 1895, moved to the State Capitol (today the collection is in the Society's museum in Denver). The Wetherills, the beneficiaries of this unexpected windfall, went back to digging at Mesa Verde. Artifact collecting offered them the benefits of excitement and adventure, with the added prospects of considerable profit. Its advantages outweighed those of ranching and farming.

Mason spoke for all of them when he concluded: "Our previous work had been carried out more to satisfy our own curiosity than for any other purpose, but this time it was a business

proposition. In no work I ever did are one's expectations so stimulated —something new and strange being uncovered every little while." Such a commercial attitude might shock today's archaeologists, but the times of 1889–90 were very different, and these were pioneers just beginning to feel their way. The editor of *The Archeologist*, in the February, 1894, issue, frankly addressed the question: "The sale of a whole collection, or part of it, so long as complete finds are not split, is always proper. Single specimens, bought of dealers, may be sold with a free conscience, also complete finds."[5]

The Wetherills actually proved to be much more conscientious in their archaeological activities than their Mesa Verde predecessors had been. Richard explained in an April 7, 1890, letter: "We recognize the fact, the principal scientific value of collections existed in the circumstances of their

Balcony House had been visited by several parties when Nordenskiold took this photo. John Wetherill is sitting in the center.
Courtesy: Mesa Verde National Park

original position, or reference to the implements or objects with which they are associated, and we worked accordingly, with a view to throw as much light upon this subject as possible. . . ."[6] The second collection was followed by two more early in the 1890s, all of which eventually found their way into museum holdings.

Exploring and collecting, exciting as they were at times, also had their tedious side. Columbia University professor T. Mitchell Prudden, who dug with the Wetherills off and on from the mid-1890s through the next twenty years, recalled entering "upon the search in the choking dust heaps which the ages have strewn over all the ruins, and under the piles of fallen masonry." The sun was unrelenting, the dust cloyed insufferably, and tons of stones resisted displacement.[7] These summer adventures assuredly gave the tall, slightly balding physician and professor the relief he sought from his teaching responsibilities. He grew to love the Southwest.

As the Wetherills explored, dug, and exhibited, news of their discoveries spread wide. Almost immediately, more visitors began to appear at the Alamo Ranch, wanting tours. One of them was Frederick Chapin, an author, confirmed traveler, and enthusiastic mountaineer who had been visiting Colorado—primarily Estes Park— for years. He arrived at Durango on September 18, after "ascents of Pike's Peak and Mt. Sneffles," and went on to Alamo Ranch the next day. He returned the next year for a second tour. His articles and his 1892 book, *The Land of the Cliff-Dwellers*, called further attention to Mesa Verde. The thirty-seven-year-old Chapin thought of his investigation of the antiquities as a "variation from mountain climbing," but he used his skills for "scaling cliffs" to reach the "fortresses."

Chapin thoroughly enjoyed himself and recounted his experiences with a vigor that captivated readers. From the time of his arrival at the Alamo Ranch until he returned there from his camp at the ruins, each day brought new adventures. Chapin found several ways to reach the mesa top, including the Wetherill's Crinkley Edge Trail, later known as the infamous Knife Edge. One path led down into the Mancos Canyon until it intersected an Indian trail; another went west across the Mancos Valley to Point Lookout and then up a cattle path. The third, pioneered by Chapin in September, 1890, ascended from the Montezuma Valley. No matter which route was chosen, a trip without pack animals was out of the question. Provisions for several days had to be accommodated. And no matter how one reached the top, one arrived hot and thirsty, with water in short supply.

Richard Wetherill served as Chapin's guide. They had a brief confrontation with the Utes, who demanded a toll for the privilege of crossing the mesa. Wetherill refused to pay and nothing came of the incident, a fortunate ending because the party was armed with only a "rickety revolver." Richard's earlier friendship with the Utes did not prevent trouble throughout this period. They claimed, and rightly so, that the ruins lay on their reservation. At least one of them feared the potential impact of the digging on their land. Chapin recorded these words: "White man dig up Moquis, make Ute sick."

Overcoming the Ute hindrance, Chapin went on to find Cliff Palace everything he had hoped: "Surely the discoverer had not over stated the beauty and magnitude of this strange ruin. There it was, occupying a great oval space under a grand cliff wonderful to behold, appearing like an immense ruined castle with dismantled towers." Across the canyon from the site, Chapin and his guide used some of the hand and toe holds of the original inhabitants to climb down to a dead tree, then used its branches as a convenient ladder. A steep gulch stopped them, but not for long, as Richard's rope rappelled them over the ledge. A few minutes more and Chapin was at last climbing into Cliff Palace.

He later toured other ruins and poked around mesa top "mounds," where he found pieces of broken pottery and arrow heads. He avidly photographed what he saw, but like many later visitors, he lost several of his best shots "from a stupid double-exposure." One of those he described as "a weird ruin, almost inaccessible." He also lost two glass plate negatives to a falling rock dislodged as he, John, and Richard were climbing out of an isolated ruin.[8] Such minor setbacks did not deter Chapin from this fascinating, strange, and for him, very romantic place.

Chapin came to Mesa Verde to experience it and to write about it. He believed his major contribution to be his photographs and his descriptions of the ruins. Chapin called national attention to what had been only a local and state sensation, and he set literary and reporting standards to which those who followed him could aspire.

As the news of the discovery spread, it attracted the attention of a slender, twenty-two-year-old Swedish tourist, Gustaf Nordenskiold. The Wetherills would host no more important visitor than this young college graduate —a student of geology, botany, and chemistry—who had already spent several summers doing field work when a strenuous 1890 expedition to Spitsbergen felled him with tuberculosis. In late May, 1891, he arrived in New York; after a southern tour, he reached Denver. It is likely that his predilection for museums brought him into contact with the early Wetherill collection, and he had certainly talked with people

Gustaf Nordenskiold, the scholarly young Swedish visitor and writer.

Courtesy: Mesa Verde National Park

who knew of Mesa Verde, including botanist Alice Eastwood, a friend of the Wetherills, who had been there in 1889. Nordenskiold, leaving Denver with a letter of introduction from Eastwood, wrote home:

I have now also a ticket down to Durango in south Colorado and back here again. I am going there to look at the cliff dwellers. [June 27]

I went by train to Durango and from there by coach to Mancos. There I stayed with a farmer named Wetherill, who drives his cattle in the tract where the cliff dwellings are, and thus knows them well. He, himself is old and stays at home while the boys drive the cattle down into the valley. I decided to go with them to a place where they camp, and then go with one of them to visit the ruins. My intention was to stay about a week at Mancos Canyon.

Now the week has gone, and I have made up my mind to stay for one or two months. [July 11][9]

That visit stretched into more than two months and produced a major impact on Mesa Verde and on Wetherill's sons, whom Nordenskiold described as cowboys, "but with a surprising degree of education."

Before he finally left in November for a tour to the Grand Canyon, Navajo country, and the Hopi villages, Nordenskiold excavated at what may be described as the "hall of fame" of Mesa Verde sites—Chapin Mesa and Wetherill Mesa. His day began at 6 A.M., when he climbed to the site with his workers and a Wetherill, quite often John:

There we dig, sketch, photograph, label finds and so on till the sun is high in the sky. Then we have dinner, a tin of corned beef and a loaf of bread is all we get, for we cannot have much with us, then we resume work again until the sun begins to sink in the west and the shadows on the side of the canyon grow long.[10]

Skunks—"horrid creatures"—threw confusion into one camp, but Nordenskiold overcame them. He also faced the continuing problem of dust, which lay so fine and deep in the inner rooms that you "couldn't dig in it for more than 15 or 20 minutes" before gasping for breath and needing fresh air, according to one of the crew, Roe Ethridge. Nothing thwarted Nordenskiold, and for the first time these ruins were examined by a trained scholar.

An easterner, William Birdsall, was another inquisitive physician who toured the Southwest as Dr. T. Mitchell Prudden had. Guided by Richard Wetherill, Birdsall reached Nordenskiold's camp and observed it for a few days. Before the year was out, he

wrote an article about the experience. Nordenskiold later, in his own book, hailed Birdsall's account as the best description "yet published." At the same time, he was somewhat aggrieved not to be given credit by Birdsall for the excavation that had been "instituted by me." [11] Sadly, omissions of that sort and professional jealousies crept early into the world of Mesa Verde archaeology.

Nordenskiold completed his field work by September 5 and returned to the Alamo Ranch to pack the artifacts into crates and barrels for shipment to Sweden. He took the loaded treasures to Durango; from there they were to be shipped by rail to the Swedish consul in New York. With that development, what had been a brilliant summer excursion suddenly turned cloudy and threatening, for when Nordenskiold reached Durango on September 8, he found himself facing objections from unnamed "authorities" to his shipping the artifacts out of the country. Believ-

ing he had satisfactorily answered their objections, he returned to the ranch late the same evening. More specimens needed to be packed, including at least one mummy. On the sixteenth, Nordenskiold sent the lot to Durango, only to have the Denver & Rio Grande Railroad refuse to handle them. The startled Swede learned that his actions had created much ado, and he was being slanderously condemned in the Durango and Denver papers. He could not believe the charges hurled at him —collecting relics illegally, damaging the cliff structures, and attempting to send a valuable collection out of the country, which was probably the core issue. He promptly and wisely retained a lawyer, who advised Nordenskiold that his accusers had little legal basis for their charges. No laws then on the books prohibited acquiring a collection or sending it out of the country; nevertheless, Nordenskiold suffered the embarrassment of arrest and interrogation on September 17, in accordance with a warrant issued at the request of the Ute Indian Agent Chas A. Bartholomew. Nordenskiold was required to post a bond of $1,000.

Durangoans were indignant over Nordenskiold's expedition, believing it to be one of looting and devastation. Denver newspapers picked up the inflammatory accusation. The *Weekly Republican* hoped that the arrest would "result in putting a stop to the looting of the cliff-dweller ruins," a sentiment echoed by the *Rocky Mountain News*. Nordenskiold, in desperation, got in touch with the Swedish minister to the United States, who approached the State Department, which then investigated the case.[12] A hornet's nest of emotion was stirred up in the process.

Two weeks later, Nordenskiold appeared in District Court, only to find the complaints had been dismissed. Local residents, to their chagrin, had discovered that no prohibitory statutes existed. The Ute agent, Bartholomew, did not attend the hearings, although he had created some of the trouble. He gave the excuse that Indians had lied to him about Nordenskiold's activities and that they were now satisfied that the "graves of their people are not desecrated."

A month of Nordenskiold's time in America had been lost, not to mention the money spent on legal fees, and this gentle man had suffered "much unpleasantness." The only benefit to emanate from this sordid affair was the two weeks' delay of Nordenskiold's departure, which allowed him to return to Mesa Verde to photograph (he was an outstanding photographer), take measurements, and draw plans of the ruins. And there his studies ended.[13] Understandably, Nordenskiold felt persecuted, but there was little to do but recover his specimens and ship them to New York. The *Republican* of October 8 launched one last blast, demanding a law (state or federal) to protect these ruins, lest "practically everything of historical value" be removed.

The issues raised by Nordenskiold's misadventures would not be resolved easily. Wealthy Americans were "looting" Europe in search of antiquities to collect and display, and the British had a worldwide empire from which to gather relics. Some of this gathering was done in the name of preservation, but much of it was designed to enhance private collections. Going beyond the issue of local and state chauvinism, Coloradans had focused on the question of what the best place was to display and preserve the Mesa Verde material. Would scholarship and visitation be better served by keeping the collection near its origin or in Europe? Ideally, the answer would have been the former; however, the lack of finances and, to a lesser degree, of professional museum staff put Colorado in

Cliff Palace, as Nordenskiold photographed it in 1891. It is located on Chapin Mesa, which Norden- skiold named after another early visitor, Frederick Chapin. Courtesy: Mesa Verde National Park

second place. Neither the state nor the federal government seemed prepared to sponsor an expedition like Nordenskiold's or to undertake protection of the sites.

Nordenskiold's abrupt visit had raised all these questions. Coloradans and Americans in general would have to hear more and read more and feel their way cautiously to find the answers to them. Nordenskiold had underscored the urgency of the matter, but more time would be needed to attract popular concern and support.

The concern that had been shown by Durangoans was commendable, but the treatment of Nordenskiold had bordered on the contemptible. Two years later, Nordenskiold's monumental work, *The Cliff Dwellers of the Mesa Verde*, was published, forever solidifying his place in archaeology and in the park's history. The book was the first extensive examination and photographic record of Mesa Verde prehistory and until 1964 was the only description of the Wetherill Mesa ruins. His expedition, the first conscientious attempt to excavate and record Mesa Verde archaeology systematically, proved to be a milestone in American archaeology. As Robert and Florence Lister later wrote: "While these modern studies greatly augment and refine the record of the past, in no way do they detract from the solid achievements of the young man from Stockholm who came West to regain his health and left behind a permanent memorial to the American people." [14] Richard Wetherill appreciated what his friend had accomplished, as did the rest of the Wetherill family. Richard wrote on December 31, 1893, that everyone who had seen the volume "thinks it the finest thing of its kind." [15]

For the Wetherills, too, the time of active work at Mesa Verde was drawing to a close. That Nordenskiold's painstaking field methods had not been lost upon them was evident in their later expeditions. They and their friend had pioneered in excavation work at Mesa Verde and had brought the ancient dwellings to the world's attention. Although their methods were unquestionably crude by contemporary standards, they cannot be faulted for them. Al spoke for all when he wrote about those years:

> The cliff-dwelling work was much more exciting than hunting gold (and I have done both), because we never knew what we might find next. We had started in as just ordinary pothunters, but, as work progressed along that sort of questionable business, we developed quite a bit of scientific knowledge by careful work and comparisons.

A fair evaluation of their efforts was made by William Birdsall in 1891: "Although not professed archaeolo-

Gustav Norden-skiold took this photograph of the Alamo Ranch, where he, and many later visitors, started their Mesa Verde trips.
Courtesy: Mesa Verde National Park

gists, they have amassed a very large collection of the remains of the cliff dwellers and are in possession of a vast number of observations and facts concerning them." [16]

For the rest of the 1890s, the Wetherills turned to making a profit from their discoveries, not unusual for Americans of the nineteenth century. The Alamo Ranch became, in a manner of speaking, a Mancos Valley dude ranch, to which a tourist could come and, for two-dollars-a-day board and room, rest or take a day's guided trip to the ruins for five dollars. The three-day trip to visit a large number of ruins evoked the reassurance that those "unaccustomed to such mode of living need have no fear of danger or discomfort." The "hardy, resourceful, well-informed" Wetherills, as T. Mitchell Prudden described them, would handle all problems. Richard also acquired a partner during this time, photographer Charles B. Lang, and went into

the business of selling photographs at the ranch. He still sold relics, on at least one occasion on consignment for a friend. Some of his brothers moved away; marriage had added to their responsibilities, and the ranch and guide business did not provide enough income for all.

During the Mancos gold excitement in 1893, guests reclining leisurely in hammocks strung between cottonwood trees could watch the boys operating a sluice box (with what success, no one can say). More breathtaking for the people the Wetherills guided into Mesa Verde was the Crinkley Edge Trail, with its narrow ledge precariously carved between cliffs above and cliffs below and angled toward the valley floor. [17]

Visitors kept coming, more each year. They delighted in the adventures they found at Mesa Verde. Walter Jakway went there in 1899 or 1900 as a small boy, and over eighty years later,

he still remembered the experience vividly.

We took many artifacts like corn grinders out with us. I recall climbing a long steep ladder to the main veranda. The boys would put a ¼ stick of dynamite with a cap and fuse and throw it in to rout out the rattle snakes which were thick. Then we went in to explore the old buildings. A large stone slab was removed from one small room and four skeletons were standing there. [18]

Alice Palmer Henderson complained that bathing turned out to be a luxury. Just as well, she decided, because of the dreadful alkali water, which "takes off what little skin the pinons leave." The ride over fearsome trails was one she never forgot.

Meanwhile, a group of Mancos young people had found something unexpected on an excursion to Cliff

Visitors to the World's Columbian Exposition of 1893 walked through this replica of McElmo Canyon's Battle Rock to see the Mesa Verde exhibit.

Courtesy: Chicago Public Library Special Collections Division

Palace. They heard "strange, uncanny sounds. So weird and unearthly were these noises that they did not tarry long, but hied them quickly home." Richard Wetherill uncovered the source —a nest of young "buzzards"! His brother Al encountered one of the first bored tourists, who was unimpressed by either the scenery or the cliff dwellings: "Oh, it's all right. But say, did you ever see the great cornfields of Iowa and Kansas?"[19]

People were enticed to come west to Mesa Verde by the 1893 World's Columbian Exposition in Chicago, despite its separation in distance and its disparity in epic from the Mancos Valley. At the Exposition—surrounded by the Palace of Fine Arts, the world's tallest Ferris wheel, the exotic "Streets of Cairo" that featured belly dancers, and the new taste treat called cotton candy —the twelve million visitors could see on the midway a reconstructed canyon of the cliff dwellers' country.

Those who could tear themselves away from the fair's hedonist attractions saw Square Tower House, Balcony House, and Cliff Palace, recreated a tenth of their size. At the end of the canyon sat a museum that included mummies, placed "so as not to offend those who did not care to look at such things." Several pamphlets tempted further study. A much smaller collection of relics had also been included in Colorado's 1893 exhibit.

All "offensive" concerns aside, the exhibit proved to be a crowd pleaser, as did Richard Wetherill, who left Mancos in mid-September to act "as a ruin sharp." In Chicago he first saw the photographs that William Henry Jackson had recently taken, which the *Mancos Times* believed would be good advertising for the Mancos Valley. After a trip to Niagara Falls, Saratoga, and Brooklyn, Richard returned home in early November.[20]

The Mesa Verde exhibit in Chicago had been sponsored by the H. Jay Smith Exploring Company, which had built a similar one the year before at the Sixth Annual Minneapolis Industrial Exposition. A Smith Company exploring party had spent six months at Mesa Verde in 1892 to collect relics and take photographs. They also brought an artist into the field to make sketches for the canvas backgrounds. Their efforts paid off. As one enthusiastic visitor to the Minneapolis exhibit proclaimed, "I've about decided to take my next outing in the region of their ruins. . . . I'd like nothing better than to do a little exploring on my own hook."[21] Others agreed with him, and on some days Mesa Verde tourists (the *Mancos Times*, June 25, 1897, called them "knights of the grip") nearly overcrowded the board sidewalks of Durango and Mancos.

Tourism's impact on nearby communities thus emerged, long before there was a park, as one of the recurring themes that would dominate the story of Mesa Verde. The economic and publicity potential was not lost on local people. Dominance would bring a tremendous boost over other urban rivals, an opportunity to overcome the region's isolation, and perhaps population and business growth. These unexpected windfalls could not be allowed to slip away without a fight, and each town's merchants and boosters hastened to see that they would not.

Mancos and Durango stood ready for the onslaught and boldly vied for the larger share of the business. Durango started out with several advantages. It was larger (an 1890 census count of 2,726 versus Mancos's 635), offered better hotels and railroad connections, and had more newspapers. Its greatest asset lay in the fact that almost all visitors to Mancos had to travel through Durango to get there. Durango had been promoting tourism almost from the moment of its birth.

The *Southwest*, back on April 14, 1883, crowed that "Durango is a great resort for pleasure and recreation generally." Durangoans considered their Animas Valley ruins to be the best available, as Frederick Chapin had discovered when he arrived in town in 1889:

It seemed difficult to obtain much information in regard to the now not far distant Mancos country. In fact, if we had not been well informed in regard to the literature of the cliff dwellings and ruined pueblos, we should have been led to turn aside and visit ruins of minor importance which exist in the lower valley of the Animas [present Aztec ruins].

Chapin doggedly persisted in his quest and finally attained the Wetherills' ranch.

Needless to say, Mancos residents resented the nature of the competition from their larger neighbor, but in the cutthroat, no-holds-barred, urban world of that era such deviousness was not without precedent. Durangoans also championed a railroad to the west, giving as one of the more progressive reasons the tapping of the Mesa Verde trade ("bound years to come to attract the curious"). The answer to their prayers was the Rio Grande Southern, constructed in 1890–91; the rails started in Durango and reached Mancos in the spring of 1891, then turned northwest toward Dolores.

Durango promptly proclaimed itself as the headquarters for visitors going on to tributary Mancos and the cliff dwellings. Durangoans once again, though, missed the opportunity to buy a Mesa Verde collection, when the Durango Archaeological and Historical Society failed in 1893 to raise the needed funds.[22] The crash of 1893, which had already gripped the community and the state, would last for five years of bitter depression.

Mancos boomers gave as good as they got and began by disputing Durango's claim to being the "livest of live towns" in southwestern Colorado. When the *Mancos Times* was opened in 1893, it gave the town a long-needed voice and instantly joined the battle. Mancos, the editor emphatically insisted on May 12, would attract a population of 3,000 before "60 days roll around." Durango would awake to that fact by finding its streets deserted and many business houses closed. "Mancos will never rival her. She will outstrip her."

Durango's press returned the barbs in kind, the ink and press paladins giving no quarter and taking no prisoners. The *Mancos Times* railed on August 18, "not one single citizen has a good or kind word to say of their neighbor denizens of the 'Smelter City' as they are pleased to term their five-cent-beer burg." Mancos gave more than lip service to the campaign for supremacy. The Hotel Lemmon offered free bus rides to and from all trains, as well as guides, animals, bedding, food, and camp equipage to tourists to the Mancos Cliff Dwellings and the gold mines. Confidence was spurred by more than just Mesa Verde —Mancos was going through a gold excitement that it hoped would equal that of Cripple Creek, the current mining wonder on the Colorado and the national scene. There would be no such luck: The nearby La Plata Mountains promised much, delivered little.

But Mancos did not need to hang its community head in shame; it held aces in the Mesa Verde game. It was nearer to the cliff dwellings, and the best trails left from its front door. The renowned Wetherill clan lived and worked nearby, bringing publicity and fame to the Mancos Valley. Even so, when Louise Switzgable desired to visit the ruins, she found no literature or pamphlets available to explain how to reach the area. She finally wrote the Mancos station master to receive information; he put her in touch with a guide. Louise ultimately reached Mancos safely. Departing for Mesa Verde, she found that "quite a crowd from this little village surrounded our going to see us off." [23]

As the 1890s drew to a close, the *Times* prolonged the battle, attacking both Durango and a new threat from the west—Cortez. Much more than just visitors to Mesa Verde raised the ante. Some tourists, the editor believed, would also invest in land, stock, and businesses, bringing a needed bonus for the Mancos Valley. Neighboring Cortez attempted to join the fray in 1899, but that town suffered from a major handicap—no railroad connections. Its only slim hopes for transportation rested with a stage line to link the village with the railroad at Dolores. Even so, Sterl Thomas promoted his guide service, good water, and "everything comfortable" for the fifteen-mile trip to the ruins, "the nearest and most picturesque route."[24] The youngest, smallest (population 332), and most isolated of the three competitors, Cortez gave no serious challenge for monopoly of the Mesa Verde business.

In the more bitter Durango-Mancos rivalry, Mancos had more at stake, since it had only Mesa Verde to distinguish it from a score of similar southwestern Colorado villages. Al Wetherill remembered it as a "cow town." With the Wetherills and its nearer location, Mancos could hold its own for the moment against a larger, more aggressive rival, but it never came near to reaching the *Times*'s overly optimistic forecasts.

As these two fought on, the Rio Grande Southern and its parent company, the Denver & Rio Grande Railroad (D&RG), promoted. Railroads furnished the fastest, most comfortable means to reach the ruins, and they provided the only continuing regional and national promotion. Advertisements and pamphlets boasted of the "wonderful HOMES OF THE CLIFF DWELLER," the magnificent scenery, and the wonders of this great agricultural region and added glowing praises for Mancos and Durango. All the bombast, of course, profited the railroad coffers. The D&RG also tied itself to the Wetherills, stressing to readers that not only the railroad but also the pioneer family would gladly furnish information and promptly make necessary arrangements.[25] To make the cliff dwellings a popular attraction, railroad support was essential, and it came readily.

The end result of all this promotion produced more "knights of the grip"—and more vandalism of ruins throughout the whole area. Americans craved souvenirs to take home; damage, intentional or not, followed in their wake at the ruins. The accelerating rate of visitation created fears that soon a priceless heritage would disappear. Did anyone care about Mesa Verde, or was this to be considered solely as a matter of business and profit? Was this only a short-term means to the ultimate end of helping to settle southwestern Colorado?

CHAPTER THREE

Women to the Rescue

Once the Wetherills had demonstrated that a successful find held more potential income than did a year's labor on the farm or ranch, the scramble for the dollar started. B. K. Wetherill warned the Smithsonian in a March 3, 1890, letter that "the valleys of Mancos and Montezuma have been pretty thoroughly dug over, it being about the only means of support of quite a number of people." Of course, not everyone dug and destroyed for money. Some sought additions to their personal collections; others viewed their outings as a novel way to spend a Sunday afternoon or a couple of days. Regardless of the motive, the end result was the same —destruction of irretrievable archaeological evidence or, at the very least, damage to a site.

T. Mitchell Prudden observed that by the mid-1890s settlers were organizing picnics at the ruins on Sundays and holidays for the primary purpose of digging. A story current at that time was that a banker in a nearby town "grub staked" men to dig in the ruins, supplying them with food and equipment for a percentage of the profits on artifacts they sold. These pothunters, or "Sunday-diggers," hiked far into Mesa Verde, leaving behind a "rusty old can" or some other memento of their presence in a ruin that more often than not had been severely damaged.[1] Their trail often led to Durango, where there was a ready market for pothunters' wares. A Mesa Verde mummy was even featured in a county fair parade.

Dark days these for Mesa Verde, even though the hard times locally and the pressing need for new income during the depression made them understandable. The lure of adventure, added to the profit motive, made the ruins almost irresistible. Life at home, on the farm, or on the ranch rarely provided so much excitement.

B. K. Wetherill was not the only one to buck the general trend and warn that ultimate destruction and irreplaceable loss would be the outcome of uncontrolled access. From the federal government level (U.S. Geological Survey and Secretary of the Interior Ethan A. Hitchcock), from organizations such as the Smithsonian Institution, and from private individuals protests arose against looting and vandalism. Colorado historian Frank Hall advocated that the ruins be "religiously preserved, not wantonly destroyed," and T. Mitchell Prudden lauded the Wetherills for being "most eager and persistent in preserving from harm the great ruins of the Mesa Verde as well as others."

Early preservation efforts were confronted by a wall of public indifference that created the need for a variety of solutions. Frederick Chapin, as early as 1889, had proposed the intriguing possibility that Cliff Palace "be converted into a museum and filled with relics of the lost people and become one of the attractions of southern Colorado."

Establishment of a state or national park constituted a more general approach. The Colorado Historical Society favored a state park; Nordenskiold's attorney, Ben W. Ritter, preferred a national park. Prudden called it a national disgrace that the U.S. government had made no effort to save the relics, and in 1896 he called for a national park at Mesa Verde. Three years later, the *Mancos Times* followed suit, calling the national park idea "laudable" and urging every public-spirited Colorado citizen to support it.[2] Those citizens needed more time to think about it.

Random attempts also were made to involve the federal government. As early as May, 1882, the New England Genealogical Society sent a memorial to the U.S. Senate, "praying" Congress to preserve some of the extinct cities. After the discovery of Mesa Verde, the Colorado legislature and several other local groups requested preservation

of the prehistoric ruins, but all their efforts came to naught.

The situation demanded a leader determined to stay the course in the face of setbacks and public apathy. Previous efforts, though well intentioned, had lacked that determination. Finally all the essential ingredients were brought together by a dedicated woman, the irrepressible Virginia McClurg, and the followers she recruited in a campaign that lasted for over a decade. McClurg's interest in Mesa Verde dated back to her visits (as Virginia Donaghe) in 1882 and 1886. In the 1890s, she turned into a one-woman crusade, passionately devoted to saving the ruins and creating a park. She launched an emotional campaign in Colorado to awaken the public, and her message was soon transmitted to the rest of the American public.

This was not the first time a determined woman had coaxed the public to support preservation. Forty years

Virginia McClurg, who led the fight for the park; at the moment of victory, she saw her triumph slip away.
Courtesy: Pioneers' Museum, Colorado Springs

earlier the shy, crippled southern gentlewoman Ann Pamela Cunningham had founded the Mount Vernon Ladies' Association of the Union to save George Washington's Potomac River home. She had organized committees in various states, overcome discouragements with perseverance and courage, and succeeded in purchasing the plantation buildings and grounds in 1859. The Civil War intervened, but Cunningham and her association were able to preserve Mount Vernon for posterity. They set a sterling example of what women could accomplish.

In 1894, Virginia McClurg gave a lecture series in Denver; at the conclusion a petition for the preservation of prehistoric ruins was drawn up and enthusiastically signed by those present. Off it went to Washington, where congressional apathy led to its quick demise. Disgusted, but not discouraged, McClurg vowed to continue her campaign. In 1897 she traveled to the Pueblo, Colorado, convention of the Colorado Federation of Women's Clubs, to plead with that group to make the cliff dwellings one of its projects. She was successful; the women responded wholeheartedly by organizing a fourteen-member committee with McClurg as chairman.

Having enlisted this eager support, McClurg unhesitatingly and boldly lobbied to win her goal. Colorado had granted women the right to vote in 1893, so it seemed the state would be receptive to women's taking an active role in previously male-dominated activities. Even so, this Victorian lady's aggressiveness and determination surprised many; she would not be deterred.

She talked with the Colorado senators, Edward Wolcott and Henry Teller, pressuring them for support. President and Mrs. William McKinley both received letters stating the need "to make it the most interesting park in the

United States. Then all can explore our wonderland, but none can destroy or take away." In return, she received a letter from an assistant secretary to the president asking that McClurg kindly take her request to the Secretary of the Interior, rather than bothering the president or his wife. Undaunted by this rebuff, writer and poet McClurg feverishly wrote articles, gave speeches (some featuring that new wonder, "stereopticon" views), and attempted to raise money. With perpetual energy and a martyr's dedication, Virginia McClurg enthusiastically pleaded and promoted.

> The Cliff place is the prey of the spoiler, soon it will be too late to guard these monuments. . . . We will act as custodians of specific ruins while the matter of national preservation . . . [is] pending. . . . for it is a noble work and not the least illustrious upon the roll of presidents will be the name of him who is the first to protect the oldest aboriginal monuments of the United States.[3]

She slowly awakened Americans and kept Mesa Verde fresh in the public mind.

At first the most appealing idea seemed to be making the committee of the Colorado Federation custodians of Mesa Verde while a national preservation act slowly worked its way through Congress—somewhat along the lines of the Mount Vernon effort. The urgency for preservation had become acute, as McClurg well knew and repeatedly warned, and some expeditious, inexpensive stopgap measure had to be found. Putting her talents to practical use, McClurg worked to get an accurate survey and hoped to have Indian police guard the ruins. The *Denver Republican*, however, warned that to do so would be unpopular, even though "practical and economical,"

because southwest Coloradans wanted to save the ruins while at the same time removing the only Indians extant in the vicinity, the Utes. With the Utes relocated elsewhere—anywhere—their land could be opened for settlement by people who considered themselves more progressive. Given that profit could be generated from interest in these ruins and relics, the Utes seemed to be only a hindrance. Old ideas died hard.

This predicament, as it turned out, brought one of the unexpected results of the growing interest in the cliff dwellers. Tension between the newcomers and the Utes had come with settlement, reflecting the centuries-old struggle over who would dominate. Over the most recent generation, relic collecting and exploration had produced new appreciation for the ancient people, if not for the Utes. Virginia McClurg and her backers promoted this amelioration of attitudes, and as an unintentional result, opinions began to change on a wider front. Perhaps Indians were not, after all, the barbarians of yesterday. Might it not be conceivable that westerners would come to appreciate their contemporary neighbors, just as they were learning to value an earlier Indian culture?

These philosophical questions were tangential to the main one: establishment of a park to preserve the cliff dwellings. Pursuing that goal, McClurg and Durangoan Alice Bishop, an early visitor to Mesa Verde and a park supporter, traveled to Mancos in 1899 and then on to Ute headquarters at Navajo Springs in Mancos Canyon. There they met with the old and experienced Southern Ute leader, Ignacio, and Acowitz, the same one who had befriended the Wetherills. Through an interpreter, McClurg made an offer of a thirty-year lease for the land encompassing the ruins at $300 annual rent, with the Utes retaining grazing rights (a compromise that eased the consciences of these women, who felt guilty about removing the Indians from their own land). The Utes would also be granted the right to appoint special policemen for the park.

All these concessions meant little to the practical Ignacio, who stunned the women by suggesting that the entire $9,000 rent be "plunked down at one pop." That demand proved to be too much of a pop—the conference ended without a meeting of minds. McClurg then toured Mesa Verde, ablaze in its "autumn dress of gold and crimson," to inspect sites and conditions of ruins and to look for sources of water.[4]

The setback with Ignacio only temporarily disconcerted McClurg. She returned to the fundamental question: Who should control Mesa Verde? Even though she feared that under federal protection all relics of the cliff dwellings would belong to the Smithsonian, she was not convinced that a state park would be any better. Certainly not one run by a state like Colorado, McClurg sarcastically warned, "that considers closing its institutions of learning and cannot care for her blind, poor and insane." McClurg's dire predictions did not come to pass, however, and her moment of bitterness soon passed. When she returned to the question at hand, she knew what she wanted: "No, let this be the women's park."

In the meantime a survey had been made and a map drawn. A circular was sent to every town in Colorado that had a Women's Club, "innumerable letters" were written, and lobbying was undertaken in Washington. What McClurg wanted was Ute and government consent for a park; then the next step would be the construction of wagon roads and trails, a restoration project, excavation of relics, and, finally, a hotel.[5]

With vigor and innate stubbornness, Virginia McClurg forged ahead.

McClurg was a natural leader who was able to attract an equally dedicated and determined corps of women to her cause and had a knack for arousing interest and enthusiasm among those she described as the "wealthy class who must have some outlet for their suppressed zeal."

The cultured and energetic Lucy Peabody, who became McClurg's lieutenant in the battle, led the fight in Washington, D.C., where she had previously worked and still retained excellent connections. She had come to Colorado as a bride in 1887 and now, in her thirties, was in the midst of a very active "public and private life." She had become deeply interested in ethnology while working in Washington, so it was natural that Lucy Peabody would turn to the fascinating Southwest and quickly be caught up in McClurg's excitement over Mesa Verde.

Behind McClurg and Peabody stood a loyal, hard-working cadre of women. Ella McNeil, the wife of one of Colorado's prominent bankers, worked in Washington, D.C., and Colorado. Ella Adams, the wife of former governor Alva Adams, joined the cause, as did Luna A. Thatcher of the Thatcher banking family and an energetic host of Durango women that included Alice Bishop; her mother, Jeanette Scoville; and Estelle Camp, McNeil's sister-in-law. Perhaps the most outspoken of the group was Helen Stoiber of Silverton, Colorado. Although her imperious manner created enmity, that never bothered her, and she fought the battle to the end with enthusiasm and her husband's mining money.

Most of the early supporters came from Colorado; later recruits joined from outside the state. Natalie Hammond, for example, the wife of noted mining engineer John Hays Hammond, visited the ruins, went on the lecture tour, and donated money to clean up and enlarge what became known as Hammond Spring near Spruce Tree House.[6] That these determined women faced an uphill struggle was a reality that did not seem to deter them.

Work within the Colorado Federation of Women's Clubs was acceptable to a point, but a single-issue organization was to be preferred. In May, 1900, articles of incorporation for the Colorado Cliff Dwellings Association were filed (the initiation fee was two dollars; yearly membership was one dollar). The obvious leadership emerged: McClurg was selected regent and Peabody the first vice-regent. Chapters in California, Arizona, Utah, and New York eventually joined the organization. With a new vehicle and an old goal, the women plunged ahead. Some husbands also played an active role in Colorado, where men were welcome to join. Al Wetherill represented the local chapter at Mancos. The California chapter, however, limited membership to "cultured Christian women."

As the women pushed forward, they found themselves in the mainstream of one of the major women's projects of the 1890s, the club movement. Clubs had multiplied, splintered, and federated at an energetic pace throughout the preceding twenty years. When the century turned, a vocal, visible collection of clubs had spread from the east coast to the west with a network of local, state, and national organizations. Like Virginia McClurg's product, the various clubs provided thousands of middle- and upper-class women, usually white, native-born Americans, the chance to be active outside of the home and to work toward common goals. Members supported worthy projects, raised funds, and acquired for themselves an avenue for social activism in civic affairs. These organizations also provided educational and leadership outlets that were often unavailable to women of that generation and enriched the quality of members' lives.

Indeed, before long such clubs became a symbol of social activism for their members. As a later scholar, Nancy Woloch, wrote, they united in the conviction that women as women had something distinctive and significant to contribute collectively to public life.[7]

It may be that many of the Mesa Verde women were not aware of their role in the larger movement, as more pressing and immediate goals occupied their attention. One of those involved negotiating with the Utes about the land on which the cliff dwellings lay. The discussions met with one stumbling block after another. In 1900, four Durangoans, led by the veteran Alice Bishop, traveled by train to Mancos and then overland by buggy to Navajo Springs. There they met with Ute leaders and their agent and reached a tentative agreement on a lease. Estelle Camp never forgot the aftermath. The joyous Utes "staged a wild drunk, dancing and shouting about the store building all through the night." Unfortunately for the terrified, and utterly proper, Victorian women, the Secretary of the Interior refused to accept their treaty. They had no authority, and as far as Washington was concerned, a majority of the tribe had not authorized the lease. A redrafted treaty was submitted the next year, only to be rejected once more. The infuriated McClurg exploded, "The department fondly imagines that Weeminuche Utes sit at ease at their agency, pens and blotting paper in hand, ready to sign leases, but such is not the case."[8]

Washington's bureaucratic road blocks forced the Association to focus more of its attention there. Lucy

Peabody and her capital connections provided the perfect solution, and her selection as chairman of the legislative committee was propitious. She left "no stone unturned" in her efforts. The federal government so far had shown little interest in preservation, except for the 1879 Act of Congress that specified that all collections made by parties for the government must be housed in the National Museum in Washington. And a special agent had been sent to southwestern Colorado in December, 1899, at the request of several Durangoans, to make a careful evaluation of the actual situation.[9] Nothing had come of those endeavors—neither the law nor the investigation benefited the Association.

With Peabody as their legislative leader, the women turned to promoting the introduction of park bills in both the House and the Senate. They found some important and willing con-gressional allies. Congressman John Shafroth, one of the most progressive Coloradans of his generation, devoted himself to this cause and to that of woman's suffrage, thereby endearing himself to the women of Colorado. This Missouri-born, University of Michigan–educated lawyer had first been elected to the House of Representatives in 1894. Now a House veteran, he had introduced national park bills in 1901 and in the two sessions following, only to meet defeat in committee hearings. Senator Edward Wolcott's efforts had gone no further.[10] Shafroth also fought for "good roads," a vital requirement for Colorado and for the welfare of the park should it come to fruition.

Undeterred by Washington's reluctance, the women redoubled their efforts. They attacked the "knockers," who believed a park campaign could not succeed, and they pressed ahead

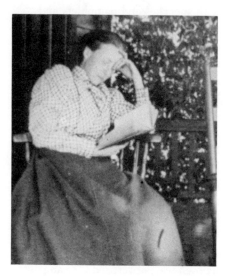

Estelle Camp was one of the Durango women who joined in the effort to create the park.
Courtesy: Author's Collection

with speeches and pamphlets and with obvious confidence in their ultimate success. McClurg wrote to Vice-President Theodore Roosevelt, who responded much more favorably than had the president.

One method the women used to raise money was to have members ask their friends and acquaintances to contribute ten cents. "No one minds giving 10 cents and besides it makes the laudable work of the association known," wrote McClurg. They also sponsored rummage sales and other fund raisers.[11] Each undertaking, in its own way, advertised the campaign; McClurg was right about the results of publicity. The careful laying of the ground work would, it was hoped, pay off in eventual benefits.

Nothing caught the press's attention more than did a tour to Mesa Verde, which the Association sponsored for a "distinguished party of ladies and gentlemen" in September, 1901. The group included a correspondent for the *New York Herald* and some leading archaeologists and scientists; McClurg, Peabody, McNeil, and other Association members conducted the tour for the opportunity it offered to tell the story of their fight. They rendezvoused in Durango, where Estelle Camp and the Reading Club met them at the depot. A tour of the city was followed by a "delightful" evening reception. Next day, it was on to Mancos and then to Mesa Verde, under the guidance of Al Wetherill and Charles B. Kelly. This was the "most interesting and influential body of people" yet to visit the cliff dwellings, claimed the *Mancos Times*. The writer optimistically added that the party would advertise the ruins more extensively than anyone ever had before and that hundreds of tourists would be induced to come to Mancos —a statement showing that hope never died in Mancos.

Not all of those expectations would come to pass, but Professor Jesse Fewkes, one of the party who did rally to the cause, was destined to play a significant role in the future park. Denver and New York newspapers gave the trip ample coverage; that particular goal of McClurg had been achieved.[12]

The celebrity tour proved to be the last hurrah for the Wetherills in the ongoing Mesa Verde story. Benjamin Wetherill had died in November, 1898, naming Richard his heir-at-law, but Richard now lived at Pueblo Bonito in Chaco Canyon, several days' ride to the south. Al and his mother lived at the ranch and carried on the work, but they faced debts, and times were not good for local ranching. Tourists still came, but others, especially Charles Kelly, now competed for a share of the guide service business. The ranch slowly declined, along with the Wetherill fortunes in the Mancos Valley, and in 1901, when a mortgage payment was overdue, a judgment was obtained against the property. After Al tried in vain to raise the money, the Alamo Ranch was sold at public auction in February, 1902.[13] Circumstances had changed; following the Mesa Verde excitement, the Wetherill brothers had turned elsewhere to explore and dig and then move away. Their interest in the Mancos Valley naturally declined.

With tourism on the increase, Charles Kelly, better known as C. B., certainly competed for the Wetherill guide service. Having come to Mancos in 1886, Kelly was almost as much of an old-timer as were his competitors, the Wetherills. From his "up-to-date" livery stable in Mancos, he guided visitors to Mesa Verde, and if the *Mancos Times* reporting can be trusted, by 1900 he was more than holding his own against Al and the Alamo.[14] A veteran of the Leadville, Colorado, silver excitement and the freighting business, this "good man" had some fascinating stories to tell his guests at the cabin he built opposite Spruce Tree House. The popular Kelly was an active member of the Mancos Hose Company and one of the region's noted race-horse owners.

Both Al and C. B. could have used a better road to the ruins. Mancos people also wanted a wagon road into the "heart of the region" to increase travel and to give them an advantage in the rivalry with their urban neighbors. No one had yet blinked in that ongoing faceoff. When visitors were told in Durango that "they could drive from Durango to Cliff Palace in carriages, thus avoiding the tedious horse-back ride from Mancos," the *Mancos Times*, June 14, 1901, exploded, "These things are laughable, but extremely annoying." Nor did the editor appreciate Cortez's claim that it was located twelve miles nearer to the cliff dwellings than Mancos. The facts did not bear that out, the *Mancos Times* (June 28) piously reported, and furthermore the "foot trail" from Cortez was much worse, and the guide "gets lost every time" he attempts the trip.

Sterl Thomas, the guide in question, did not actually get lost; the Mancos people could be as careless with the facts as their rivals. Montrose photographer Thomas McKee experienced one of Thomas's trips in 1900. He left this account of his long day's journey to Spruce Tree House.

> We left Cortez and went southwest to an old trail which we followed, traveling east on the rim rock of the mesa on the north side, and really it was no trail at all, as to show itself and none whatever going down to Spruce Tree House; the underbrush, and the cedar and pinion trees were thick and made it hard to travel through the wilderness of forest with pack horses and our own saddle horses.[15]

When he got there, he endured the traditional lack of good water, as he

*Early guide
and first ranger
Charles Kelly
with part of his
"string."*
Courtesy: Jean Bader

Kelly's cabin, near Spruce Tree House, provided the first accommodations at Mesa Verde.
Courtesy: Mesa Verde National Park

A group of early-day Mesa Verde visitors outside Kelly's cabin.
Courtesy: Jean Bader

toured the ruins and took his photographs. Twelve-year-old Minnie Hickman took the same trip four years later and retained similar memories. Their accounts emphasized why Cortez was a poor choice as a jumping-off place. Mancos boosters cheered the disadvantages of Cortez, but the trip from the Mancos side, though easier, still held some challenges.[16]

The adventures did not end upon reaching the ruins. Minnie remembered that one of her party was hit on the head by a rock as he climbed into Spruce Tree House. Effie Eldredge was embarrassed by the "ridiculous overalls" the ladies had to wear, and she waited until the very last moment to put them on. Victorian decorum had to be maintained even here, so she and her sister Gladys retired to the sage brush, changed, "giggled over the attire," and then rode toward Mesa Verde.

Up at sunrise, stiff and sore, they consumed a hearty breakfast and prepared for the day's touring. Fearful that mice would run up her legs, Gladys tied shoe laces tightly around her pants at the ankles, and off she went to see the sights. No mice ruined her day, but the embarrassment of getting stuck in Spruce Tree House almost did. With a minimum of effort, she was extricated from her predicament. The party had lunch in the "court yard of Cliff Palace, amid broken stones and adobe." Only Effie, among the ladies, climbed the "rickety log ladder" and rope into Balcony House. While returning to their cabin (built near Spruce Tree House by Kelly to provide at least a rough frontier kind of comfort), the guide killed three rattlesnakes. Effie and her friends could only imagine hot baths and soft beds while they tidied their hair; Mesa Verde did not provide many Victorian amenities.[17] A meal of beans and salt pork and an early bedtime awaited them at the conclusion of their vigorous day.

The women of the Cliff Dwellings Association were working hard in the meantime to change this primitiveness and to save the ruins. They received a boost in 1903, when Congress authorized negotiations with the Utes. Back went the redoubtable Alice Bishop and her friends for another powwow, at which the Utes once again agreed to a lease. Something then happened that is undocumented, and the next year Senator Thomas Patterson and Virginia McClurg visited the Utes, who now claimed that the government had treated them unfairly. They objected to the rations they received and the failure of irrigation water to reach the reservation, in accordance with treaty obligations. Everything eventually was worked out, and Congress would ratify the agreement in 1906.[18] The treaty came too late, however, to be of much help in preservation or in attaining a major breakthrough toward creation of the park.

*Climbing up the
canyon walls and
into the ruins was
an adventure in
the pre-park days.*
Courtesy: Jean Bader

Another attempt in 1904 to create a park died when the House failed to act after the Senate passed the bill. But in losing, the cause won publicity and public attention. For example, that same year the government published a pamphlet about the prehistoric ruins of the Southwest. It forthrightly emphasized that preservation needed to be, and was becoming, a matter of much concern for the American people. More important, the author believed that no barriers hindered the "speedy accomplishment" of turning this awareness into saving the ruins.

The women must have wondered where such confidence came from after the setbacks they had suffered in Washington. They could not be displeased, however, by the author's praise of Mesa Verde as offering the finest specimens of "true cliff dwellings." The clincher came with the statement that a national park established

there would "be of great educational value." The pamphlet favored the name Colorado Cliff Dwellings National Park; others suggested different titles.[19] By whatever name it would be called, the cherished park seemed to be closer to becoming a reality, even though it still lay tantalizingly just beyond the Association's reach.

Vandalism and relic removal continued unabated all the while. So did damage as tourists wandered about; even the most careful contributed their unintended share. The need for action loomed more urgently than it had a decade before, repeatedly warned McClurg, Peabody, and the others in 1904. Time was working against them; if anything was to be preserved for the American people to see and for archaeologists to study, then action had to be taken now—not promised for tomorrow.

CHAPTER FOUR

Victory

Slowly, steadily, Washington's political climate came around to favoring the idea of a park at Mesa Verde. Congressman John Shafroth's yeoman efforts on behalf of the park paid dividends as the legislative sessions rolled by. He had educated fellow House members sufficiently to change congressional attitudes, but he had earlier warned Virginia McClurg that turning the ruins over to the state or to the women would create vehement opposition from the Smithsonian Institution and from the archaeological societies. McClurg, Lucy Peabody, and the others had worked to overcome that opposition, in the face of strong doubts outside of Colorado that their plans could succeed. The death of Senator Henry Teller's park bill in 1904 showed the depth of feeling. In that case, the issue was not the creation of the park itself, but who would have the right to excavate the ruins. The Smithsonian sought to retain that privilege. When the opposing sides failed to compromise, the bill died.[1]

In 1905, the Association members geared up for another try. A new urgency drove them—newcomers to Colorado were laying claim to 160-acre homestead sites in several canyons, a potential complication of the ownership issue. As these homesteaders struggled for a toehold, giving their names to Prater, Morefield, and Waters canyons in the process, they pushed the Association women into high gear to achieve their prize.[2] Each in his or her own way, the homesteader and the society woman chased the best of all worlds at the end of the western rainbow.

Shafroth had been correct in his assessment that it would be easier to pass a bill creating a national park than one creating a state park, and, with some reservations, McClurg finally concurred. Shafroth, however, no longer sat in the House, and despite the best efforts of Colorado Representative Herschel Hogg, one of Colorado's leading attorneys and a Telluride resident, the 1905 bill died on the floor after it came out of committee. On the state front, the Historical Society backed Hogg's bill unreservedly, as did several archaeological societies throughout the country.[3] Although another session and another year had passed with success as elusive as ever, park support had grown in and out of Congress. The women stood on the threshold of victory when 1906 arrived.

Years of lobbying, promoting, and educating now started to pay rich dividends. From President Theodore Roosevelt to his Secretary of the Interior, through Congress to the Colorado people, the mood seemed to favor the national park plan. The women also reaped benefits from the now thriving conservation movement, which had caught the general public's attention as never before. For the past thirty years or so, Americans had been hearing and reading more and more about the general theme of conservation of natural resources, with particular emphasis on the future of forests and agriculture. In the arid west, these two subjects often translated into water issues.

With the popular Roosevelt in the White House, using the office as a "bully pulpit" for one of his favorite subjects, conservation came into favor as never before. Within the larger movement arose individuals who supported conservation not so much to protect watersheds or to assure America of future timber reserves but as a way to preserve wilderness areas for their inherent aesthetic, spiritual, and moral values. The two factions were accommodated nicely in the national park movement, although the seeds of dispute were sown for later disagreements between those who would favor the concept of multiple use of resources and those who would argue for preservation. At Mesa Verde, this particular conflict would erupt over the issue of whether grazing and coal mining should be allowed.

As early as the 1860s and 1870s, the wonders of Yellowstone and Yosemite had been called to the attention of Americans. As a result, the former was set aside as a park, and the latter was given to the state of California, which acted as a trustee for the federal government until Yosemite, too, eventually gained park status. The precedent for preservation had thereby been established, and in the following years various groups pushed to preserve other scenic sites. The supporters of Mesa Verde moved within this ground swell of interest, although they stressed the cultural and historic attributes of their potential park, not its natural wonders.

The Roosevelt era provided the best opportunity the conservationists had ever enjoyed for arousing support and for winning some of the battles they had been waging. Journalists and reporters, politicians and public officials, easterners and westerners, became more aware, more informed, and more involved, although the increased interest did not necessarily transfer into advocacy and action on behalf of conservation.

The push to preserve the Mesa Verde ruins clearly benefited from the popularity of the larger national movement. Now, everything seemed to be coming together, thanks to hard work and some fortunate circumstances over which the women and their supporters could exercise no control.

Hogg introduced another Mesa Verde National Park bill in December, 1905, in the House; Senator Thomas Patterson followed suit in January, 1906, in the Senate. Both bills survived committee votes, the point at which so many earlier bills had died. Once more, pressure was brought to bear.

The Nebraska Academy of Sciences, the Colorado Equal Suffrage Association, the Davenport (Iowa) Academy of Sciences, the Pueblo Business Men's Association, the Colorado State Forestry Association, "men of high character" (professors and scholars), and "learned" women all endorsed and urged passage of the bill. Colorado governor Jesse McDonald wrote: "The People of Colorado, and I believe of the entire West, would be glad to see this bill favorably reported upon by your committee [senate], as we are quite anxious that this historical place be properly protected."[4] Testimony in support of the bill called attention to the national significance of the ruins, the destruction that had already occurred, the unfit nature of the land for agriculture and its classification as "poor range at the best," and the potential tourist market. Proponents claimed that a park "would bring money into such towns as Durango and Mancos."

Once again, the bills slowly wound their way through the congressional labyrinth, while the members of the Association anxiously watched and awaited the outcome.

This time the political atmosphere had changed, for a very significant reason. A second major bill was under discussion: an antiquities bill that would preserve historic and prehistoric ruins or monuments on government lands. It, too, had been introduced earlier, only to die, and it, too, had attracted more support, more interest, and more publicity even when it failed. It was ardent conservationist Iowa Representative John Lacey who introduced the antiquities bill. Like Shafroth and others, Lacey had long supported historic preservation. It had been a long, drawn-out struggle to achieve agreement among all the interested parties. Noted southwestern archaeologist Edgar Hewett, who had worked persistently to protect important regional ruins, found it easy to support enthusiastically both the park and the preservation efforts and to rally his friends to the cause. Hewett was at the peak of his career; the one-time college president and skilled writer had the ability to create a scholarly and, at the same time, a popular account of the prehistoric ruins, which caught the attention of both academia and the general public.

Each bill complemented the other, since their goals overlapped. Some of the resolutions and endorsements supported both the park bill and the antiquities bill. Mesa Verde was, perhaps, the more emotional issue, but the antiquities bill raised a broader-based following, because of its benefits for the whole country, as opposed to one state in particular. As the women fought for Mesa Verde, they plowed the ground for the more sweeping antiquities idea at the same time. Antiquities advocates later returned the favor, rallying to support the specific park concept. It was a winning partnership—a two-front advance toward a common goal.

In 1906, when both bills went before the House Public Lands Committee, John Lacey was its chairman. Senator Patterson carried the cause to the Senate by sponsoring an identical effort.[5] The bills moved ahead at the typical tortoise pace, but they did move, with no major obstacles in their path. Beyond Congress sat the enthusiastic President Theodore Roosevelt, a conservationist, a historian, and an ardent supporter of all that the two bills proposed.

After nearly a quarter of a century of pleading, cajoling, and never-say-die lobbying by McClurg, and a decade's worth of effort by most of the others, victory lay only a few short weeks, or months at most, away. At this auspicious moment, the Association fell apart when its leaders began assaulting each other with rancorous name-calling over the old issue of state control versus federal control.

The sudden discovery that none of the major cliff dwellings was situated within the boundaries of the proposed park certainly proved embarrassing but did not pose an insoluble problem. An amendment to the bill was introduced to include in the park's jurisdiction all the ruins within five miles of the boundary. The issue should have rested there, but Virginia McClurg changed her mind or—more accurately—"reversed her position" and returned to her beloved idea of a state park, which would be comfortably controlled by the Association. Such an arrangement would, in effect, place the cliff dwellings under her personal control.

No question of the cause surrounded this change of heart—at the moment of victory, the once-allied Peabody and McClurg fell to fighting over the spoils. These two determined, independent, and strong-willed women had pledged themselves to a common cause in Mesa Verde; as the struggle for it continued, they could not completely contain their individualism. The split, which could have been predicted, had been long in coming.

Lucy Peabody, with her Washington connections, ardently supported the national park idea, while McClurg had been won over only by circumstances. Each had gathered her supporters within the Association, but for a time the rift had been smoothed over for the sake of the common aims. However, the Colorado Cliff Dwellings Association had refused, back in November, 1905, to endorse officially Hogg's bill, because it gave exclusive control of the national park to the Secretary of the Interior, something Secretary Ethan A. Hitchcock had pushed for. The refusal also hinted at the problem of the non-included cliff dwellings.[6] This lack of endorsement by the Association had escaped attention during the hubbub of the next couple of months.

Then in February, 1906, McClurg came out openly against the bill, and all hell broke loose in the Association. Emotions and opinions that once had been suppressed now burst into public view, in the face of numerous denials of a split in the ranks. Both factions rapidly issued statements, attacking and denying; the public witnessed a dismaying dissolution of unity. Peabody and McClurg battled it out in the press and outside of it, catching Representative Hogg, among others, in the cross fire. At one time he had supported McClurg. The following charges are typical of the exchanges in the struggle:

> Meat in the coconut is that [Mc-Clurg] is loath to relinquish the prestige she has gained by reason of her interest in preserving these ruins.

> [Hogg's] backbones belong rather to antediluvian dinosaurs than modern legislators.

> The action of the Colorado Cliff Dwellers Association, however, may result in the defeat of this bill as well as the one that proposes to put it under feminine and individual control, and the state may be left in the lurch.[7]

All the slander made for gossipy press in February, 1906, and for weeks thereafter the Denver newspapers reported the turmoil. The infighting, as one member commented, "precipitated a warm fight."

McClurg was attacked for putting her prestige too much on the line and conducting a personal vendetta against Peabody, when the park should have been of primary importance, and was castigated for blinding herself to the fact that preservation belonged to the government and not to a volunteer

*Lucy Peabody
as she appeared
years after she
played a role in
the Mesa Verde
story.*
Courtesy: Colorado
Historical Society

association of women to "manage it according to feminine ideas." McClurg responded heatedly, pointing with great glee to the women who maintained and operated Washington's Mount Vernon and charging that very "few members of the Association" had pressed for the national park.

McClurg's distrust of national control was shared by other women, in particular the women of Mount Vernon. It reflected a legitimate fear, as women did not even have the vote in most places yet. Perhaps she also feared putting matters in the hands of the far-off federal government with its "faceless bureaucracy." Lucy Peabody, more experienced at working with and within the government, obviously did not share such feelings or fears. Peabody continued to support publicly the national park concept, pointing to Yellowstone as an example of what the federal government could do with direct supervision. McClurg countered rather unconvincingly that Mesa Verde would "not thrive" under either state or federal control. Prompted by the belief that only her plan could succeed, she sent an open letter to the *Rocky Mountain News*, which published the letter on March 11, 1906. After graciously praising Peabody and others for their excellent work, McClurg expressed resentment of the slurs and mudslinging and thanked the *Denver Post* for supporting her. She again attacked the Hogg bill, claiming that the Association never had any national park policy, and pled for the issue to be kept out of politics. She also threw in a new twist by accusing the Peabody people of wanting the Utes removed so that those with "covetous eyes" could seize Indian land.[8]

The accusations, half-truths, and mudslinging sullied the park campaign; the women chose up sides and pressed ahead with tattered banners. As it turned out, Virginia won the battle, but

Lucy won the war. Peabody resigned from the Association, taking her followers with her and leaving Regent McClurg with a decimated membership and a discredited cause. Even the *Denver Post* (Feb. 23, 1906), which had praised McClurg, now proclaimed that Mesa Verde belonged to the world, not to any single organization. With a touch of sarcasm, a little misidentification, and a large dose of truth, the writer asked, "In fifty years from now who will care or know anything about the Cliff Dwellings Protective Association?" Prophetically, the article stated, "In fifty years from now if the government of the United States takes care of those Cliff Dwellings, the whole world will know of them." The Colorado press stayed involved, not only because of local interest in the cause but also because of the urban rivalries that had begun with Mancos, Cortez, and Durango vying for the tourist trade. Bigger stakes now brought Denver,

Colorado Springs, and Pueblo into the competition for their share of the glory. Some of the Denver support for Peabody reflected a desire to detract some attention from McClurg's Colorado Springs and her Pueblo supporters.

Countering the stories coming out of Colorado took some effort. Edgar Hewett and others managed to defuse some of their effects. Hewett's four-week visit to Mesa Verde in March and April, 1906, inspired a long, enthusiastic letter that restated the value of the Mesa Verde archaeological district and warned of the continuing "irreparable damage" occurring every year. He supported the amended park bill and believed that no injustice would be done to the Utes, since both they and the park would be under the jurisdiction of the Department of the Interior.[9]

Fortunately, while the women fought it out, Congress paid more attention to Hewett's type of continued backing. The House and Senate bills were

pushed onward, as was the companion piece of legislation, the Antiquities Act, which moved a little faster and was signed by the president on June 8, 1906.

The Senate and the House both approved the Mesa Verde National Park bill later in June, and on the twenty-ninth President Theodore Roosevelt signed it. Section one carefully defined the park boundaries; section two provided that all prehistoric ruins within five miles of the park boundaries be "hereby placed under the custodianship of the Secretary of the Interior," who also had "exclusive control" of Mesa Verde National Park. The secretary was authorized to permit examination, excavations, and other gathering of objects, provided that they always "are undertaken only for the benefit of some reputable museum, university, college, or other recognized scientific or educational institution." Finally, to protect the ruins from vandalism, a fine of not more than one thousand dollars or imprisonment of not longer than twelve months could be imposed on anyone guilty of violating the ruins.[10] Curiously, this law established a much harsher set of penalties than did the Antiquities Act. The long struggle was at last over. The federal government now would chart the future of Colorado's first national park.

Mesa Verde joined an illustrious group of six national parks that included the already far-famed Yellowstone and Yosemite as well as Sequoia, General Grant, Mount Rainier, and Crater Lake. Unfortunately, during the previous four years, three new parks had been set aside that did not measure up to the others' high standards. This was possible because of the lack of a congressional policy to govern the establishment of parks and of an agency to screen park proposals. Of these three inferior parks—Wind Cave, Sullys Hill, and Platt—only Wind

Cave still exists as a national park.[11] Political pressure, local chauvinism, and misguided enthusiasm had been allowed to rule. The need for a regulatory agency was urgent, but no action came immediately. Some people undoubtedly saw Mesa Verde as of little more consequence than its recently born contemporaries. Some of the same methods had been used to press for its creation, albeit on a broader national level. Fortunately for Mesa Verde, its significance put it on a par with Yellowstone. Now its supporters had to develop that potential.

Southwestern Coloradans backed the creation of the park with far more enthusiasm than they supported nearby national forests. Mesa Verde National Park displaced few people, threatened no potential private interests, and promised ongoing benefits for the region. On the other hand, creation of national forests—for example, Mesa Verde's neighboring San Juan National

Forest in 1905—ended time-honored frontier traditions that allowed public utilization of natural resources with minimum payment and little or no government regulation. Local residents could envision the closing or federal management of grazing, mineral, and timber lands. They did not want to encourage that trend. The West's ambivalent relationship with the federal government never was more clearly shown than in this corner of Colorado.

The Colorado press's reaction to the momentous event seemed relatively subdued, perhaps because the emotional fight of the past few months had spent its energy. Mancos, however, fully appreciated what had happened; that community had struck a potential gold mine. "Mancos is IT. Mesa Verde National Park," hailed the *Mancos Times-Tribune*. The editor thought this might be just the needed spring tonic to energize the community and revive it from the economic blues. He envi-

Main Street in Mancos, 1917, during the town's heyday as the starting point for trips to Mesa Verde.
Courtesy: Mesa Verde National Park

sioned publicity, visitors, a first-class hotel, increased sales for farmers and ranchers, and "thousands of dollars" in government contracts. Mancos, he bubbled, harbored within a very short radius every resource to make it a "first class town." It only remained for the residents to "shake off your lethargy of mind and body, roll up your sleeves and get out and help turn something up." Not satisfied, the editor admonished: "Let us remember that cities are made, not grown, and the making depends upon the citizens themselves."[12]

Of all the Colorado communities, little Mancos best understood what Mesa Verde could mean economically. It obviously had the most to gain, with Cortez out of the running and Durango apparently too far away to take real advantage of this opportunity. Mancos determined to turn Mesa Verde and the accompanying publicity windfall into an economic energizer that would spark the village's attainment of "city"

status. Local surveyors had already won a contract to run the boundary line between the park and the Ute reservation. What Mancos gained, so did the region, the state, and the country. One newspaper reporter caught that spirit: "Hats off to the women of the association, and three cheers for Uncle Sam."

Unfortunately, the women could hardly hear the cheers, nor had they much spirit for merry-making. Virginia McClurg, who had led the Association, had lost; Lucy Peabody, on the outside looking in, had won. Adherents of both women carried on the petty fight for months, justifying their own cause and attacking that of the others. The public victory, like the congressional one, went to Peabody. The American Anthropological Association extended to her its first-ever public vote of thanks for "her valuable services . . . [and] untiring effort," with no mention of McClurg. The press hailed

Peabody as the "Mother of Mesa Verde National Park," and the "gifted and charming" Lucy (whose husband was the brother of Colorado's former governor James Peabody) earned a bright star in the family's Colorado heritage: "Perhaps, no woman in the country has more thorough and profound knowledge of Archaeology, Anthropology and Ethnology, than this earnest, able, enthusiastic student of scientific research. Colorado, the whole Nation, owes her a debt of gratitude."[13]

McClurg's supporters tried in vain to balance the story; their effort was doomed almost from the start by McClurg's decision not to support the national park. The *Denver Times* eventually recognized her contribution to the park's creation, attributing the achievement "in largest measure to her patient, continuous and self-denying work, covering a quarter century." She had been the "moving spirit," who failed to finish the race and who lost out before the cheering started. Virginia McClurg, unable to rise above the personal jealousies and the clash of personalities that had exploded over the past year, stood forlornly and bitterly on the sidelines for the victory celebration.[14] Although the breakdown of leadership did not fatally affect the park's establishment, it did handicap McClurg personally, and she never recovered from the setback. It would be over forty years before the last echoes of this feud were heard.

In spite of the sad ending to their story, the women had laid the foundation for Mesa Verde National Park and could be justly proud of what they had set in motion. From their first interest in the idea to the final battle, they stood in the vanguard, never retreating. The park they created brought with it a multitude of blessings, including the Antiquities Act, a new interest in archaeology, increased public awareness of the non-European past of North America, and the creation of four archaeological national monuments (Chaco Canyon, Bandelier, Hovenweep, and Aztec Ruins) in the Four Corners area in less than twenty years. Some of the characters in the Mesa Verde story also fought to preserve other areas. Hewett, for example, was instrumental in the Chaco Canyon designation.[15]

Mesa Verde had not been the first archaeological site to be set aside —that claim belonged to Arizona's Casa Grande, which had become a national monument in 1889, just as the Wetherills were exhibiting their first collection. Mesa Verde became the first national park, however, and as such was the crown jewel in the attempt to arouse the public's interest in preserving more sites. As a result, the Southwest would eventually boast of more archaeological national parks and monuments than all the rest of the country. The Mesa Verde struggle was also part of the ongoing establishment of federal regulations to protect antiquities.[16]

An evolution of western attitudes was an unexpected result of the campaign to create a park. More respect was being shown to the Utes than ever before, although they languished yet some distance from full equality in twentieth-century America. For the ancient peoples, the day of appreciation had finally come. Westerners were changing, and Colorado writer Eugene Parsons sensed that change as early as 1906, when he wrote: "Hitherto Westerners have been too busy making a living and getting rich to bother their heads much about cliff dwellings and cave homes, but the time will come when men and women will feel a curiosity to know something of the prehistoric past of the Southwest."[17] The greatest legacies left by the women who fought this good fight were the arousal of awareness, the stimulation of concern, and the motivation for action. Their park had achieved those things and more. The movement had been a watershed struggle in the fight to preserve America's cultural heritage. There would be no turning back now; Mesa Verde had set too valuable a precedent for future national parks, which would benefit mightily from the battle that had just been waged.

CHAPTER FIVE

Trials and Tribulations

Mesa Verde National Park so far existed only as a bare-bones promise on a piece of paper in Washington, D.C. The reality lay in the isolated canyons and on the mesa-top lands in far distant southwestern Colorado. Now it was up to the government to integrate the promise with the reality to create the country's first cultural park—a dream nurtured into life.

The natural first step, the appointment of a superintendent, was taken on October 8, 1906, when the Secretary of the Interior designated the Southern Ute agent, William Leonard, acting superintendent. Charles Werner followed him in May, 1907. A search

was under way, in the meantime, for a permanent candidate. Regarding this individual, Leonard suggested that "a very liberal salary would be necessary as a man qualified for the duties would not care to isolate himself at a point so distant from civilization." A "caretaker" approach to management, which Leonard believed to be the answer to budgeting problems, left the park pretty much in limbo, just as it had always been. Leonard did make an inspection tour soon after his appointment and posted typewritten placards at major ruins and at Spruce Tree camp to inform the public of the Antiquities Act and the penalties for violating it.

Deeming that action insufficient, he requested that the government furnish printed placards. It would take more than those, however; Leonard warned: "To prevent depredations by organized bands of looters and tourists, a forest ranger should be stationed in the Park all the time, to patrol it."[1] The park's first winter descended soon afterward, bringing chilly days and snow and an end to that year's tourism.

Business men and women in Montezuma and La Plata counties eagerly awaited the coming spring. When they read that 26,000 visitors had passed through Yellowstone National Park in 1905, they began to calculate what that would mean in dollars and cents. Over the course of the winter, they envisioned the great influx of tourist dollars that would be generated by "way of advertising by the entire surrounding country." The golden promise of the American West seemed to be at hand.

The situation in Washington looked less sanguine. The appointment of a permanent superintendent had hit a snag. Virginia McClurg supported her husband, Gilbert, for the job; Lucy Peabody favored Hans Randolph, a major in the Colorado State Militia. In light of the bitter animosities, it would have been more diplomatic to select a neutral third party, but Randolph was appointed on August 3, 1907, and Peabody had won round two. The elated Peabody hailed Randolph as a "true son of Colorado," an opinion with which the *Denver Times* heartily concurred.[2] The paper pointedly suggested that all those who "wish to see

the park beautified and improved and properly officered" should join it in supporting Randolph.

Another defeat proved to be too much for Virginia McClurg; in her disgust she did the rather foolish thing of supporting the building of a fake cliff dwelling in Manitou Springs, a neighbor of her beloved Colorado Springs. A "professor" Ashenhurst, who devised the idea, had "excavated" a ruin on private land south of Dolores, Colorado, and shipped what he found, along with stones, to Manitou Springs. Here Harold Ashenhurst, a young Texan who headed the Ashenhurst Amusement Company, busied himself in constructing a reproduction of a cliff dwelling at "the head of beautiful Phantom Canyon."

McClurg had become interested in Ashenhurst's idea soon after she lost the park fight, and she had become a company stockholder. The reaction

of the Association to her involvement in such a scheme generated this headline in the *Rocky Mountain News* (Oct. 25, 1906): "Society Women of Colorado Are Rent in Twain." Many members saw the Ashenhurst project as inconsistent "with the dignity of the Association" and "unscientific and hurtful" to the state. In November, in a movement spearheaded by the Durango women, who were not just a little perturbed over the creation of a rival tourist attraction, forty members resigned. That number included almost the entire Pueblo group, which was also angry about McClurg's changing of the annual meeting to Colorado Springs. One unidentified member lamented "that women interested in affairs could descend to such petty bickering."

Anyone who had watched the women sow the wind during the previous two years could have foreseen the coming whirlwind. Undaunted, McClurg claimed that the members had resigned because of politics, not because of the imitation cliff dwelling flap.[3] Her protests had no effect. The once strong Colorado Cliff Dwellings Association dwindled to include only Virginia and her loyal supporters.

The Manitou Springs replica haunted Mesa Verde for the next half century. McClurg's support gave it a semblance of credibility that Ashenhurst, stingingly referred to as a "medicine show operator," could not bestow. Although McClurg never intended the replica to be anything but an imitation to interest visitors who could not undertake the "arduous" trip to Mesa Verde, Ashenhurst had other ideas. Soon the replica was being promoted as an original, to the everlasting distress of archaeologists and park personnel.

McClurg's early contributions to Mesa Verde could not be denied. But their luster was fading now, as she tenaciously fought to maintain her reputation and her position of leadership. The Association made one more positive contribution when it raised one thousand dollars to restore Balcony House, which Virginia had visited so many years before. Young archaeologist Jesse Nusbaum, under the direction of Edgar Hewett, repaired the ruin in 1910. That last noble act of McClurg's came to an ignominious end eleven years later. In 1921, Nusbaum, by then the park superintendent, found at the Mancos railroad station a crated white marble marker that commemorated McClurg's and the Association's contributions to the park. McClurg pressured the National Park Service to install the marker "in the most conspicuous location for visitor observation" at Balcony House. The unfortunate Nusbaum found himself in the middle of what was still an emotional issue. As soon as the rest of the women learned about McClurg's move, they argued that other leaders merited equal recognition.[4] In the face of so much opposition and Park Service discouragement, McClurg eventually backed off, and the marker was returned to Colorado Springs.

McClurg's arch rival, Lucy Peabody, fared no better. Professor Hewett, a loyal ally in the park fight, wished to commemorate her role by renaming Square Tower House to Peabody House.[5] He proceeded to do so, but after several years and unspecified protests, the Department of the Interior rejected the designation.

While the women bickered in 1906 and 1907, Mancos prepared to greet Superintendent Randolph. Upon his arrival on September 2, 1907, he established temporary headquarters at the Mancos Hotel, which soon evolved into permanent quarters in the Bauer

Bank Building. Mancos had received the juiciest political plum in the form of park headquarters. In the race for prominence and the tourist dollars, Mancos sprinted into a strong lead over Durango and left Cortez eating its dust. The "affable, earnest" Randolph, as the *Mancos Times-Tribune* described him, did himself no harm when he warmly expressed his pleasure with what he saw "in these parts," this being his first visit.

Within thirty-six hours, he left for a tour of the park, guided by that old hand, Charles Kelly. Kelly had just returned from taking Hewett and others of the Archeological Society of America on a two-week tour. After Randolph's survey, he set himself the task of creating a park out of what remained at Mesa Verde after twenty years of vandalism and visitation. Shocked by the debris left behind by Spruce Tree House campers, he quickly sent workmen to clean up the rubbish,

and he issued an order that in the future no trash would be allowed to accumulate about the camp or to be left in the vicinity of the principal ruins.

Randolph announced that the work for the "immediate future" would center on a wagon road into and a reservoir within the park. He thereby put his finger on the two most pressing problems. As the *Denver Times* of August 11, 1907, had stated, the "timid traveler" found Mesa Verde "almost inaccessible" under the existing conditions. The establishment of a system of "good roads" and, in time, hotels and creature comforts, "inasmuch as they do not destroy the picturesque effect of the ruins," were intended to succor the "weary wayfarer." "Then indeed will the Mesa Verde National Park be second to none in the country; not even the far-famed Yellowstone Park."[6]

In the years that followed, Randolph set out to accomplish that goal, only to discover that the expense involved

weighed heavily against government demands for economy. As he tried to balance the needs of scientific work, construction, and maintenance, he constantly found himself in financial straits, with funds never adequate for all the needs of the park.

In 1907 Randolph immediately ran afoul of the Department of the Interior by recommending that the two thousand dollars set aside for preservation and repair of ruins be allotted instead to construction of roads. So urgent did he believe the matter to be that he wanted to postpone building a lodge and postpone the water improvement project in order to plow all that money into roads. On October 25, back came a letter from the acting Secretary of the Interior stating that, while the department recognized the desirability of "early construction of good roads," it did "not deem it advisable" to depart from the plan outlined for preservation and repair.[7] So Randolph cooperated with archaeologist Jesse Fewkes and extended to him "such assistance and courtesies" as would enable him to carry out the work properly.

During those early years, the superintendent hovered mostly in the background, deferring to the better-known Hewett and to the in-the-field Fewkes. Edgar Hewett's role was limited mostly to making suggestions, and he offered one practical one—to place the superintendent's headquarters at or near one of the main ruins, where it would also serve effectively to guard the park. This simple idea threw fear into Mancos, which coveted the prestige and profit that the headquarters in town would bring. The issue became a political football. Randolph endeared himself to Mancos residents by supporting their town, and he won out. Hewett also suggested, as did others, converting Cliff Palace into a museum to hold the materials excavated within the park.

For twenty years, the distinguished looking Jesse Fewkes, with his clipped white beard and broad forehead, had been working in the Southwest, Arizona in particular. Now in his sixties, the "grand old man" bounced from one bit of Mesa Verde research to another with unbridled enthusiasm. Somewhat of a romantic, he drove himself to make the "mystical red man known to the literate public." Fewkes continued to work during the summer at excavating ruins, clearing debris, and repairing ruins. He focused on Spruce Tree House in 1908 and on Cliff Palace in 1909. By the end of the second season, he could proudly report that Cliff Palace was in good enough condition to enable tourists and students "to learn much more about cliff dwellings than ever possible before the work was undertaken." He admitted with regret that most likely no other cliff dwelling in the Southwest had been more thoroughly looted for commercial purposes, with many of its relics now lost forever.[8] The *Mancos Times-Tribune*, September 3, 1909, pleased with his work, noted that the intention was not to restore the ruins to their original proportions but to "clean them out and repair them," so as to preserve them from further decay. The fact that Fewkes hired Mancos men to work on the project enhanced the paper's appreciation of him and his efforts.

Fewkes returned now and then to Mesa Verde through the early 1920s. His activities both closed and opened eras in southwestern archaeology. Fewkes's coming ended the early period of discovery and exploration of Mesa Verde, which had played such an important part in promoting scholarly and public interest in southwestern prehistory. The evolution from random pothunting, through commercial exploitation, to the awakening of scholarly interest had taken nearly two decades. Now, in a new century, the

*Jesse Fewkes
stands proudly
before Mesa
Verde's—and the
National Park
Service's—first
museum.*
Courtesy: Mesa Verde
National Park

final change had come. The serious twentieth-century scientific work can be dated from Fewkes's 1908 excavations and repairs. Fewkes was sharply (and fairly) criticized later for inadequate notes, inaccurate maps, and questionable stabilization and construction methods;[9] the criticism can be said to have launched that favorite professional sport of so many Mesa Verde archaeologists, attacking and discrediting one another. He did have the knack for attracting the public's attention. As early as May, 1908, he was presenting lectures to visitors about archaeology and the cliff dwellers. Those lectures evolved into the popular campfire talks of later years, which Fewkes also pioneered.

Superintendent Randolph devoted himself to more mundane matters, such as conducting a survey of roads and trails, present and future, and starting construction, when funds allowed. He devised budgets and asked for $32,400 in 1909, of which nearly half was for a projected wagon road. He also lobbied for government approval of a telephone line into the park from the Cortez-Mancos line. In 1907, he hired fifty-year-old Charles Kelly as the first permanent ranger, a logical choice since no one else knew more about the park. Kelly benefited further by being "a loyal Republican, and had the support of the people of this county—Montezuma." Outfitting for expeditions to the cliff dwellings had long been Kelly's specialty, but he quickly found out that working for the government was a different ball game. The next year, Washington would not allow him to put up tents to rent to visitors because he was a federal employee.[10] Temporary park rangers, almost exclusively from Mancos and Durango, were also hired during the summer to serve as guides.

The rangers proved to be a park asset; their presence cut vandalism dramatically.[11] Some progress had also been made toward alleviating the crucial water shortage. The little spring at Spruce Tree continued to be, as it had been since 1888, the single most important source of water, but its limited flow was soon overtaxed by the growing demand. To compensate, Randolph's crews constructed a dam in 1908 at the head of Spruce Tree Canyon to store water for pack and saddle animals and dug cisterns to catch and store water for tourists. Each of the next five years averaged 196 visitors per season, and the water reserves managed to hold out. Wells dug by erstwhile homesteaders along some of the trails furnished what little water was available for travelers going in and out.

Less success met efforts to improve and build roads into the park. Randolph correctly analyzed this problem as the key to unlocking the gates to a tourist rush. Handicapped by geographical isolation, Mesa Verde further discouraged twentieth-century tourists with the physical difficulties and discomforts of reaching it.

The editor of the Mancos paper fully understood these drawbacks and staunchly supported the superintendent's pleas for more funds. Over the years, Randolph slowly pushed a road up the mesa, routing it via the west side of Point Lookout and on toward the ruins. He was dismayed to find that repairs and maintenance steadily and greedily eroded his budget. He admitted in his 1910 report that the carriage road ended at the foot of the mesa; there a horseback trail joined it to a six-mile segment of carriage road on the mesa top, which had been inexpensively and easily constructed.[12] Most of the ruins were connected by horse roads, all of which Randolph promised to convert into carriage roads as soon as possible.

Over these roads traveled gradually increasing numbers of tourists. They did not come because of increased promotion, which was almost nonexistent. Only the Denver and Rio Grande Railroad and its Rio Grande Southern gave much marketing help; some was generated by articles in several national magazines. Mancos, Durango, and Cortez had no way to reach a larger market; the state promoted itself only generally, not its southwestern corner specifically.

Eva Anderson was one who made the effort to reach Mesa Verde. She was astounded when her guide started out from Mancos in a driving rainstorm. No worse for the experience, Eva reached Kelly's cabin, where conditions were much like they had been a decade before, even to digging for pottery in mesa-top ruins. She did not find much, a disappointment assuaged by the adventure of climbing the "greased pole" (an old tree trunk) and "the rope" to get into Balcony House. There

her party wandered about, "climbing over walls, crawling through narrow openings." On her way out, the guide cautioned to "hang on the rope," which Eva fearfully clutched: "I wouldn't let go of that rope for all the wealth of Standard Oil." Undeterred by that fearsome experience, she delighted in the rest of her fall tour of 1907.

That kind of grand adventure, Eva Anderson sensed, was swiftly disappearing. The guides discouraged relic searches as violations of government regulations. The promised new roads and an up-to-date hotel, in addition to the not "improbable ascent . . . [of the] touring car," made Eva glad that her visit had come "before all the romance was taken out of the trip."[13]

The next year, the most important government visitor yet to appear—Secretary of the Interior James R. Garfield —arrived at Mancos on a special Rio Grande Southern train. Accompanied by Randolph and Kelly, Garfield's party

A group of happy 1910 campers that includes the famous archaeologist Alfred Kidder (at right in the front row).
Courtesy: Museum of New Mexico

spent Colorado Day (August 1) in Mesa Verde, returning to Mancos the next day. The *Mancos Times-Tribune*, August 7, 1908, waxed eloquent over what Garfield's visit meant to future park development and to the community and its vicinity. The Secretary of the Interior, among his many duties, nominally administered the national parks and monuments, although each park was officially a separate unit unrelated to the others. This lack of central control handicapped the system, and it must have adversely affected Randolph's administration. Although he had made undeniable progress, he had been lax in many areas.

By the winter of 1910–11, rumors were swirling about Mancos and rippling beyond it regarding irregularities in the superintendent's office. Whispers about a drinking problem also circulated. Jesse Nusbaum, who had come to know Randolph when he worked on Balcony House the previous summer,

called Randolph an "out and out politician." Nusbaum later claimed that local hostility (unexplained) reached such a fever pitch that the superintendent carried a "revolver at all times." [14] The Mancos newspaper failed to provide much insight into these observations, but it did mention that the superintendent had suddenly changed park headquarters from the Bauer Bank Building to the as yet unfinished First National Building. This move lent credence to the rumor that Randolph was involved in Mancos banking rivalries. In a small community such as that one, Randolph was playing with fire when he tangled with local businessmen. The excessive drinking charge would not die, further damaging his reputation. Whatever the reasons, the next spring, Edward B. Linnen, "one of the oldest and shrewdest men in the U.S. Secret Service," arrived to investigate the goings-on.

Mancos was rife with rumors; residents began choosing sides, as Randolph went public with his defense. The superintendent offered to resign, but his offer was refused. In the end, he was suspended on vague charges of "general neglect of duty" and serving other interests during his incumbency. More specific charges involved the misappropriation of funds (probably referring to the accusations of "padding pay-rolls" by paying for work never performed) and the use of government money for private purposes. [15] Randolph was given time to prepare his defense, but to no avail; the hearing resulted in his dismissal in April, 1911.

C. B. Kelly, the local favorite to be the next superintendent, also resigned. His obvious conflict of interest resulted in Linnen's recommendation that Kelly either dispose of his stable or turn the business over to someone else. [16] The choice was not difficult—Kelly's stable and guide service promised a more profitable future than did a career as a park ranger (seventy-five dollars per month salary that summer).

So ended Mesa Verde's first era. The troubled closing scene should never overshadow the steady progress that had been made. Insufficient funding and inexperience handicapped Randolph. Nor had the federal government been as supportive as it should have been, hampered as it was by the lack of a specific agency to supervise the growing number of national parks. In a brief time span, Randolph had come face to face with nearly all the problems that would plague his successors—water shortages, stabilization of ruins, isolation, roads, promotion, and tight budgets (actually a theme of federal underfinancing and a lack of understanding on Washington's part). That this pioneering superintendent did not discover all the solutions is not surprising.

Early photographers faced many challenges at Mesa Verde. Lisle Updike is ready to take a photo of Balcony House.
Courtesy: Jackson Clark

"Mesa Verde Has Wonderful Possibilities"

An inventory of government property was required after the removal of Hans Randolph as superintendent. It provided an unexpected look at the physical side of the park. Aside from the expected signs, canteens, and the like, the inventory disclosed enough farm equipment to plow a homestead and enough household goods to equip a comfortable home. Stored at Morefield Canyon were the road grader, plow, scrapers, and other equipment to keep the roads and trails open and passable. Kelly's Livery in town housed a team of bay horses, a Studebaker mountain buckboard,

saddles, and harnesses. The Mancos office stored face towels and soap, two Underwood typewriters, a rolltop desk, and other office equipment, including maps of Colorado and of the United States. Balcony House and Cliff Palace also served as convenient storage space.

Three rangers welcomed visitors in 1911, providing them with guide service and any necessary assistance. The Department of the Interior questioned the need for two temporary rangers and for the team of horses; dispensing with these extras, it claimed, would reduce the strain on a tight budget. Attempts to control expenditures led to

lengthy correspondence and reminders that expense vouchers "be made out in duplicate."

Tightfisted Uncle Sam watchdogged both large and small items, including authorization for payment of up to twenty dollars for a suitable sign, Mesa Verde National Park, Superintendent's Office. Washington would not allow the purchase of two American flags until road construction bids came in, in order to determine whether the funds would be available. As 1911 drew to a close, Yellowstone Park's superintendent wrote to inquire if Mesa Verde would like some beavers in order to establish a colony.[1] The beavers were never given a chance, as Mesa Verde lacked adequate stream water for them. Instead of beavers, water shortages and tight finances characterized the rest of the decade at the park.

At the first national park conference —held at Yellowstone in September, 1911—Mesa Verde unexpectedly found itself the subject of criticism. Chief Geographer Robert Bradford Marshall of the U.S. Geological Survey, who called himself a "national park enthusiast," displayed little enthusiasm for Mesa Verde, which he had visited the past July.

There is nothing in this park to make it of national importance save the cliff dwellings. There is no opportunity for camping; the scenery is common to many Western States and needs no protection. The inaccessibility of the park, the long distance, and the miserable railroad accommodations make it, I think, out of the question to make this park popular to any degree in comparison with the other parks. . . . My recommendation would be to create a national monument of small acreage around the ruins—say each canyon containing the cliff houses and have the area around all the canyons converted into a national forest.[2]

Mesa Verde's Acting Superintendent Richard Wright simply and effectively answered Marshall: "To my mind the Mesa Verde Park has wonderful possibilities for development. If properly provided for and effectively administered, it should rank among the most important of the national reservations." He went on to praise its "quaint and mystic contents, its natural beauty, and its historical value."

The discussion between the two men told more about the opposing concepts of what national parks should be than anything substantial about Mesa Verde. The philosophical debate would stretch far beyond that time and place. In Marshall's opinion, the national parks should provide the scenery and the outdoor recreation to counterbalance the "rush and jam and scramble" of modern urban life. At Mesa Verde, intended to be a cultural, not a scenic, park, those attributes were of only secondary importance. Thus Mesa Verde, inherently different from the other parks, drew attention to some of the issues that had to be resolved. Both Marshall and Wright accurately pinpointed them. Marshall's ideas came to nothing, as the park fortunately still had friends who were not about to let that happen.

Various problems caught the attention of the superintendents during the following years, as the United States moved confidently through the second decade of the twentieth century. The continuous need to stabilize and repair the ruins, build roads, make reports, and live within the budget presented no new challenges. Pressure on the superintendent to appoint some favored individual to a park job remained relentless. Virginia McClurg, for example, tried unsuccessfully to have her son appointed a park ranger in 1912.

The dispute with the neighboring Utes over hunting rights continued to fester. Depending on one's point of view, hunting could be described as either poaching deer in the park or legally hunting them on the reservation. Superintendents and agents fired correspondence back and forth with little effect. They did manage to resolve another Ute issue; in 1911 the government and the tribe agreed on a land exchange that officially placed within

the park all the ruins contained in the amended five-mile zone in the 1906 act. This plan had been discussed off and on since 1907. In what amounted to almost a two-acres-for-one swap, the Utes received land elsewhere that bordered their reservation, most of it near Ute Mountain. The U.S. Geological Survey then ran one last survey; much to everyone's embarrassment, it revealed that Balcony House had been left out. The agreement had to be amended in 1913 to include the ruin.[3]

The Utes had held out against the land exchange in hopes of achieving a government settlement of a number of grievances. One Ute, Tawa, expressed the sentiment of many of his fellow tribal members when he angrily charged:

You want these houses so that the white men can come in and rob them. What does the government want [of] those old houses they will

do them no good. Let them alone. . . . Some people told me there was gold mines and coal mines and coal oil there. I guess that is why you want them. . . . They ought to treat us right and nice then it would be alright.[4]

The Ute Mountain Utes, as the neighboring group came to be known, harbored strong feelings about the transactions that led them to cede the land in the first place and then to accept the subsequent territorial adjustments. Their last hereditary chief, Jack House, pulled no punches when he was interviewed in 1967. The Utes objected to the taking of the land because, he charged, "the commissioner stole that land from the Ute. . . . They [Utes] wanted to keep it . . . because it was theirs, their own land, and they were living there."[5] Since that time, House complained, the federal government had moved and expanded the line, continually encroaching upon tribal lands.

The Ute issue faded quickly for everybody but the tribe. More critical to park operations was the aggravating shortage of funds. Thomas Rickner, appointed as Mesa Verde superintendent in 1913, complained to Congressman Edward Taylor during 1914, "As you are aware, we have put off and put off from year to year until the improvement of the park has become a joke and people here are skeptical about anything being done to make the Park what it should be."[6] Just starting a long and distinguished House career, Democrat Taylor would eventually exercise a great deal of power, but for the moment he could do very little; neither Colorado nor Mesa Verde wielded enough political clout to force open the federal coffers. This educator and lawyer from Glenwood Springs, whose congressional district included Mesa Verde, was fascinated by the park and, like John Shafroth, was an advocate of "good roads." Taylor wanted to unlock the Western Slope to the automobile.

Rickner, a genial Mancos Valley pioneer, rancher, Indian trader, and superintendent through most of the decade, had to make do with what he had. His appointment by the Wilson administration typified accepted policy at the time; he was a local Democratic wheelhorse, and park superintendencies were part of the political spoils system that attached to the winning party.[7] One of Rickner's first statements firmly put to rest any idea of moving the headquarters. He would keep it at Mancos, where he could be politically involved on the local scene. Mancos residents breathed a collective sigh of relief with that announcement. An acting superintendent and a short-term superintendent who had followed Randolph had recommended moving headquarters to Mesa Verde.

The number of visitors increased steadily until 1917–18, when wartime demands cut travel, and funding cuts completely stopped excavation. Rickner was forced to spend most of his time handling a host of tourist-related issues. His diligence resulted in a growing number of rules and regulations related to visitor conduct within the park. The guidelines of 1906 were steadily expanded to cover visitors and whatever they might bring with them to Mesa Verde.

Dogs came under the jurisdiction of park rules in 1913: Canines must not chase animals or birds or annoy "passersby." If brought into the park, dogs must be carried in wagons or leashed behind them while traveling; pets were not allowed to roam beyond camp limits. A dire warning accompanied the rules: Any dog who dared to "disregard these instructions" would be killed. The dogs' arch rivals, cats, received even shorter shrift—they were not allowed in the park at all!

Superintendent Thomas Rickner greets park guests at the eating house.

Courtesy: Mesa Verde National Park

Campers, too, had their instructions about timber cutting, fires, and camping. Warnings to all visitors dealt with such things as "disorderly conduct or bad behavior"; disturbing wild animals and birds; disposal of lighted matches, cigars, and cigarettes; gambling; and the posting or displaying of private notices or advertisements (they were prohibited). Fortunately, the penalties for humans who disobeyed ordinances were less final than those for dogs.[8] To enforce all the regulations and carry out his myriad duties, the superintendent received a salary of fifteen hundred dollars in 1913 and had to provide his own residence and one horse.

Two factors were critical to visitors' fuller enjoyment of the Mesa Verde experience: The ordeal of getting there had to be eased and the attractions in the park enhanced. Superintendents and park personnel, well aware of both needs, worked diligently for the next generation to improve roads, park interpretation, and visitor accommodations, with varied success.

Americans' love affair with the automobile by now had come to full bloom, thanks to Henry Ford's low-priced Model T, and transportation took on new meaning. The need for good roads for cars constituted a two-part problem for Mesa Verde—the roads outside the park as well as those within it. The superintendent's direct responsibility began at the entrance and extended from there throughout the park. Who was to build the roads to bring the tourist to the park entrance? Was it the responsibility of the federal government, the state, or the county? The superintendent's pleas were frustrated by the inexperience, the procrastination, and the bureaucracy that crippled road-building projects outside the park.

The first breakthrough for Mesa Verde came in 1913. After years of road construction, flag-bedecked wagons rolled all the way from Mancos to Spruce Tree House. The triumph of horse and wagon lasted only a year; in June, 1914, the road was ready for cars (some had actually made it through before then despite the road). And none too soon for some locals, who had complained to Congressman Edward Taylor earlier that they could not drive their autos into the park. Liverymen had the proverbial snowball's chance in hell to stem progress, but fearing that the improvements threatened them with a loss of business, they had also complained to their congressman. Taylor, caught in the middle, replied politely to each group. At this juncture, when optimists were already forecasting that before long more people would be coming by car than by train, the question of the feeder routes to the park became all the more critical.

The state was no more ready than the counties for the job that faced them. Not until 1889 had the state

Not until 1913 were the roads good enough to permit this first wagon, appropriately flag bedecked, to come into the park.

Courtesy: Mesa Verde National Park

legislature begun to designate state roads and appropriate money for them. La Plata and Montezuma counties were poor country cousins that attracted little of that money. It was twenty more years before Colorado got around to appointing a highway commission following lobbying by the Colorado Good Roads Association. Of the towns near Mesa Verde, Durango had the most to gain from any appropriations, since two designated state roads passed through there, one an east-west route, the other a north-south. Gravel-surfaced, they were sometimes hard to distinguish from the intersecting county lanes that disappeared into the rural hinterlands.

No matter on what type of road, the Colorado traveler had to traverse the mountains to reach Mesa Verde. Thus, accessibility was limited to non-winter months for many years to come. East of Durango, no direct route gave access to southwest Colorado until

The coming of the first automobiles on May 28, 1914, heralded a new era—including new problems—for the park.
Courtesy: Mesa Verde National Park

1916, when the single-lane road over Wolf Creek Pass (over the Continental Divide) was finally opened. At its dedication, State Highway Commissioner Thomas Ehrhart waxed eloquent when he described the road all the way from Julesburg, Colorado (near the Colorado-Nebraska border), to Durango: "I doubt if there is another highway on the earth's surface so replete with scenic grandeur and climatic variance as this great diagonal road."[9]

Some drivers never saw the wonders the Wolf Creek Pass road offered; panic-stricken, they stared straight ahead at the narrow road, wondering what they had done to deserve such a fate. So-called flatlanders had gained a new appreciation of mountain driving by the time they reached Wolf Creek Pass. Drivers had to look ahead to judge the distance between oncoming cars and the next turnout. If either driver failed to anticipate correctly, the driver of the descending car had to be prepared to back up to the narrow pockets. Although Durangoans hailed this breakthrough that ended their isolation, frightened tourists sighed with relief when the ride ended and wondered if there were a better way out. Wolf Creek Pass seemed to have been born with a treacherous reputation. Superintendent Rickner complained in October, 1919, that more visitors would come if there were some other way into and out of this section, "without going over that high pass where snows have already blocked the road."[10]

The state did not have the financial resources to meet all the cries for better roads; money flowed to political power and population, leaving underpopulated and politically impotent southwestern Colorado very much out in the cold. With or without Mesa Verde, not much help would be forthcoming.

As a result, local newspapers found a new crusade. With the car chugging down Main Street and over dusty country lanes, scaring Dobbin and Spot in the process, "good roads" seemed to be the panacea for everything. One editor ranked them right behind the church and the school in "upbuilding" man, woman, and civilization! Durango launched the crusade in the *Weekly Herald*, July 24, 1913, announcing that "Durango will be the pivotal point" from which potential roads would radiate in all directions. Such enthusiasm far outran available resources to turn that dream into surveys and gravel.

By the time the boys sailed "over there" in 1917, Mancos had caught the highway fever and envisioned itself as the hub. The local newspaper editor recommended joining the National Old Trails Association, one of many groups popular at the time that generally promoted a highway from a starting point to almost anywhere. Joining would bring needed promotion and place Mancos on every road map issued by

Beers' auto "stage" line. One of these cars lost its brakes and took a wild drive down the Point Lookout grade, coming to a stop several miles out in the valley.

Courtesy: Mesa Verde National Park

the association, in this case along a route from Washington, D.C., to Los Angeles. A year later, organizers of the Santa Fe Trail Association came to town to enlist members for the great "trans-continental highway" coming out of Kansas City. Remembering their history, a local group organized the Spanish Trails Association, which eventually stretched from eastern Colorado to Mesa Verde. They did succeed in naming the east-west highway into Durango and Mancos the Spanish Trail. Boosters attended conventions, praised good roads, exchanged ideas, and waited for the millennium.[11] It did not dawn.

Durango and La Plata County gained a step on their rivals, Mancos and Montezuma, by more actively promoting themselves; they also had a broader-based economy and a stronger tax base. Colorado, in fact, in 1918 named La Plata County as one of the leaders in "construction of good roads." Few travelers would have concurred in that assessment after bumping over dusty dirt and gravel roads, which sometimes seemed more like well-rutted Spanish trails than highways. As the 1920s neared, adventuresome tourists came by car; comfort and convenience still rode with the train.

But the people did come, by whatever means, arriving at park headquarters in Mancos and inquiring about the route to Mesa Verde. At this point, visitors could elect to go into the park with one of Kelly's tours, or they could travel on their own. Regardless, they were in for a thrill, as the 1915 Mesa Verde pamphlet frankly warned:

The trip over the Government road should be taken only by parties who are experienced in the handling and controlling of horses and should not be attempted in seasons when rainfall in quantity occurs. The road is very narrow in places and makes sharp turns. . . . The road is frequently weakened by washes which render passage in some places very dangerous. All strangers traversing this route should be accompanied by an experienced guide.

Rickner, well aware of the problem, had told the Mancos Commercial Club back in January, 1914, that the one need that overshadowed all others was "the completion of an adequate highway into the Park."[12] Recognition did not produce a remedy during this decade. Travelers continued to undertake the thrilling trip to the mesa top over steep dirt roads.

The future arrived with the first automobile caravan to enter Mesa Verde, a year after the wagons had done so. Those Studebakers, Hupmobiles, Reos, and Fords took an unrecorded length of time, which encompassed numerous stops for pic-

Cortez wanted to have a greater role in Mesa Verde's development, but that destiny was years away in this photo, c. 1910–12.
Courtesy: William Winkler

*By the turn of the
century, smoke
from Durango's
smelter hovered
over the town,
which hoped
to become the
region's tourist
center.*

Courtesy: Durango
Herald

tures, to reach Spruce Tree camp on May 28, 1914. They raced out in only three hours. Most important, all this activity took place in one day! The trip was made in relative ease and comfort and with unprecedented speed.

As fast as they went (twenty miles per hour or better under the right conditions), the cars moved more slowly than did the implementation of government rules to regulate them. Only two weeks before that first trip, a single-trip fee of one dollar and a five-dollar season pass had already been set, along with a six-miles-per-hour speed limit for the ascent and a maximum of fifteen for the straight stretches on top. The horse retained the right of way, and drivers were required to honk their horns at every bend of the road. If a team of horses approached, motor vehicles (these rules also applied to cycles) had to take the outer edge of the roadway, regardless of the direction in which they were moving, and turn

off their engines.[13] Old Dobbin would reign as king for a short time longer.

With the car came careless drivers and inevitable accidents; the first fatality occurred in September, 1917. Even with their problems, the noisy, underpowered cars heralded a new day for the park. In 1916, the number of visitors more than doubled, to 1,385, and the next year the figure topped 2,200. Those numbers, for just two years, included over half of all the people who had visited Mesa Verde since it opened. Rickner pointed out the obvious: In 1916, 364 automobiles had traveled into the park, 180 more than in the previous season.[14] The opening of Wolf Creek Pass, despite its fearsome reputation, had provided the necessary access from the populated east slope and beyond.

A park survey in 1918 indicated where Mesa Verde's 371 auto-driving tourists had come from. Seventy-six percent were from Colorado; another

10 percent drove from the three neighboring states of Utah, New Mexico, and Arizona. Of all the remaining states, only Kansas had more than ten cars in the park. Road conditions and car limitations pretty much prohibited travelers' coming from great distances.

The car's impact on national parks proved immediate, from creating demands for more road repair to the greater need for a telephone line. By the end of World War I, automobile travel superseded all other forms, not just in Mesa Verde but throughout all the parks. Change was inevitable. The day visit came into vogue, there were more campers (the 1919 report of the National Park Service stated that over half of the motorists carried camping equipment), and smaller numbers of tourists came by rail.[15] With the completion of the telephone line from Mancos to Spruce Tree camp in 1915, Rickner could proudly boast that a tourist no longer had to travel beyond

Today's drivers cannot appreciate the good old days! The Kelly-French "Stage" is shown mired in a mud hole in Morefield Canyon.

Courtesy: Mesa Verde National Park

the reach of the long-distance telephone. Of more immediate practical service were the five call boxes along the road, which allowed immediate access to help and information.

To meet new demands, improvements had to be made in the park. In 1911, Washington had approved the employment of a temporary ranger whose wife would be hired as a cook for guests. She was authorized to charge seventy-five cents per meal. This innovation evolved into the granting of concessionaire privileges in 1913. C. B. Kelly quickly secured the transportation concession, which by 1915 included "auto livery" at a cost of twenty-five dollars for two passengers (five dollars for each additional person) for a one-day trip.

Oddie Jeep, Superintendent Rickner's daughter and the wife of ranger Fred Jeep, had the campground concession and operated the campground from 1914 until 1929. Steady improvements soon eradicated traces of Kelly's primitive cabins and tents. The permanent camp across the canyon from Spruce Tree House was enlarged, and electric lights were installed; the park supplied its own power plant. A public campground was added later.

Another addition was a museum. An old log cabin, at one time a ranger station, served to house the artifacts and exhibits that were being collected. As far back as 1908, superintendents had encouraged the plan for a museum, because "it has been a matter of wonder to tourists, and a disappointment to them, that there was no collection for that place."[16] In the spring of 1918, with new wall and floor cases and twelve framed enlargements of photographs of Mesa Verde scenes and ruins in place, the museum opened, the first one in a national park.

The honor was a logical one—more than any of the other parks, Mesa Verde needed interpretation to facilitate understanding and appreciation of its uniqueness. The scenic attractions that predominated in Yellowstone and Yosemite national parks could be appreciated without much explanation, but to savor the substance of Mesa Verde, one had to know something about the Anasazi and their world. Interpretive campfire programs gained instant popularity, and no one performed better than Jesse Fewkes, when he told the story of the cliff dwellers. Even the grand old man of Mesa Verde was taken aback, however, when a young woman asked in all seriousness, "Why in the world did the Cliff Dwellers build their homes so far from the railroads?" This inquiry has evolved over the years into one of the classic examples of a "tourist question."

One of the changes the average visitor was not likely to notice (nor fully appreciate if he or she did) was the creation of the National Park Service in 1916. Up to that time, each of the

Among Jesse Fewkes's contributions were the popular campfire talks. He sits fifth from the left in this 1915 group.

Courtesy: Mesa Verde National Park

Jesse Fewkes conducted the excavation of Far View House in 1916. He also took this photo.
Courtesy: Mesa Verde National Park

twelve national parks had still operated as a separate unit under the Secretary of the Interior, an obviously inefficient, unwieldy system without central control and coordination. Pressure had been building for years within Congress and without to create a national parks office or bureau. The National Parks Act was finally passed and signed by President Woodrow Wilson.[17] Mesa Verde had at last found a home in government, for better or for worse.

There would be no immediate relief from some of the pressing problems. It would take a while for the National Park Service and its director, Stephen Mather—an amazingly energetic and successful miner/businessman, who loved the outdoors and the park concept—to organize and operate. All of the national parks, in varying degrees, shared Mesa Verde's problems and the need for improved park facilities and park management, better promotion, and a better-trained ranger staff.

Mather and his coworkers had a major job before them.

When inspector John Hill visited Mesa Verde in September, 1917, he was unimpressed with Oddie Jeep's operation: "The camp outfit is very crude. . . . The grounds of the camp are littered with logs, brush, road making tools, etc." Assistant Park Service Director Horace Albright also toured Mesa Verde that September and made some recommendations to Mrs. Jeep that shed light on what the service expected of its concessionaires. The tent furnishings, which then included a bed, a dresser, a straight chair, a wash bowl, and pitchers, needed to be supplemented with a rocking chair, a slop jar, a large rug, and a kerosene lamp. If these were added, Mrs. Jeep would be allowed to increase rates to four dollars per day. "I want you to know that I feel a deep personal interest in the success of your enterprise, as I fully appreciate the amount of thought and energy that

you have put into your park business," Albright tactfully wrote in May, 1918. Everything apparently worked out to his satisfaction, because Park Service inspectors, the next August, glowingly praised the Spruce Tree camp, including the meals: "Meals served at this camp are worthy of special mention. The idea of the general quality of service may be gained from the fact that fresh cream was served with the fruit and cereals. Fresh fruit was served as well." [18]

The quiet evolution of the concessionaire policy in Mesa Verde and the selection of individuals to provide services stand in marked contrast to some other national parks. Yellowstone and Yosemite had a long history of concession troubles that ranged from dishonest, unscrupulous concessionaires to the establishment of saloons and the fencing of park lands. Mesa Verde National Park may have profited from their experiences; more likely, its isolation and its seemingly limited potential subdued interest in it for all but a handful of locals who were willing to work within the economic constraints. For years, the theory that competition would keep prices down and the quality of services up had brought a swarm of concessionaires to Yellowstone and Yosemite. Few made much money. Through sheer luck or business acumen, Mesa Verde avoided this particular headache. Director Mather did not, however, escape concession controversies. They engaged his attention from the first and continued to nettle the National Park Service.[19]

Meanwhile, the rangers inspected ruins, enforced rules, and provided service, information, and help for visitors. Saddle horses were available for those who wanted to ride to the ruins in that fashion. Some enterprising children of park employees offered guide service, for a small fee, to those who wished to tour the sites by car.

Archaeologist Jesse Nusbaum was not happy with their efforts: "The interpretive story these kids (5 to 12 or 13 years of age) told the visitors was out of this world." He also accused Jeep and Rickner of purposely omitting signs from roads and trails in order to force visitors to hire guides, most of whom were their children or their relatives.

These accusations would later come back to haunt Rickner, but for the moment he had other things besides visitors to worry about. One was the question of private holdings within park boundaries. This was a minor issue at Mesa Verde, as the amount in question was only about 400 acres of patented land. Over the years it was gradually reduced. Another problem for the superintendent was the question of private development of Mesa Verde's natural resources: grazing and coal mining. This caused more concern. As the Wetherills had demonstrated,

the canyons and the mesa had long been used for open range. This practice continued unrestricted during the first years of the park; then, in 1910, the Secretary of the Interior established a permit system based upon a fee per head of cattle. None of the leases allowed grazing on or by the ruins, nor did they prohibit "free or convenient access" by the public. Washington's position was that "unless you know of some good reason to the contrary, permits will not be granted for grazing of sheep on lands within the park." Nevertheless, sheep did graze in Waters Canyon in 1911 under provisions of an earlier lease. The superintendent informed the secretary that the owner moved them every three days to prevent sod from being destroyed or damaged. The sheepman persisted, however, in overstocking his leased ground and soon found his permit suspended, thus ending that phase of grazing.

In the years following, it was exclusively cattle that munched on park grass; during the peak year of 1918, the over two thousand head nearly equaled the number of visitors. War-time patriotic fervor had put increased demands on all national parks to allow more grazing, timber cutting, and even the slaughtering of buffalo and elk in Yellowstone to provide meat for the "boys." Mesa Verde complied, though it was not pressured as much as some other parks.

Superintendent Rickner retained his popularity with the local ranchers because of his generous granting of permits; however, he was not blind to the benefits for the park—extra help in maintaining order and additional fire watches. Protests against political favoritism and overgrazing (Nusbaum as early as 1907 had observed the effects of uncontrolled grazing) sur-faced by the end of the decade, along with questions about whether this was the proper use for a national park.

Rickner persisted in his practices. He managed to find a tourist attraction in the fact that cattle bunched near water places: "More photographs have been attempted of cattle seen along the drive than almost any other feature of the park." [20]

Coal mining in Mesa Verde was another issue. It had long been known that coal existed in the region, and in the period from 1906 to 1910 pressure was brought to bear by the Colorado congressional delegation to permit mining within the park. The argument ran that isolated Montezuma County residents needed the mines in order to lower the price of coal, which other-wise had to be shipped in, first by train and then by wagon. To make the idea more palatable to conservationists, who were a vocal group on the national scene at the time, it was suggested that royalties be used for park improve-ment. Several congressional attempts to allow mining failed, including one

that was vetoed by President William Howard Taft on the grounds that the bill would impede park management. Not until 1910 was the Secretary of the Interior authorized to grant leases and permits for the use of land and park resources. Action was delayed to allow a mineral survey to determine exactly what the park contained. As early as 1907, Hans Randolph had undertaken an inspection tour with that very pur-pose in mind.

Several leases were ultimately issued; George Todd, the most active miner, had been one of those who forced the mining issue. Todd had opened a mine on Ute land barely west of the park, actually operating on a small scale before the park was established; eventually, he dug under the boundary. Along with other lessees, Todd paid a ten-cent-per-ton royalty; he found the mine to be of limited potential: "I am having to figure awful close to make the proposition pay its way." He also complained of arduous mining conditions, a poor grade of bituminous coal, and a limited market. Fortunately, his operations never became large (for instance, production was 661 tons in 1912 and 474 tons in 1915) and inflicted only minimal environmental damage that was far from the visited ruins. Coal mining intensified the conflict about the basic purpose of parks; no solution came forth in the 1910s.[21]

Publicity for Mesa Verde increased during that decade, a reflection of Americans' growing interest in parks. Newspapers and magazines carried feature stories about the cliff dwellings and encouraged visitation. An article on Mesa Verde in the Marfa, Texas, *New Era* in 1916 explained the government's philosophy: "Uncle Sam wants the people of the United States to use their national parks and become acquainted with their splendors. Why have great national playgrounds unless the people play in them."

Horace Albright's 1917 visit gave the park a publicity shot that came all too rarely. Newspapers picked up his remarks that Mesa Verde was "in the front rank of the world's most magnificent scenic wonders." He went on to say that "it has a distinction all its own," and he predicted no limit to the numbers of visitors in future years.[22] The park would now receive, the Denver press hoped, the government attention it had long deserved.

The Denver & Rio Grande expanded its promotion efforts, even as the automobile doomed the railroad's tourist future. Its leaders wholeheartedly agreed with the statement by Great Northern president Louis Hill at the 1911 National Park Conference: "Every passenger that goes to the national parks, wherever he may be, represents practically a net earning."[23]

Before the train became a fleeting memory, Willa Cather, just entering the peak years of her illustrious career as a novelist, penned this poignant account of a 1915 train ride from Denver to Mancos:

You leave Denver in the evening, over the Denver & Rio Grande. From the time when your train crawls out of La Veta pass at about 4 in the morning, until you reach Durango at nightfall, there is not a dull moment. All day you are among high mountains, swinging back and forth between Colorado and New Mexico, with the Sangre de Cristo and the Culebra ranges always in sight until you cross the continental divide at Cumbres and begin the wild scurry down the westward slope.

That particular branch of the Denver & Rio Grande is called the Whip-lash, and most of the way you can signal to the engineers from the rear car. You stay all night at Durango. In the morning you take another train

Willa Cather thoroughly enjoyed her visit to the park.
Courtesy: Helen Cather Southwick

for Mancos; a friendly train with invariably friendly passengers and a conductor who has been on that run for fourteen years and who can give you all sorts of helpful information.

Within a generation, railroad tourism would be gone, as would Cather's beloved world of Mancos; Cather stayed there six days, instead of the one she intended. She was exhilarated by the ride, the town, and its people.

The streets are lined with trees, the yards are a riot of giant sage and Indian paint brush, shaded with cedars; the wheat fields are veritable cloth of gold and the whole town is buried in sweet clover. . . . Not once while I was in Mancos, indoors or out, was there a moment when I could not smell the sweet clover.[24]

And although the Model T, the "war to end all wars," and the "roaring twenties" bespoke the end of this era, which faded ever so quietly into a gentle afterglow of nostalgia, the national park that so impressed Cather would go on to a prosperous future. The Department of the Interior began to publish pamphlets, giving the tourists all the information they could possibly want. To meet the changing times, it also published eagerly sought after automobile maps.

In 1915, Mesa Verde acquired a companion national park in Colorado. After more than a decade of discussions and five years of intensive lobbying, Rocky Mountain National Park came into being. Attempts to preserve this mountainous wonderland had faced less opposition than that encountered by Virginia McClurg and her backers. After local obstacles had been overcome, the biggest one arose in the form of the U.S. Forest Service, which resisted the surrender of its control over the region. Park advocates decried what they saw as a lack of protection given to nature and the granting of too-lenient rights by the Forest Service for grazing, mining, and timber cutting. The park proponents finally prevailed, and President Woodrow Wilson signed the park bill into law on January 26.[25]

Mesa Verde's impact on the establishment of Rocky Mountain National Park appears to have been minimal at most. Although this has not been clearly established, the supporters of Rocky Mountain may have learned something of determination, lobbying, and other persuasive methods from the women of Mesa Verde. Rocky Mountain's backers, in support of their cause, could point to the economic impact of tourism locally on La Plata and Montezuma counties, but Yellowstone, older and more popular, provided a much better example of that. And in fact, before 1915 many times more people had already visited Estes Park and hiked the surrounding mountains that would be included in Rocky Mountain National Park than had ever braved the canyons of Mesa Verde.

The obvious ties that connected the two Colorado parks came from politicians. Congressman Edward Taylor, as early as 1910, had prepared a park bill and had skillfully presented the case for Rocky Mountain National Park in the years that followed, besides guiding the final bill through the House. Former representative and governor John Shafroth testified on behalf of the bill.

Mesa Verde was both hindered and helped by the creation of Rocky Mountain National Park in 1915. The father of that project, Enos Mills, boosted both parks and wrote Rickner after a visit to Mesa Verde: "I have commended your work highly to the 'powers that be.' I gave both the Associated Press and the *Denver Post* an interview which will call attention to this park."[26] Colorado had now doubled its national park attractions, but Mesa

Verde's isolation and the difficulty of travel quickly put it behind its younger rival in popularity and in visitor totals. Travelers tended to head for well-known Denver first; the beautiful drive from there to Estes Park and thence to Rocky Mountain National Park could be accomplished in less than a day. Mesa Verde could not compete with convenience.

Coloradans exuded pride in 1917 when the young Rocky Mountain National Park enticed more visitors than any other national park. With Mesa Verde and Rocky Mountain national parks and Wheeler and Colorado national monuments, Colorado had become the "center of the tourist industry in the United States," crowed the *Rocky Mountain News*. The same article analyzed why the older of the two parks trailed the newcomer so badly. It was perplexing, the writer stated, that Mesa Verde had acquired a reputation for not being easily accessible, with no satisfactory visitor accommodations and with an unattractive location in mountain-desert country. "Only ruins" were there to entice the traveler. How such a "completely mistaken impression" could "seize the mind of man," he did not know.[27]

Movies came to play a significant role in attracting tourists to Mesa Verde. This new wonder, which rivaled the car in popularity, held great potential for publicity, an advantage the Department of Interior quickly recognized. But the new phenomenon brought problems with it. The department finally advised Rickner in December, 1915, that motion picture permits had to come from Washington. Some unspecified complication precipitated the correspondence: "This whole moving picture business last summer lacked definite organization, and I am now trying to straighten out the tangle."[28]

A later filming took place in early September, 1917, when Virginia McClurg and her Cliff Dwellings Association raised their last hurrah with a pageant, "The Marriage of the Dawn and the Moon." McClurg wrote, costumed, and directed the play, which was based on an old Hopi legend. Once again, she held center stage. Set in Spruce Tree House, with most of the cast from Mancos, the entire performance was filmed to be "shown in thousands" of theaters all over the country. Following the most "pretentious pageant" ever undertaken in Colorado, the guests sat down to a banquet of roast calf, roast sheep, baked ears of maize, and trays of peaches. Virginia's idea was to reproduce the Indian "staples" of the region.[29] Whether the movie actually proved to be a great advertisement for Mesa Verde, as hoped, has been lost to history. One of the movie "directors" remarked that, with a "little more time devoted to practice," the pageant would make a great success. Wartime

Virginia Mc-Clurg's "The Marriage of the Dawn and the Moon," the first of Mesa Verde's pageants.
Courtesy: Colorado Historical Society

limitations and changing public attitudes, however, doomed "Marriage" to the dustbin of history.

When the 1920s opened, Mesa Verde was entering a new era. Gone, along with McClurg and her Association, were the Wetherills and the days of horses and wagons. Ahead lay the domain of the automobile, the tourist, the flapper, and postwar America. Specifically for Mesa Verde, this era meant its evolution into a professionally operated park and the emergence of Jesse Nusbaum as the man who dominated its development and shaped it in his image more than any other individual.

The Nusbaum Years

Jesse Nusbaum became superintendent of Mesa Verde National Park on May 21, 1921. Although Nusbaum's appointment attracted little attention from Americans caught up in what would be known as the roaring twenties, his presence dominated the next phase of the park's history. The lanky thirty-two-year-old Nusbaum, the first trained archaeologist to attain the office of superintendent, had worked at Mesa Verde as early as 1907. He and another promising young archaeologist, Alfred V. Kidder, had come with Jesse Fewkes to survey and to photograph ruins. And Nusbaum was the one who completed the Balcony House work for Virginia McClurg.

Interested in archaeology since his boyhood in Greeley, Colorado (where he spent hours poring over Nordenskiold's text and photographs), Nusbaum had gained wide experience from digging in Central America and the Southwest. In the years to come one of his major accomplishments would be the upgrading of archaeological research, when he could find the time to devote to it. Those precious hours would become available only in the winter, when snow closed the park roads.[1]

By 1921, at the time of his appointment, Nusbaum had acquired a variety of experiences upon which to draw, and he needed them all. Once again, the administration of Mesa Verde had foundered on the rocks of incompetence: Thomas Rickner's superintendency had collapsed under charges of nepotism, cronyism, and partisan politics. One visitor even accused Mancos and Cortez people of entering the park without reporting themselves and of flouting the rules and regulations. Sunday seemed to be a day devoted to revelry. Someone else criticized the lack of protection for the ruins and the inadequate visitors' services and facilities.

Jesse Nusbaum inherited a peck of troubles, which he described succinctly as an "unholy mess." The removal of Rickner did not put everything to rights. Chief ranger Fred Jeep, Rick ner's son-in-law, lingered on, continuing his practice of illegally excavating park ruins ("pot hunting," Nusbaum disparagingly called it). His wife, Oddie, ran the concessions, and most of the other jobs were held by relatives of the Rickners and the Jeeps. To make matters worse, the highlights of Nusbaum's telephone calls rapidly surfaced on the streets of Mancos. He soon found out why—Rickner's daughter was the operator. Nusbaum immediately requested a replacement for her.[2]

In a letter to a friend, dated June, 1922, Nusbaum revealed his trying situation. Jeep, he observed, was a sick man, having fallen victim to a large overdose of wood alcohol (bootleggers operated everywhere, flagrantly defying the law of prohibition). Jeep's son wreaked his share of havoc, too, including scribbling over the park register, throwing ashes across the recently scrubbed museum floor, and

"raising hell in general." Several of Jeep's friends, whom Nusbaum refused to rehire, spent the winter in Mancos recounting how the superintendent had cheated them out of their pay. Nusbaum had had enough. He fired Jeep in 1922, citing a variety of reasons. Nusbaum admitted that he never again "would accept an appointment where a family had intermingled interests." He rose to the challenge: "We are here to win out, put this park in the best shape possible and make every visitor a continual booster for it."[3]

All of Nusbaum's considerable skills would be required to achieve the "best shape possible" in the park's administration; there would be no time for archaeology for the moment. Nusbaum had seen signs of what he would be in for during a disconcerting grilling in Washington by Colorado's senior senator, Republican Lawrence Phipps. At one time a partner of Andrew Carnegie, Phipps had come to Denver in

1901. Already a millionaire, he came not to make money, "but to invest in health and happiness . . . to hunt and to fish." This conservative businessman seemed much more concerned about Nusbaum's politics than about his qualifications.[4] Phipps begrudgingly concurred in the appointment, but Nusbaum would hear from him again.

Willing to rush in where angels feared to tread, Nusbaum quickly announced that park headquarters would be moved to Spruce Tree camp, where he would also build the superintendent's home. Mancos rose up in righteous anger; letters were dispatched to Phipps, and Nusbaum soon received a call from the irate senator. In no uncertain terms, the senator admonished him to return promptly to Mancos, "It's your responsibility to run the park and attend to Republican lines in that region and let the ranger run the Park." Risking his job, Jesse replied that he had pledged to administer the park in the public interest and that he planned to devote his full time to that responsibility.[5] Nusbaum prevailed, and the headquarters stayed in Mesa Verde.

The first project, the superintendent's home, was designed and built by Nusbaum, who based it on Hopi architecture. He also made the furniture along the simple lines of New Mexico's earliest Spanish colonial style. The Nusbaums lived first in a tent, then in a ranger's cottage. Finally, in mid-March, 1922, they moved into their uncompleted new home. They, and one other employee, were the first people to winter in the park, their only links to the outside world being a forty-mile pack trail and the slender telephone wire.

"We observed Christmas [1921] in great style, having sent in a pack outfit to Mancos several days before for packages that had arrived, Christmas supplies, mail, etc." A decorated tree, a turkey dinner, and wreaths made of red cedar branches with purple berries added to the festivities of the only day Nusbaum took off all month. Work on the house claimed all of his time. During brief spare moments, the family managed to squeeze in skating on the reservoir and sledding. One of the heaviest snow seasons in years locked the Nusbaums in the park.[6]

The house was a triumph. When curious tourists clamored to see it inside and out, the Nusbaums bowed to their wishes and opened it for public tours. Overly aggressive individuals inevitably strained their hospitality beyond tolerable limits; in 1925, Park Service Director Stephen Mather, at Nusbaum's urging, ended the open-door policy: "A man's home is his castle and the superintendents of our parks and their families are entitled to, and should have, that privacy in their own homes that any other citizen is entitled to."[7] Surviving the flap over moving the headquarters and

Visiting Cliff Palace was more of an adventure in the "olden days."
Courtesy: Mesa Verde National Park

completing his home freed Nusbaum to put his stamp on the administration and development of the park.

Grazing, after first being reduced, came to an end in 1927, over the strong objections of local cattlemen. Its demise was long overdue because of the damage it caused. Nusbaum described it this way: "The cattle were eating the place up, trampling down shrubbery, browsing, trailing over muddy roads, jumping up the banks of road slopes, tearing them down, and rolling rocks into the road in the process." Jesse had been warned that tampering with grazing permits "was extremely hazardous, very much like professional suicide," but he was not deterred. "We are not in the cattle business," Nusbaum announced emphatically. Angered locals had suffered another blow to the long-established practice of favoritism. Rickner had actually allowed his friends and in-laws to graze their cattle without paying a fee.[8] The recipients of his favors quite naturally preferred a less professional, more political superintendent.

Coal mining also drew to a close, but with less emotion. This time Nusbaum's job was smoothed by the meagerness of the deposits (only one lessee attempted to operate in the early 1920s, but without success) and the fact that improved roads and trucking made transporting coal to Cortez easier and cheaper. The superintendent discovered that the coal actually came from the adjoining Ute lands, and he shifted whatever royalties accrued to them. In a small way, the question of coal mining at Mesa Verde helped to force a resolution of the larger issue of mining in the parks. By a 1920 act, Congress had ended the activities of prospectors and miners in the national parks; in 1931, a bill specifically prohibited mining in Mesa Verde. Over the years since, mining interests have exerted pressure to open park lands.[9] Mesa Verde, however, has not been one of their targeted areas—its mineral potential is too limited to generate much interest.

Nusbaum was also faced with the ongoing water problems. Increased visitation had once more put pressure on the supply; stop-gap measures, consisting of a gas engine and a pump, combined with a water tower near the lodge, allowed the park to accommodate needs into the 1920s. But the vexing impediment to park prosperity would not go away, and again it threatened to inhibit the visitors' enjoyment and limit the campers' stay. The direct relationship between water supply and visitation remained grimly evident.

Moving forcefully in the face of the usual shortages of funds, the superintendent installed a new pumping plant, constructed dams to impound spring runoff, and built large tanks and an underground cistern for storage. One of the more interesting innovations came with an acre-sized catchment, covered with galvanized sheet metal, which was connected to tanks to catch, filter, and store rain water.[10] In desperation, a second catchment unit was built, but visitors' demands still exceeded the water supply. By 1930, the forecast of acute water shortages forced the planning process to begin all over again. Some people began to understand why the Anasazi had left!

Resolving the grazing and mining issues out of the three most pressing problems, and staying nearly even with the third, would have satisfied most men, but Nusbaum had only begun. He rapidly moved on to improving the park experience for the visitors. No more youngsters gave tours; regularly scheduled morning and afternoon auto caravan trips to the ruins, conducted by rangers, took their place. No more people scampered over the ruins and picked up shards at will, if the super-intendent could prevent it. Signs were posted to instruct visitors, and evening campfire talks enlightened them on the park's attractions and its history.

Upgrading the professionalism of the rangers became one of the superintendent's first priorities. Although the program was designed to please the public, it elicited at least one complaint from a contrary tourist, who said that a ranger "used too big words." Nusbaum investigated and ascertained that the ranger had been "conscientiously" carrying out his duty; it was recommended that he simply refrain from using "unusual and obscure words."

When the 1927 season arrived, the park was open from May 15 to November 1. Car trips were scheduled for 8:00 A.M. and 1:15 P.M. sharp, with no deviations in time allowed. Shorter trips, at 10:00 A.M. and at 3:30 P.M., accommodated latecomers. The daily fee of one dollar allowed tourists to come in as early as 5:00 A.M., and they could now drive faster, as the speed limit had been increased to twelve miles per hour on the hills and twenty-five miles per hour on the open stretches. Wagon teams still retained the right of way, but cars no longer had to stop as long as they passed the horses at less than eight miles per hour. That restriction held little significance —horses had become rarer than automobiles had been before the war.

Free public campgrounds lured the campers away from Mrs. Jeep, and for the first time, they were well marked and easily found. Campers, admonished to "leave your camp site clean when you leave the park," did not always obey, forcing park employees to clean up after them. Everyone was warned to conserve water, not to bathe in the park's reservoirs, and to abide by all the other rules and regulations.[11] Mesa Verde had come of age as a professionally operated and administered park.

Most of the changes in the park can be attributed to the car, a mixed blessing, indeed. Its use contributed growing numbers of visitors; they came at greater velocity but not always with an increased appreciation of what they saw. The use of automobiles had produced that breed of tourists who trailed a cloud of dust in their hurry to cover as many miles and visit as many places as possible in the shortest time. What could be experienced and enjoyed along the way began to seem to be of little consequence.

The automobile, better roads, and camping facilities brought vacations and Mesa Verde within the economic reach of almost everyone. The impetus was reflected dramatically in park attendance, which jumped to over 16,800 in 1928 (six times what it had been in 1920), a record that stood until 1931. Nevertheless, isolation, relatively weak promotional efforts,

and no nearby major population center continued to affect visitation to Mesa Verde; Rocky Mountain National Park attendance in 1928 topped 250,000. Mesa Verde's unique role as a cultural park also hurt it. While park advocates and other Americans were debating the functions that parks should serve—a "people's playground" versus a nature experience, for example—Mesa Verde sat on the sidelines.[12] It was evident that more American vacationers than ever were traveling west, but it was by no means clear what was enticing them there. If attendance figures can serve as indicators, it seems safe to assume that scenery, recreation, and mountains outclassed mesas, history, and cliff dwellings in influencing vacation plans.

Visitors' reactions to Mesa Verde provide interesting reading. A sampling from the 1920s included these: "The Cliff dwellings should be counted as one of the Wonders of the World,"

"Good retreat for honeymooners," "A most interesting and educational park full of romance and thrills," and "Today is the realization of a ten year ambition. . . . Hats off to Mesa Verde."[13]

Jesse Nusbaum worked unstintingly during these years; nothing stopped or even slowed him once he had made up his mind to do something. Almost nothing, that is. Government reports were known to have driven him nearly to distraction. He complained repeatedly about "useless" reports, until he finally exploded to the director after being informed that other park superintendents complied: "I admit I have been negligent in the matter—I would rather be doing the work—helping with it, no matter how strenuous, than writing reports to Washington telling how much 'I' was accomplishing." Sometimes he successfully cut through red tape. Nusbaum sparred several

Rangers conducted automobile tours that started from the museum. As this August, 1929, scene shows, crowds could become a problem.
Courtesy: Mesa Verde National Park

A little adventure still lay in wait for the tourist of the 1920s who climbed down to some of the less-developed sites.

Courtesy: Western Historical Collections, University of Colorado

rounds with the Post Office Department before gaining a park post office in 1924, which would be open during the tourist season.

With less struggle, he secured a weather station for the park, but he did not need measuring devices to tell him that inclement weather adversely affected visitation. The years 1921, 1923, and 1929 proved to be especially bad in that respect. The worst was 1929, when visitor numbers dropped by over 2,000. A severe winter took its toll. It was followed in July and August by rains that left the highways "literal seas of mud." Every piece of park equipment, plus men and teams, came to the rescue, but nothing brought lasting relief until the sun broke through.[14]

Less important matters also demanded their share of Nusbaum's attention. He reported the use of rifles to shoot down slabs of rock that overhung trails and threatened to fall on visitors. The Utes pestered Nusbaum to some degree with their "poaching," but all in all, he seems to have had good rapport with his neighbors. Nusbaum noted in 1921 that, for the first time, he had spotted elk in the park, a nice addition to the deer, coyotes, and smaller animals that were already there. Because of Nusbaum's efforts, a tennis court was built for employees, who needed some recreational diversion other than observing tourists and nature.

The public's evening hours were enriched by the lectures given by Nusbaum in his "beautiful, deep resonant voice" and by a new feature of the campfire talks, a Navajo sing. Navajos from the nearby reservation constituted more than ninety percent of the park's unskilled labor force during the 1920s. They brought their families with them and lived in government-built hogans. As one author suggested, "how much more interesting is a place . . . where one can see the civilization and culture of tribes that have disappeared, as well as that of those who are still in the flesh."[15] These Navajos proved to be excellent workmen on both park and archaeological projects. They also clung to their own ways, as Superintendent Nusbaum understood: "Navahos drift in thru the snow to work for a few days when we have it to do for them . . . get their checks, go to the trading post and secure what they desired when they came here to get the wherewithal to purchase it." Over the succeeding years, the Navajos became an integral part of the park.

Nusbaum appreciated the Navajos and understood their culture far better than did most of his contemporaries. Sympathizing with the economic plight of their life on the reservation, he worked to provide jobs within the park and built the hogans for them as a thoughtful gesture to ease the cultural shock. While the Navajos gained experience and income, the Utes re-

By the 1920s the main ruins had been stabilized and the rubble had been removed, making sites easier to visit. This is Cliff Palace.
Courtesy: Amon Carter Museum

mained on the outside. Perhaps the Utes' dissatisfaction with boundaries and land may have made the superintendent reluctant to hire them or discouraged them from working for him.

Jesse continued to encounter the same intermittent problems with his Ute neighbors that had characterized previous years. Nuisance-type aggravations strained the relationship. Untended campfires, poaching, and cutting timber, for example, forced Nusbaum to throw an unexplained "scare into them" in 1926. In a letter to the director in May, he said he believed that his action would "make them more particular in the future, both as to fires and cutting green timber and to hunting on Park lands." The park's relentless affliction during the next three decades would be the failure of both sides to negotiate with tolerance and understanding, thereby reinforcing an unfortunate heritage.

Thanks to Jesse
Nusbaum's ef-
forts in the 1920s,
Navajos found
the park an im-
portant source of
employment.
*Courtesy: Mesa Verde
National Park*

One of the most immediate of Nusbaum's concerns had been the lack of medical facilities within the park to treat employees and visitors. Nusbaum and his wife, Aileen (a nurse), successfully lobbied the surgeon general and Congress for medical supplies and tents and finally for a small hospital. Congress, recognizing Aileen's efforts in establishing a first aid tent, in nursing patients, and in designing the structure, named the new hospital the Aileen Nusbaum Hospital. When it opened in 1926, it included six beds (three rooms), a doctor's office, an operating room, and a kitchen. Small monthly salary deductions underwrote employees' costs; tourists paid according to a list of posted fees. Typical injuries and illnesses treated during June, 1926, included insect bites, bruised muscles, sore throats, and injured feet, ankles, and fingers[16]—just about everything that might be expected from out-of-shape tourists hiking and climbing at an altitude of seven thousand feet. It was obviously important to have medical services available.

Even with Nusbaum's avid interest in the park and his own physical efforts on its behalf, the pace of archaeological excavation at Mesa Verde slackened from that of the previous two decades and went into low gear for the next thirty years. The spectacular ruins had already been dug, and funding had become less available than it had been in the earlier days of discovery. Nusbaum learned about some of those days firsthand when the still hale and active old-timer William Henry Jackson visited the park in 1921 to retrace some of his steps of a generation before. He also donated a set of his early photographs, much to the superintendent's delight.

Mesa Verde did contribute core samples from some well-preserved timbers, which helped University of Arizona astronomer Andrew E. Douglass develop a tree-ring calendric chart. Working from the theory that trees' annual growth rings could be correlated in order, from the present backward as far as samples could be collected, Douglass set to work. His new field, called dendrochronology, consumed decades of patient effort. When completed in 1929, it proved to be a resounding success, and for the first time, Mesa Verde and southwestern sites could be closely dated.

Although archaeological work did not progress as hoped, the crusade for a better museum succeeded brilliantly. The original log cabin and its collections, which Nusbaum first saw in 1921, dismayed him. To make matters worse, Jeep claimed the displays as his personal property, a contention Nusbaum emphatically disputed. He prevailed and forced Jeep to hand over his key and desist from digging.[17] Such actions did little to endear the superintendent to the Jeeps or to their friends.

Nusbaum had hardly finished building his house before he launched a campaign to build a fireproof museum and upgrade the collections.

This campaign exhibited Jesse Nusbaum at his charming best. He easily won over his friends, who introduced him to some of the country's wealthier families. California held riches to tap, and Nusbaum was able to secure from Mrs. Stella Leviston of San Francisco a gift sufficient to start the building and from Mrs. Mary Sedgwick of Berkeley enough to underwrite a small expedition to gather materials to be placed therein. His reputation and personality enabled him to operate smoothly and confidently in these fund-raising endeavors, the most famous of which involved John D. Rockefeller, Jr.[18] The slight, handsome, fifty-year-old Rockefeller was deeply committed to preservation and conservation, as his involvement at Jackson Hole, Wyoming, and Williamsburg, Virginia,

testified. In both cases, he saved part of America's heritage, wilderness, and colonial history.

On a hot Thursday morning—July 3, 1924—Nusbaum drove into Mancos to meet the Rockefeller party and escort them to Mesa Verde. Watching out the window of the old park office, where he was waiting, he suddenly saw two Packards turn down Main Street and head toward the park in a cloud of dust:

> I pursued them at once but because of drought and dusty conditions, I was unable to safely pass the rear car for about five miles. I tooted my exhaust siren, and this car slowed to let me pass, then followed me closely until I hailed and stopped the lead car, after passing and stopping just ahead of it.

The Rockefeller sons seemed disappointed at first that the car with the

siren had not been the sheriff coming to arrest their father for speeding! After that disconcerting incident, Nusbaum led the Rockefellers through the wonders of Mesa Verde. The party visited the museum and the park headquarters, toured the ruins, savored a steak fry ("the choicest T-bone steaks available") in a special cave location above Balcony House, and (shades of Virginia McClurg!) saw a pageant at Spruce Tree House presented by Aileen Nusbaum and others. One of the girls waiting tables that summer was unfavorably impressed by her special guests; "they had on the worst looking old clothes you ever saw in your life."[19] Amid the distractions, Jesse found time to discuss the park and its future with his guest.

Rockefeller enjoyed everything immensely, and out of the visit grew a warm friendship and a team effort, with Rockefeller providing the finances and Nusbaum the skill and field supervision. Rockefeller donated the money to complete a four-room section of the museum; both men hoped that the government would then be motivated to appropriate funds to finish the entire structure. (It was fortunate that neither man held his breath, because it was not until 1936 that Washington finally came through with an appropriation.) Although the building's completion was delayed, Nusbaum forged ahead with his efforts to compile a reference library to complement the museum holdings. His architectural contributions would eventually be recognized for what they were, a "pace setter" example of blending buildings into the park setting.

Perhaps of more immediate significance, from 1924 to 1929 Rockefeller underwrote Nusbaum's winter expeditions into remote areas of the park. Often working through badly disarranged remains left by earlier diggers, Nusbaum and his workers re-covered many items for display in the museum, thereby increasing the public's appreciation and understanding of the fascinating Anasazi and their Mesa Verde world. Nusbaum lacked a trained crew, so he taught his apprentices the required skills and techniques. His stepson, Deric, received his first archaeological training here, as did others. The Rockefeller-Nusbaum partnership improved the museum, upgraded the specimens on display, broadened the knowledge of Mesa Verde's prehistory, and served as an ideal public-private partnership. Both Mesa Verde and the American public profited from it.

Two years after Rockefeller's visit, the Nusbaums served as hosts to Sweden's Crown Prince and Princess. The young couple felt at home when they were greeted by a prominent display of their countryman Nordenskiold's book and photographs. In what was becoming almost a V.I.P. tradition, they took in a ceremonial play and feasted at a "beefsteak fry" at Sun Temple. The ordinary tourist, however, missed out on the "royal treatment." Amy Thompson remembered the pervasive dust, the "awesome sight" from the Knife Edge Road, and on the hot, dusty walk to Spruce Tree House, the "tin can [that] sat at the side of that spring, and the weary traveler could quench his thirst with a deep swig from it."[20]

Both celebrities and regular tourists found the park's accommodations steadily improving. With no expansion room at the old location, in 1923 Spruce Tree Lodge, cottages, and tents were moved to a site across the road from the museum and the park headquarters. New cottages and tents would be added later. Improvement and enlargement were sorely needed; Nusbaum estimated that 60 percent of the visitors in 1923 used the facilities. A visitor in 1927 paid $1.00 for meals and $4.00 per night in a tent, or $4.50

*John D. Rocke-
feller, nattily
attired in his bow
tie, surveys Cliff
Palace in 1924.
He and Jesse Nus-
baum formed an
ideal partnership.*
Courtesy: Western
History Department,
Denver Public Library

Jesse Nusbaum (far right) and his crew at the Step Cave Excavation, 1926. His step-son, Deric, stands third from the left; to his left is future superin-tendent Marshall Finnan.

Courtesy: Mesa Verde National Park

in a cottage; slightly less if a friend or two shared the accommodations.[21] The attractive, "full of pep" Oddie Jeep ran the concessions during these years, managing to overcome some of her animosity toward the superintendent. Nusbaum's firing of her husband had not started them off as the best of friends, but Nusbaum did on occasion praise her for her excellent seasonal service. She succeeded in infuriating him when she sold some prehistoric pottery. He fired off a strong letter of protest, reminding her that such transactions were prohibited, as she had been told before her late husband left the park.[22]

Internal park problems did not trouble visitors, who kept coming in ever larger numbers each year. In 1923 this popularity elicited a new rival to challenge Durango and Cortez as the gateway to Mesa Verde: Gallup, New Mexico, and its patron, the Santa Fe Railroad, made a bid for the honor.

The Santa Fe had promoted the Southwest for many years, even featuring Indians in its advertising campaigns; the park and the train seemed a natural alliance. Cortez hoped to improve its position, too, since the auto stages from the Gallup train depot came right through the town, carrying with them the Swedish royalty, among others. The three-day round trip between Gallup and Mesa Verde cost $40 per person in 1927. However, the road, never good at its best, seldom earned travelers' praise, and it was this drawback, more than any other, that discouraged the popularity of the new gateway.

J. O. Morris, who ran the "stage," did not serve Gallup's cause well, either. One woman passenger complained that "she had been handled like a piece of luggage, that Morris did not speak six words to her from Shiprock into Gallup." The misanthropic driver also managed to embroil himself in an argument with the Fred Harvey management personnel, who described him as "arrogant and over-bearing, and has poor equipment and does not keep his regular schedule." The Harvey Houses and the Santa Fe Railroad had been "married" for decades, promoting themselves and the Southwest. Morris countered by accusing the firm of not giving to him business that was rightly his. The fact that Fred Harvey was considering establishing a rival service out of Santa Fe might have colored its opinion; whatever the reason for the dissension, poor Nusbaum found himself caught in the middle. In the end, there was little to quarrel over—the day of the railroad was fast receding, and the highway north from Gallup to Cortez remained almost impassable in places. After a 1928 trip, Nusbaum cursed the section of it that ran from the state line to Cortez as "one hour of grief and ruts and chuck holes and bouncing all over the road."[23]

Cortez's hopes faded again. Mancos,

too, had suffered a nearly fatal set-back when Nusbaum moved the park headquarters into Mesa Verde. As train travel declined, Mancos's importance receded further, despite its continued bold claim that "Mancos is the Gateway to MESA VERDE NATIONAL PARK." Durango gained a little superiority each year. The automobile put Durango in the day-trip orbit to the park, and for the tourist, it offered advantages rivals could not match: more accommodations, better transportation outlets, and a greater variety of things to see and do. Mancos would have to hustle before its neighbor took away its prime source of outside income.

Isolation continued to affect Mesa Verde adversely; no major east-west highway came anywhere near the park. State roads, however, did improve because of a major construction program begun in 1922 under the aegis of the new State Highway Department. The park matched the state's efforts by re-building the abandoned Knife Edge Road, which it opened in 1923, calling it (without exaggeration) "one of the most spectacular drives in America." The next generation of tourists called it by other names, many of them less than complimentary. It terrified, thrilled, challenged, and awed travelers, in turn. The road was "benched in," so that a sliding car would go into the ditch rather than over the edge. Nus-baum remembered how the bad condition of the road had once benefited Mesa Verde. The chief engineer of the National Park Service had become so scared in 1925, when his car slid on the clay-shale roadway, that he forthwith supported the superintendent's request for graveling the road.[24]

Some drivers questioned the reopening of the Knife Edge Road, as opposed to some other safer but less spectacular route. Politics and topography dic-tated the selection. The sometimes unpredictable and still dissatisfied Utes blocked a southern path down the Mancos Canyon and up a side canyon. Mesa Verde's northern cliffs and steep slopes discouraged even the most opti-mistic engineer from planning a route to scale them. There seemed to be no other choice for the National Park Service, so the decision was made. Park personnel and visitors would be haunted by that decision for a genera-tion.

More cars each season added to the difficulties with which the park person-nel had to contend. Vehicles overheated on the steep grades, burned their brakes out going down, and suffered power losses at the seven thousand to eight thousand feet elevations; those with gravity gas feeds sometimes had to back up the hill, if fuel ran low in the tank.[25]

Through all the crises, Nusbaum

enthusiastically promoted the park in his lectures, his writing, and his work.

> Work is our first, middle and last name on this park, and the same name on Sunday and holidays most of the year, with little regard for the time piece—so little in my own case that I have not carried a watch since I have been here until Aileen gave me one for Xmas this year.[26]

Nusbaum's prose approached the poetic when he discussed or described Mesa Verde; he could write well, when he chose to do so. Those nagging government reports failed to inspire his best literary efforts; his everlasting procrastination in producing them disgruntled his superiors throughout his career.

Aileen and Deric Nusbaum trailed only a step or two behind Jesse in their promotion of Mesa Verde. She pro-

Reaching Mesa Verde had become somewhat easier by the mid-1920s. Shown is future Highway 160 leading west out of Durango.
Courtesy: Center of Southwest Studies, Fort Lewis College

Immediately inside the park, the infamous Knife Edge Road loomed ahead, a fearsome ascent even for old hands. Careless motorists soon found themselves in trouble.

Courtesy: Mesa Verde National Park

duced her play several times and wrote articles; her son, with his mother's help, produced *Deric in Mesa Verde*, a classic account of a boy's growing up in the park. This interesting story revealed something of Jesse Nusbaum, as in Deric's statement, "I am not allowed to dig in the Park, but if I find anything lying around I bring it to the Museum."[27]

Jesse Nusbaum fought misinformation about the park as vigorously as he promoted it. From the one-shot, off-the-mark rumor of a park water shortage, which a Continental Oil gas station in Durango had spread in 1927, to the ongoing Manitou cliff dwelling scam, Jesse rode to the park's rescue. "Each year I get more 'Red-Headed' than ever," he exploded, when describing his reaction to the Manitou cliff dwellings fraud. This operation now advertised itself as an exact and scientific reproduction of Spruce Tree House, Cliff Palace, and Balcony House and asked "Why visit Mesa Verde when you can see it all here for a dollar?" Why go to a "region even now difficult of access," when Manitou Springs was as accessible? Nusbaum pulled no punches when he wrote to Director Mather: "I resented their reproduction even under the original plan, long before I became superintendent of this Park." He accurately perceived the real threat it posed to Mesa Verde: "It really works a great hardship on this Park to be forced to compete with such a combination, with their constant 'Bally-Hoo' near a great tourist center like Colorado Springs."

He came near to getting his revenge. In 1922, the proprietor of the Manitou dwellings had announced that he was headed for Mesa Verde to excavate new material. Nusbaum, tipped off by a friend, lay in wait with his staff. The man and his wife eventually appeared, registering themselves from Rock Springs, Wyoming. That deception confounded nobody—a ranger silently shadowed them throughout their visit. "They were given several fine chances to 'start something' in the excavation line if they dared do so, but I guess that they knew their game was up," Jesse wrote somewhat disappointedly. He later attempted to prosecute this same man for mail fraud (for fraudulent advertising) but was advised that he had no case.[28] Jesse Nusbaum had met his match, and this problem from the McClurg era lived on to harass park officials.

Nusbaum persevered through every setback. His clash with the Rickner-Jeep crowd got him into more trouble with Senator Phipps, who tried in 1923 and 1925 to remove the superintendent. Phipps supported his request with letters from Mancos residents, who charged Nusbaum with various forms of mismanagement and, among other things, with not paying attention to ordinary people, "only the wealthy and intellectual." Director Mather, disgusted by the pettiness and the politics and appreciative of Nusbaum's contributions, stood loyally by him; Phipps lost every round.

The other Colorado senator jumped into the action in a slightly different manner. Rice Means, who had been elected with Ku Klux Klan support, came to the park during the heyday of the Klan in the mid-1920s. That visit prompted local Klansmen to invite the superintendent to join the organization, which would then conduct a parade and an initiation ceremony at the Sun Temple. Nusbaum refused emphatically and promptly prepared to break up any torchlight parade and cross burning,

to the extent of arming some of his employees with pick handles. Nothing untoward happened, and the Klan members departed.[29]

That incident displayed Nusbaum at his forceful best. His accomplishments during the decade were legion. He quickly brought Mesa Verde to organizational parity with other parks, and his considerable personal charm had its effect on people in a variety of ways. He ended the grazing and mining threats and called a halt to a brief lumbering attempt. He succeeded in avoiding some problems common to other national parks: Wildlife management was never a big issue here, nor did anyone ever suggest building a

dam! Visitor totals moved ever upward but never as fast as in Rocky Mountain National Park.[30] By 1930, largely because of its active superintendent, Mesa Verde National Park was very different from what it had been ten years before, in everything from maintenance to visitor experience.

Nusbaum had administered and developed his park into a jewel of the park system. He concurred with the sentiments of Representative Edward Taylor, who called Mesa Verde "America's greatest historical asset. This park is entirely unique."[31] Mesa Verde had finally come of age, thanks to the determined and dedicated work of Jesse Nusbaum.

CHAPTER EIGHT

"To Get Away from It All"

Do Indians fall in love like we do?

What did they do for toilets?

How many cliff dwellings are there in Mesa Verde that have not as yet been found?

Don't you think that the constant climbing over these cliffs might cause the cliff dwellers to develop suction cups on their hands and feet?[1]

Those were some of the questions asked of startled park rangers during the 1930s, in all sincerity. Experienced ranger Don Watson called the question-and-answer game a battle of wits between himself and his tour group; he rated the last question in the list above as the "best" of the 1935 season. American tourists can be unintentionally funny. The 1930s were not a particularly humorous decade for most Americans, but nevertheless they kept coming to southwestern Colorado to see the country's best-known collection of cliff dwellings. What they saw was a park in the process of change.

An era came to an end when Jesse Nusbaum stepped down as superintendent in 1931, ending an outstandingly progressive decade of leadership. He resigned to become director of the Laboratory of Anthropology at Santa Fe, New Mexico. Before taking that job, he had been granted a leave of absence, which made the parting from Mesa Verde less abrupt. His departure did not break his ties to the park; Nusbaum would return twice in the next fifteen years, as superintendent from 1936 to 1939 and again during World War II.

He left behind a much stronger administration and a park much better managed than the one he had taken over ten years earlier. Director Horace Albright praised him, "Jesse was an archeologist and one of the best superintendents we ever had." Superintendent Robert Heyder echoed those sentiments in 1987 when he said Nusbaum was "probably the most significant superintendent we have ever had or will have. To me, he was the most important person in the development of the park."[2] Mesa Verde had come to maturity under Nusbaum's leadership —his successors could build on that solid foundation in the years ahead.

The immediate problem that affected the park, as well as the country as a whole, was the Great Depression, which came officially with the October, 1929, stock market crash. Southwestern Colorado temporarily avoided the shock waves emanating from it. Not until the summer and fall of 1930 did the real impact hit, and once it grabbed hold, it hung on tenaciously for the next decade. Mining, agriculture, and business slumped, then plummeted, into the worst times in memory. The effects of the Depression can best be understood in personal terms. Etched in one woman's memory years later was the sight of her mother, with tears in her eyes and anguish in her voice, as she was forced to explain that there was no money for the treasured nickel ice cream cone. For young Durangoan C. Coyne Thompson, the search for a job turned out badly: "You couldn't get a job because people, like on the farms, could not afford to feed you, so you couldn't work for room and board."

For Mesa Verde, the Depression meant fewer visitors and a decreased budget, as the Depression reached its nadir in 1932–33. Financial straits translated into a mimeographed annual report in 1932 (limited number of copies), an 8⅓ percent salary cut, and a 10 percent reduction for construction. The superintendent described the obsession with the subject, when he said that "the word economy has risen from obscurity to a prominent place in the thoughts and speech of all Americans."

The economic impact of the decline of tourism soon hit the local businesses and the park concessionaire.

The decrease in visitors (not until 1934 was the 1931 number surpassed) had a successional impact on park enterprises; in the words of Superintendent Marshall Finnan in 1932, "There has been a decided tendency on the part of the traveling public to seek the most economical type of accommodations which has resulted in a material decrease in operators' revenues."[3] Despite the early decline in numbers, the Depression did not curtail visitation after the mid-1930s as much as the economic severity of the times might have suggested it would. The gradual improvement of the local and national economy helped put people back on the road, but it was more than that. The public saw the national parks as one of the best tourist bargains available to them and may have perceived the parks as offering a temporary haven from the harsh realities of the times. By the end of the 1939 season, even though the park still suffered from its isolation and

During the Depression years, camping allowed some travelers to trim expenses. Camping conditions had improved significantly since the 1890s.
Courtesy: Mesa Verde National Park

Visitors were arriving in buses in the 1930s. It is June, 1934, and Conoco's up-to-date bus has a whole parking lot to itself.

Courtesy: Mesa Verde National Park

poor roads, "a hell of a trip in and out of there," Mesa Verde visitor totals had reached 32,000. In spite of the encouraging upswing in attendance, this was only one-tenth of the Rocky Mountain National Park visitation.

By the 1930s, visitors were coming from all 48 states and territories, as well as from foreign countries (24 in 1932 and 13 in 1939, as war neared). National Park Director Horace Albright could proclaim proudly that Mesa Verde was fast attracting both national and international interest. Each year, the percentage of Colorado visitors decreased, as other states gained in numbers.

Among Coloradans, Mesa Verde became a popular destination for local high school students on their so-called sneak day, an annual senior ritual. Silverton teacher Fury Dalla remembered that the kids "wanted to go," even when they had to leave at 6:00 A.M. to arrive in the park before noon.

Durangoan Phyllis Jones did not have to depart quite so early for her class's "senior sneak," which included parents, teachers, and plenty of food. She recalled vividly the unpaved Knife Edge Road: "It was beautiful and treacherous. It wasn't very wide." The class was divided into tour groups, each with a guide. "No one stopped at the top and *looked* down, we all *went* down. We saw some houses that have long since been closed to the public."[4]

Regardless of who they were or where they came from, visitors to Mesa Verde found a park that was better managed and more attractive than the one that had been seen by their contemporaries as few as a dozen years earlier. The Depression could not roll back the achievements of the Nusbaum years.

Jesse Nusbaum's legacy permeated the park. The prohibition against grazing meant that a "delight of wild flowers" once again greeted arrivals in May and June. That was justification enough, believed Director Albright, to deny a Mancos rancher's request for limited grazing: "From our standpoint there doesn't seem to be a solitary reason why we should again permit such use of park resources."[5] The water supply improved with the completion of a deep well drilling project in 1933 and the integration of all the park sources into a single system in the years that followed. These improvements, unfortunately, did not end the problem for all time—there were shortages again in 1936 and notices were posted urging conservation.

A new entrance station and a new campfire circle probably did not elicit exclamations of delight from park visitors; nevertheless, they contributed to the pleasure of tourists' visits, as did the introduction in 1935 of a radio communication system throughout the park. The direct benefits of an ongoing road improvement program were more appreciated, though little had been done to alleviate apprehension around the Knife Edge. By late 1935, most of the park roads were graveled. The rest, it was promised, within a "short time" would be covered with a layer of oiled gravel to end the "annoyance of mud and dust."

One improvement of benefit to visitors, though most would have been unaware of the magnitude of the change, was the upgrading of the educational and interpretive programs and the advancement in professionalism of the seasonal rangers and the permanent staff. The evolution had been slow but steady, beginning with the park's first political and local appointments and extending to the trained and knowledgeable rangers of the 1930s. The turning point had come with Nusbaum, who personally selected, trained, and indoctrinated his staff. The seasonal rangers usually came from the ranks of college students specializing in southwestern archaeology or some other archaeological major.

Specialists, such as a park naturalist, also joined the staff. In 1930, naturalist Paul Franke was placed in charge of the educational and nature work. (A few years later, this former teacher and school superintendent became park superintendent.) He took an important educational step by publishing *Mesa Verde Notes*, which featured stories of everything from prehistoric people to flora and fauna in the park. The staff in 1930 consisted of seven permanent and fifteen seasonal employees, the latter primarily ranger guides. Depending on park needs, laborers were employed on a temporary basis.

Tourists did appreciate the continuous upgrading of the museum. Although it was perhaps not quite what the *Colorado Yearbook 1935–36* claimed—"the largest and most comprehensive" exhibit of Mesa Verde archaeology available anywhere—it did offer the best display yet seen in the park. An attempt to improve it further by purchasing the Nordenskiold collection failed; otherwise, it expanded steadily. Among the exhibits that generated the most acclaim were the dioramas, which were finally completed in 1939 after several years of detailed, meticulous work. If finger prints and nose prints on glass can serve as indicators, the Spruce Tree House diorama and an exhibit about cliff dwellers' diseases, as evidenced by their bones, won hands down as the most popular museum attractions of 1939. The diorama glass became smudged so quickly during the peak season that it had to be cleaned as often as every two hours. A natural history museum, opened in 1940, doubled the potential enjoyment for the public and added a new dimension to the park's interpretation. Visitors could also inspect the experimental corn field, which marked its twentieth year in 1938; it had had only two crop failures during that time.[6] The Anasazi had probably done no better, at a time when the success or failure of crops meant feast or famine.

The Mesa Verde pamphlets published by the National Park Service told visitors explicitly what they could and could not do. They were warned that one rule would be "strictly enforced": No person could enter a cliff dwelling unless accompanied by a ranger or a ranger naturalist. Those planning only a one-day visit were urged not to attempt all the climbing trips, because they were "very strenuous" and could cause strained and aching muscles. *"Headwork, rather than footwork, leads to an understanding of the Mesa Verde."*[7]

The Depression retarded, but never halted, park operations at Mesa Verde. In the spring, the park was readied for its opening, and ruins repair work was started. Increased visitation meant that thousands of feet tramped by a site,

a process that structurally damaged the fragile ruins and made painfully apparent the need to replace some of Fewkes's earlier reconstruction work. Under the direction of noted archaeologist Earl Morris, badly needed stabilization was begun. In 1934, a permanent stabilization team created "an economy, both in money and in results accomplished."[8] Morris's skillful repair work would serve as a model for future projects, as the park raced against time to save its heritage. Tourists came and went all the while, generally unaware of all the preservation activity going on in the canyons and on the mesa. Each fall, the exhausted staff prepared for the closing of the park as another season passed into history.

During the tourist season the park staff had to contend with vandalism, petty and otherwise. The old familiar urge to see one's name in public places lured many people into trouble, including Denverite Dolores Houck, who left

her address as well! In a stern letter, she was asked to pay for the cost of sanding and repainting the "viewpoint" box cover. Her alternative was to prepare to stand trial! "The circumstance of finding your name and address at a prominent and much visited location of this national park will, I am certain, prove embarrassing for you. It is certainly disturbing to us. What sort of a park would we have if each visitor inscribed his name and address or his mark herein. . . ." Five high school students from nearby Bayfield, Colorado, also found out about the long arm of federal jurisdiction when they defaced one of the walls of Spruce Tree House.

Cameras stolen from cars, names inscribed on ruins, joyriding in U.S. government trucks—malice and mischief of this kind disrupted the regimen of the superintendents. The problem became so bad in 1938 that Paul Franke wrote to J. Edgar Hoover to ask for F.B.I. help. He expressed regret at bothering Hoover on so trivial a matter, but he was "extremely annoyed by the cases of petty thievery."[9] The bureau's response has been lost.

Employees were reminded on several occasions not to abuse the use of the telephone with extended conversations and to pay personal toll charges "within 24 hours." When electrical home appliances interfered with radio newscasts, the topic created serious discussion at the September 5, 1939, staff meeting. With the world situation deteriorating around them and newspapers arriving belatedly, park management decided that newscasts and programs "should not be subject to this interference." In the days that followed, the staff switched on their static-free radios to hear grim war news from Poland and other parts of Europe.

Of less import were the purchase of a Ping-Pong table and the building of a ski run and a new tennis court. These additions upgraded the limited recreational facilities available to the staff and, at least in the realm of Ping-Pong, allowed some players to "develop into quite a group of champions." The tennis court caused almost more trouble than it was worth, first in construction delays, then in repairs.

Phantoms from the past rose up to haunt the present. From time to time, an old-timer would appear, claiming that he had made the first discovery of the ruins. "Publicity seekers," a disgusted Finnan called them, bemoaning the dearth of pioneer records to rebut such pretensions. One who had been intimately involved in the discovery and development of Mesa Verde, Charlie Mason, came to the park for the last time in 1935 and related his adventures of nearly fifty years ago; within a year he was dead.[10]

Staff conference minutes from June through August, 1936, provide a sampling of typical administrative problems and issues that had to be dealt with. Vandalism, the need to keep the grounds "neat and clean," and the low water reserves came up for discussion. Complaints about mosquitoes, flies, and odors in the camping and headquarters areas received a hearing, were investigated and, it is hoped, were ultimately resolved. Improper parking and cars driven into trees prompted deliberation of campground problems. "Stray cats in the park" caused consternation. Their presence in itself was a mystery, since domestic felines had always been banned by federal regulation. Somehow, the ingenious creatures circumvented one of the park's oldest rules. Other subjects for discussion included arrangements for the fall school term and the need for a community church.[11] Mesa Verde had its own elementary school; high school students had to go elsewhere.

The inevitable life of bureaucracy tormented some of the staff. Charles

Quaintance, a naturalist assistant, was transferred to Mesa Verde from Rocky Mountain National Park in December, 1934. After only three months, he complained to the chief of the wildlife division that there were no "problems to study" and that his position did not give him time to study wildlife itself: "My training and leaning is for work as a field naturalist, rather than for office work." He apologized for not submitting his February report on time, explaining that the typist had been diverted by other administrative work.[12]

The superintendent sometimes became embroiled in unanticipated emotional issues. In 1939, for instance, long-time "outstanding" friend of the park Edward Taylor supported an attempt to change the name from Mesa Verde to Cliff Dwellings National Park, exactly what the women's group had suggested forty years before. "Mesa Verde" seemed meaningless, Congress-man Taylor argued; Cliff Dwellings would tell the world what the park was all about. Nusbaum hied himself off to Washington to meet with Taylor, there to impress upon him the fact that the name Mesa Verde had been in the public, the historic, and the scientific mind since 1873 and that a change would require "very careful consideration."

Bolstered by National Park Service support, Nusbaum also carried with him letters from local citizens who opposed the change. Durango banker A. M. Camp tackled the matter more directly by writing his congress-man. Mesa Verde, he contended, was "romantic Spanish nomenclature, reflecting the charm of the southwest," and, furthermore, the name Cliff Dwellings represented nothing specific. Tourists might pass up the park thinking, "Oh, I saw cliff dwellings in New Mexico and Arizona." In the face of persistent persuasion, Taylor threw in the towel, writing "Friend Nusbaum" that as long as substantial opposition stood against a change, which it did overwhelmingly, he would take no action. However, he warned, "At the same time, I will prophesy that such a change will be made sometime in the future." Nusbaum won another concession for his beloved Mesa Verde.[13] There had also been a brief flurry of interest in naming it the Edward T. Taylor National Park in recognition of the congressman's "years of useful public service." That idea died in infancy.

Franklin Roosevelt's administration had the same tremendous impact on Mesa Verde that it did on other American institutions. Elected in 1932 to try to jump-start the country into moving again, Roosevelt launched a sweeping New Deal program, and federal agencies proliferated. The Rural Electrification Administration, for example, brought electricity into southwestern Colorado and the park, a long-sought improvement. Ranger Kenny Ross pinpointed what this meant:

> That was an experience in the late thirties and early forties to see the lights go on all over the country. Driving back and forth it was very striking. It happened over a period of many months, first a light way out by Pleasant View, then another blinked on somewhere else. It was interesting, you realized something was going on, the country was moving out of the real pioneering life into the modern world.[14]

Tourists driving that same road probably did not take time to philosophize about the changes going on around them—they were concentrating too hard on staying as far away from the edge as they could. A night trip would have been out of the question.

One of the most popular programs with the president, and with the voters as well, was the Civilian Conservation Corps (C.C.C.), an effort to take unemployed young men off the streets and out of the towns and put them to work. The C.C.C. soon had more than a quarter of a million youths working under army officers to clear forests, plant trees, improve roads, and perform other useful tasks. Over two and one-half million young men eventually found employment through the C.C.C. at a total cost of some $3 billion. Mesa Verde, and all other national parks, provided natural sites for these kinds of activities. Fortunately for Mesa Verde, a six-year development plan had already gotten under way when the C.C.C. appeared on the scene; all the superintendent had to do was turn over some of the projects to it.

The C.C.C. camps located in the park truly symbolized the program. The first C.C.C. camp was established in May, 1933, in Prater Canyon; it was abandoned the next year when year-round camps were constructed on Chapin Mesa, slightly over a mile north of park headquarters. In the first years, two camps stood there side by side, but in 1937 they merged into one. Wooden buildings—barracks, infirmary, mess hall, recreational hall, quarters for officers—gave the camp the appearance of a military post.

The C.C.C.'s real reason for existence lay not in building camps but in giving young men a new start in life. With high hopes, they came to Mesa Verde National Park (most of them aged eighteen to twenty-three) from Mancos, Durango, and the surrounding area, as well as from Oklahoma, Texas, and Arizona. They had been unemployed, many of them on relief rolls. The C.C.C. men signed on for a six-month tour. After a one- to two-week conditioning period and time to recover from inoculations, they worked a forty-hour week (less transportation time) on various projects within

The coming of the Civilian Conservation Corps introduced a new era for Mesa Verde. The boys shown in this photo are cleaning their plates near the mess hall.
Courtesy: Mesa Verde National Park

the park. They earned thirty dollars a month, of which twenty-five dollars were sent home. For those without families, the army held the money in a savings account until the individual's discharge.[15]

The purpose of the program was twofold—to help the park and the individual. Young men, many of them disadvantaged by the hard times, were given a rare opportunity for education, recreation, social activity, a job, acquiring skills, and—according to the flowery editor of *Mesa Verde Notes*— "a chance to live in the great outdoors, to feel the body develop and the muscles grow taut under the impulse of hard work, and to earn money with their own hands; that is what the C.C.C. is offering the Colorado boys in the camp." It would be virtually impossible to single out a park activity that was not affected by C.C.C. money, personnel, and program.

Before the camps shut down in 1942, the C.C.C. crews constructed and remodeled buildings, ran surveys, improved roads, landscaped, did maintenance work, built furniture, operated the switchboard, helped excavate pithouses, and carried out insect control programs; the list stretched endlessly. They fought fires, one of their most dangerous tasks. In 1934, Mesa Verde suffered severe fire damage—2,229 acres were burned in one major and four small fires. One C.C.C. camper, stationed in the rear to fight spot fires, found it hard to concentrate on the fire: "We hadn't anything to eat until we finally took some cheese and bread" from one of the crews up front.[16] Abetted by extremely dry conditions and strong, hot winds, that fire resisted control by almost one thousand men, and it left scars on the western end of the park that endure to this day.

The C.C.C. projects that were most obvious to visitors dealt with the museum, where the young men arranged exhibits, including the dioramas, rebuilt pots from shards, and catalogued collections. Their endeavors there "stand as a lasting monument to the CCC at Mesa Verde."

John McNamara and Coyne Thompson were two of the young men who joined the C.C.C., because "that was the only job, there were not any jobs available." Their experiences encompassed both the good and the bad. John worked in the sandstone quarry for a while:

They would drill holes, put steel wedges and double jack it out. About twenty of us at a certain command would swing and it only took a couple of swings before the whole block fell out. Then the stone masons who were members of the camp would cut them into blocks. Then we

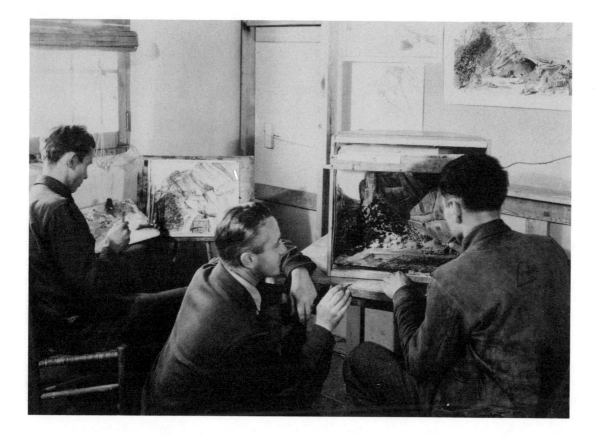

Among the
projects the
C.C.C. worked
on were the diora-
mas. Two future
superintendents,
Meredith Guillet
and Paul Franke,
and Kenny Ross
are shown here
busily making
plans.
*Courtesy: Mesa Verde
National Park*

would load it on trucks. One thing about the CCC camp, I always said, you earned every damn bit of money you got.

Thompson was not a part of that project, nor of the road crew "chain gangs." His first assignment was "the bug detail on the trees that were infested with bugs. From that I went into the excavating of ruins." Reveille came at 6:00 A.M., followed by breakfast, and then it was off to the work detail. "The food was pretty good, really pretty good," according to Coyne, who went on to add with a laugh, "We had cooks and they had bakers. And guys had KP."

About their contact with Park Service people, both said with amusement, "We met them all the time. They didn't work with us—they were in a higher class of nobility than we were." Reflecting on their experiences, they agreed that "it was a growing up education.

By the time you left, you were able to cope with the world at large. It was a good experience, there wasn't any doubt about it." [17]

Another C.C.C. veteran, Robert Beers, concurred with the assessment of the other two with regard to the worth of the program. He had worked on the road, in the office, and on the bug eradication detail. As he reviewed his service, however, he remembered most fondly the porcupine crew. Its job was to hunt porcupines, which damaged trees by their eating habits; the results were mixed: "I don't know if there was truly an invasion of porcupines up there or not, but some naturalist decided they ought to control the porcupine. We had our 22's from home and we'd go out, primarily at night. I don't think we ever shot very many." Although they posed no serious threat to the pesky porcupines, the C.C.C. boys probably were the culprits who smuggled the cats into the park. A

kitten held great appeal as a pet in the spartan barracks.

The C.C.C. publications, *Kiva Krier* and *Cliff Dwellers*, give further glimpses of life in the park and the camp. Sports, dances, movies, and parties enlivened leisure hours. Basketball and softball (a baseball diamond had been built) were popular sports, but football was abolished by order of the district commander after two players suffered injuries during a game in the 1934 season. Weekly movies, featuring such all-time Park Service favorites as *Glimpses of Yosemite* and *Beavers*, came around in regular cycles; fortunately, the audience changed as enlistments ended. Holiday meals for those who remained in camp offered special treats. An enthusiastic writer, in the December 25, 1937, *Cliff Dweller*, raved about the previous Thanksgiving's dinner: a "swell meal," which earned nothing but praises from the guests and corpsmen. "Everyone ate and ate until not room for so much as even a last bit of dandy mince pie."[18]

Economic benefits were bestowed by the corps beyond the realms of Mesa Verde because of the money sent home to parents, the men hired as supervisors, and the supplies and materials purchased for use on park projects. Those purchases came as a godsend to hard-pressed merchants. Durango's Jackson Hardware sold all the buckets, axes, and ropes it had in stock during the great Wetherill Mesa fire of 1934. Tourists, too, spent money beyond Mesa Verde, the average estimated to be about ten dollars per day per person in the late 1930s. Because a two-day stay was almost mandatory, the dollars pumped into the local economy amounted to "no small sum," as one analyst pointed out.[19] All these benefits brought some relief from the Depression that still lay on towns and farms.

Everything was not as sanguine in the C.C.C. camps as it might have appeared to be—or as the nation ardently wished it. Yellowstone officials faced a discipline crisis in 1933 with street-wise New York enrollees, which resulted in a strike, the discharging of ringleaders, and one death before the situation calmed. Mesa Verde was fortunate to confront only what might have been expected—some drinking and disruption in neighboring communities at dances and other social activities. One escapade in Dolores, however, led to the arrest and jailing of several C.C.C. campers. Their friends took a truck over and freed them by lifting the building off its foundations and dropping it into the river. The result was "quite a stink raised about it."[20]

The Depression and the coming of the New Deal made an impact throughout the National Park Service as well as at Mesa Verde. The C.C.C. boys were employed everywhere, and federal money underwrote a multitude of projects. Thanks to Roosevelt's interest

and the needs created by hard times, the parks got a boost they would not have received otherwise. They served as an economic refuge, an unforeseen blessing in those dark days.[21]

In the middle of this traumatic decade, Durango came out the winner over declining Mancos in their battle for supremacy. With a broader-based economy, Durango was better able to weather the crisis, while Mancos suffered a disheartening setback when the railroad's tourist transportation collapsed. Alvene and Fury Dalla, who remembered Mancos firsthand, described it as "a very little town at the time, a little farming community." Its population of 748 in 1940 paled in comparison to Durango's 5,400. With improved highways, which included the formidable Wolf Creek Pass, Durango appeared to have a bright future as a tourist center.

Durango—larger, wealthier, and feistily aggressive—swamped its one-time rival with a more dynamic advertising program. Maps showed Durango as the center of southwestern Colorado; Mancos was nowhere in sight. Durango also had a radio station, three times as many hotels and restaurants as Mancos, and an airport. Will Rogers landed there in 1935 and took off the next day to circle Mesa Verde on his way to Los Angeles. Durango, not Mancos, was featured in Rogers's newspaper column. The Mancos paper could only mention that he had flown over; the brief item spoke volumes about the community's position. Mancos no longer controlled its own destiny.

Durango would not reign unchallenged. As Mancos declined, Cortez made another bid for recognition. The future of Cortez depended upon highway improvements to the west, south, and north. The possibilities for bringing in tourists from the trains running through Gallup lasted only a short while; the decline in passenger traffic hurt the Santa Fe Railroad as much as it did the Rio Grande Southern. Eventually the future of both communities rode with the automobile and with improved feeder roads to tap the tourist traffic on such U.S. highways as Route 66 through Gallup. Unfortunately, the best efforts of both the Gallup and the Cortez Chambers of Commerce failed to achieve the improvement and oiling of a key highway, Route 666, between the two towns.[22] The driver wending his way to Cortez still found that near-frontier road conditions made an adventure of crossing the Navajo reservation in New Mexico.

To the northwest, Utah was awakening to the drawing power of Mesa Verde and to its tourist potential. The Lions Club of Moab, Utah, believed that highway signs could promote the park and Utah communities. In a 1935 letter to Superintendent Ernest Leavitt, the club regretted that it found itself "quite badly embarrassed financially," and it begged for help from Mesa Verde. Leavitt advised the Lions that he was required to expend his appropriations within the park boundaries, but he encouraged them in their project. Montrose, Colorado, proposed a similar idea with an interesting twist—it wanted to be promoted as lying on the shortest route between Yellowstone and Mesa Verde.[23] Expectations exceeded realities in all cases. There was no doubt, though, that Durango would confront new rivals in the years ahead.

Tourists entering the park, regardless of the direction from which they came, found a major change in the management of park concessions in the late 1930s. In 1929, the Mesa Verde Park Company, a subsidiary of the Denver & Rio Grande Western (a new name reflecting the railroad's 1921 reorganization), had bought out Oddie Jeep. The new company took over with high hopes and a great deal of planning, only to fall victim to the Depression and to the drastic decline in railroad travelers. In addition, its innkeeping fell far short of earlier standards; one of the workers said the style was "more or less old fashioned . . . with everything sort of formal." That image did not accommodate well to the new generation of the 1930s; public tastes were changing. Not all the blame could be laid to the parent D&RGW; the same thing happened in Yellowstone, where the hotel business collapsed. By 1937, the Mesa Verde Park Company had declared bankruptcy. In June of that year, Ansel Hall took over the operation, and for four decades, his Mesa Verde Company ran the park concessions.[24]

The Halls had been encouraged to come to Mesa Verde by Jesse Nusbaum, back again as superintendent. Ansel's wife, June, was apprehensive about what they had purchased: "When we bought it, there were noth-ing but wooden cabins down in the headquarters area. . . . They had two bathtubs in a little bath house." But both Halls saw the potential and set to work.[25]

Ansel Hall, a rare combination of romantic idealist and practical businessman, would be the dominant figure in the future concessionaire developments of Mesa Verde. A graduate of the University of California with a degree in forestry (a member of the school's first class with that major), Hall had hired on with the National Park Service as a ranger with a decided interest in the interpretive possibilities of parks. Now forty-one years old, he had advanced rapidly in the National Park Service to become Chief Naturalist and Chief Forester. When another career advancement was offered, he decided he did not wish to move his family to Washington, D.C. His catholic interests—photography, forestry, museums, nature, and education—had served him well and would continue to do so in the park.[26] Never before had the Mesa Verde concessions been in such good hands. Among the first things Hall did was to open a store, stocked full of groceries and fresh meat, for park residents and visitors. Nusbaum promptly recommended to his employees that they shop there; since it was "established to meet your demands—it merits your patronage."

In January, 1938, when Jesse Nusbaum went to Washington to a parks conference, he discussed the changes he had seen and what prospects the future held. Whereas the parks had once been platted to meet the needs of very limited and slow-moving traffic, now its problems came from the speed and volume of automobiles. This intrusion brought into question the proper use of parks, heretofore interpreted to be to provide reasonable and restrictive access for visitors, with shelter, food, safety, and sanitary facilities available

The Mancos Shale under Knife Edge Road tended to slide, which did little to bolster tourists' confidence. Fortunately, this slide came in November, 1941, after the park had closed for the season.

Courtesy: Mesa Verde National Park

to the public. These things, centralized on Chapin Mesa, had formed the core of Mesa Verde's program, along with what Nusbaum termed the "wilderness concept." Because of its single highway entrance, Nusbaum pointed out, Mesa Verde remained largely a wilderness of precipitous canyons and intervening mesa lands. With great foresight, he spoke to future generations: "The perpetuation and preservation unimpaired of wilderness values of national parks continue as its most potent ideals and functional objectives."[27] The Depression and then World War II prevented immediate consideration of preserving a wilderness experience, but the idea did not die.

The attack on Pearl Harbor, December 7, 1941, brought the United States into World War II. These remarks, found in the January 10, 1942, monthly report, showed the depth of American feeling:

The outbreak of hostilities brought on by Japan's sneaking back-stab at our Pacific possession imposes on all of us a prime duty to assist in any way possible to eradicate predator dictatorships and greedy cliques from the face of the earth. We all stand eager and willing to do what we can to help.

In this way, Mesa Verde went to war.

More changes came quickly. The Depression had already made an impact on tourism; now the war virtually suspended park activity. Visitor totals dropped from 36,000 to 4,000, and the average stay was shorter, too (the majority raced through the park in one day). Jesse Nusbaum returned again as acting superintendent in May, 1942, and watched as employees were drafted, park funds were cut, and the C.C.C. camps were closed. One of the last camp commanders, Angelo Brewer, remembered how his family "enjoyed it very much" living there. But he soon went directly into service, and not long afterward, the army requisitioned all the supplies and equipment, even a few portable buildings that could be carried away easily. An era had ended, and Nusbaum wondered how the park would find the "forces and funds" in these dire times to replace the C.C.C. It was a "matter of grave concern," he believed.[28] However, Mesa Verde's "long established prestige for service" was maintained, the proud superintendent reported, through "generous contributions of overtime."

Park life went on with a reduced staff; the entrance checking station, for example, was not staffed after the fall of 1942. The crews maintained roads as well as circumstances permitted, and park services were continued. At least ten overnight guests were required to ensure a campfire program. Rangers

A group of sol-
diers from Camp
Carson, Colo-
rado, toured the
park in 1943
while awaiting
orders to travel to
more dangerous
fronts.
*Courtesy: Mesa Verde
National Park*

conducted only two ruins trips per day. Despite the cutbacks, visitors kept on getting themselves lost and periodic searches were undertaken, just as in years past. Rangers arrested poachers and warned speeders. Vandalism declined. Among the less important projects during this time was a prairie dog survey, conducted in 1943. The survey results indicated that no control program was needed, although rats, mice, and the "kissing bugs" were poisoned at the superintendent's home, where they had managed to become a problem.[29]

Kenny Ross described those years: "We did have tourists and we had almost no staff. For three years it was just work, day and night, to keep up." Knife Edge, he observed, still gave visitors fits. The beautiful Luise Rainer, a two-time Academy Award winner for best actress, enjoyed Mesa Verde, although "she had to have someone drive her car out. Her excuse was that on the way up she had driven on the inside, but that wasn't true, especially on the Knife Edge."

One of the young Hall girls, Robin, held slightly different memories:

> . . . the thing I remember most was that whatever you wanted to do, you couldn't do it. You could climb a tree, but climbing a cedar tree is a little bit stickery. You couldn't dig a hole, you couldn't pick flowers. . . . I remember hiking was never something that I enjoyed. In Mesa Verde to hike you had to go down, that was the easy part, coming home you had to walk up.[30]

Growing up in the park atmosphere could be difficult. One time her father received a note saying that she, her brother, and several playmates had been sliding in Calloway's barn. That incident was minor compared to the major infraction—they had also built a fire in the hand forge and had played with the blower, shooting flames almost to the ceiling!

During those years employees patriotically purchased war bonds and collected scrap metal during the various drives; they planted victory gardens, suffered through shortages and rationing, and cooperated with wartime agencies. Unlike some other parks, Mesa Verde was never used for military purposes.

One of the war-related problems that did, however, confront Nusbaum involved a demand—reminiscent of 1917—by ranchers to open the park for grazing. Patriotic ranchers (the Mancos Cattlemen's Association) claimed that this concession would help the war effort. They propounded all kinds of arguments about why grazing would not hurt the park or interfere in any way with visitation. Their one failure was underestimating Nusbaum, who more than matched the opposition at hearings held in November, 1942. He had been down this road before and forcefully presented his evidence and beliefs: "The concept of a national park—*for the benefit and enjoyment of all the people*" would not be derailed by local ranchers dressed in patriotism. He prevailed and "put a monkey-wrench in their machinery, at least for the present." The victory was not absolute; Nusbaum had to be on the lookout for illegal grazing for the remainder of the war.[31]

By spring 1945, the end of the war hovered in sight. As Americans entered a new era, so did their national park system. What lay ahead was a subject of speculation, but more changes would come, without question. What they would mean for Mesa Verde, only the future could tell. Jesse Nusbaum had an inkling—in his June 11 monthly report he noted that inquiries had already crossed his desk from both east and west coast war workers who wanted "to get away from it all."

CHAPTER NINE

A Grand Tradition

World War II ended, and within five months Jesse Nusbaum had retired for the last time as superintendent of Mesa Verde. His tenure had covered seventeen event-filled years. No one else had held the position for so long a time; no one else had contributed so much to the development of the park or done so much to shape its image. Nusbaum's retirement broke the last active personal link with the early park days and signified a changing of the guard. New faces and new ideas would chart the years ahead.

In those last months, some old matters and some new ones crossed his desk. A request by NBC to make a film for a children's television program would have been totally unforeseen in 1921 when he was first appointed. Continuing discussions about roads and plans for the postwar era sounded ever so familiar to Nusbaum—only the years had changed. In the last weeks of his administration, who should come back to haunt him but the ghosts of Virginia McClurg and Lucy Peabody. Another attempt to change the name of Square Tower House to Peabody House threatened to open up the old wounds one more time. Nusbaum opposed the plan; he had walked this trail before and knew that the friends of other deceased individuals would "rightly claim comparable recognition."[1] The discussion went on for another year, but Nusbaum's position prevailed.

As he stepped aside, perhaps the most satisfying praise of his work came from eminent planner, landscape architect, and conservationist Frederick Law Olmsted. Nusbaum reported that Olmsted told him, after a late summer visit in 1945, that "Mesa Verde's development is among the finest and most appropriate in the National Park Service. He thought our archeological museum superb—probably the most 'illuminating' he has ever visited."[2] Olmsted expressed deep satisfaction with the landscape and with the architectural development as well—the latter was something Nusbaum could certainly take credit for, along with the C.C.C. boys.

Old problems hounded the new era. Superintendent Robert Rose's staff meetings in June and July, 1946, dealt with heavy visitor traffic, equipment maintenance, and complaints about high fees charged by the Rio Grande Motor Way to transport visitors to and from Durango. One problem from the McClurg past continued to torment Mesa Verde—the Manitou cliff dwellings. A number of park visitors complained that they had been misled by falsehoods about Mesa Verde—for instance, that a trip to the ruins necessitated a horseback ride of many miles over poor trails with no guides. The Manitou Springs folks also boasted that the ruins "can't compare with theirs." The superintendent lamented that, despite many past attempts by Mesa Verde personnel to minimize or

correct this situation, little had been accomplished. These fake ruins were still represented as genuine by the private owners: "Evidently their oral advertising continues as unscrupulous as ever. Of course, persons who subsequently come to Mesa Verde 'see the light.' "

Although that issue would not be resolved soon, the long-standing one involving water was finally overcome. The time required to move from satisfaction in July, 1946, in just "holding their own" to finding a solution covered only four years. Prior to the war, a plan for piping water from the La Plata Mountains had been proposed, and surveys had been run. Money had actually been appropriated in 1942 for a thirty-mile pipeline, but the matter lay dormant until 1949 because of its nondefense nature and other curtailments. Construction started in 1949, and the pipeline was finished the next year, along with a million-gallon reservoir for storage.

The new West Mancos Water Supply System made the old sheet-metal catchments, deep well, Spruce Tree spring pump, and other equipment obsolete. They were all removed, and the area was restored as nearly as possible to its natural condition.[3] For the first time since the early years of the century, the pump house, the pipe, and the other paraphernalia did not interfere with visitors' appreciation of Spruce Tree House.

A subject of concern at the staff meeting of July 22, 1946, was porcupine damage. The C.C.C. boys, of course, had tangled with the quilled creatures many times. After the war, however, procedures for dealing with park wildlife took on greater importance. Acceptable practice no longer allowed random hunting of porcupines. Population studies were carried out; even though the end result of trapping or killing might be similar to earlier actions, a conscious acknowledgment

With the return of peace, Americans took to the road. This photo of a 1947 tour indicates the size of the crowds that had come to the park.
Courtesy: Mesa Verde National Park

was made that now an ecological balance had to be struck between man and wildlife. As in the late 1940s and 1950s, wildlife management took on new meaning throughout the entire park system.

Wildlife within the national parks had always been important, but more so in Yellowstone and Rocky Mountain, for example, than in Mesa Verde. Predator control and overpopulation had never been a cause for concern in Mesa Verde, nor had visitors generally expected to see a variety of wildlife roaming within the park as part of their experience. It was mountain lions that put the subject into front-page headlines for Mesa Verde. Local ranchers charged that the predators were killing cattle and sheep, then using the park as a sanctuary to escape retribution. Hunters joined in the chorus of complaints, charging that the pesky cougars were also slaughtering deer. In the winter of 1947–48, the topic moved

up from the Cortez paper to Denver's *Rocky Mountain News* and from the superintendent to the regional director of the National Park Service. Rose and his staff, realizing that nothing would be gained by fighting their battles in the press, quietly endeavored to explain the park's policies to local groups and individuals. Most perplexing to all concerned was the fact that no reliable observations of mountain lions had been made in the park in the past two years, although a tourist claimed to have seen one the previous July.

The park staff concluded that mountain lions did not represent "an increasing menace to livestock and game," nor was Mesa Verde a breeding place for predators that intelligently used the park as a refuge, while raiding private herds of choice livestock. In the end, emotion died and the controversy faded away; rumors and histrionics had not been translated into long-run pressure.

Even before this uproar, wildlife matters had been garnering attention. Surveys and management policies came to be part of the park's program. The number of deer, ever increasing, created the biggest problem. They played havoc with attempts to raise a test field of corn, among other things. Porcupines continued to damage trees as they foraged for food. Other parks faced much greater problems than these and sheltered more varied animal populations than the deer, coyotes, skunks, porcupines, jack rabbits, and occasional mountain lions, badgers, elk, mountain sheep, and bobcats observed by visitors and park staff.[4]

In these postwar years, the park and nearby communities attained new heights of rapprochement. For example, the park staff built a float for Durango's Spanish Trails Fiesta parade in August, 1946. Superintendent Rose complimented his personnel for the "splendid spirit" they exhibited in building the display, which depicted a prehistoric cliff dwelling. Rose had encouraged the construction because of the "goodwill [that] participation in this important San Juan Basin event creates for Mesa Verde." The feeling was mutual; with increased attendance (over 52,000 in 1947, 150,000 in 1954, and 200,000 four years later), the park had rapidly assumed a major role in the local economy.

Both Durango and Cortez barreled into a boom after the war, thanks to oil, natural gas, and uranium. Durango held on to its lead as a tourist center, because it still had better transportation connections, more varied tourist attractions, and a wider variety of accommodations, but both communities became more oriented toward tourists, each providing a strip of restaurants and motels to tempt the road-weary traveler.[5] The chambers of commerce leaders cheered tourism, and newspapers and radio stations promoted it.

A major reason that Mesa Verde visitation jumped (and why, paradoxically, Cortez lagged behind Durango) was the steady improvement of highways, except those to the west of Cortez. Even before the war's end, plans had been made to improve the Four Corners highway system. Cortez's Chamber of Commerce led the fight to improve the road to Gallup, with Nusbaum enthusiastically supporting its efforts. Proponents argued that a better road would make it easier to transport war-needed agricultural products south from Montezuma County to the railroad at Gallup, but it is obvious that they were looking forward to the postwar tourist trade with equal relish. Hopes for quick action hit a snag when protests mounted from Aztec, New Mexico, which found itself off the route and threatened with a loss of business. Aztec managed to delay the project for one year, but it was a doomed effort to preserve the status quo, just as the one by the liverymen of Mancos had been earlier. Neither could stop progress in order to protect local interests. By the end of 1946, the road between Cortez and Gallup had been realigned, resurfaced, and oiled; Cortez had acquired one needed artery to the outside. Without a pause, the Cortez chamber pushed to improve the roads into Utah and called for the surfacing and oiling of Wolf Creek Pass. One might question why Cortez would concern itself with Wolf Creek, which would aid its rival, Durango. Chamber officials optimistically believed that an improved Wolf Creek Pass would give Cortez fine roads to Mesa Verde, Yellowstone, and beyond. "We have been in the wilds long enough and are getting out," asserted the chamber's secretary.[6]

Progressive attitudes could not mask urban jealousies, which continued to infect all these communities. Durango vied with Cortez for tourist supremacy, as always, with challenges from Gallup, Shiprock, and Aztec, New Mexico, as well as any other town within a day's drive of Mesa Verde. Each was determined to attract its share, and then some, of the tourist business, and each wanted to be sure none of the others infringed upon its rights. With more at stake now, emotions intensified. It would be a battle to the end.

The Navajo Trail Association remained as the only regional effort of any consequence, and it continued to boost attractions along Highway 160. Superintendent Rose strongly backed the group's efforts, understanding that unity promised more than fractionalism: "We all appreciate your continued interest in all communities, including ours, located upon, and close to, our Navajo Trail." Regrettably, few local residents had that perspective; their individual interests outweighed regional benefits.

The rivalries of the towns became a moot point when highway construction was taken out of local and state hands as the federal government assumed the major responsibility. The development of the natural resources of the Four Corners region as part of war demands, and then for defense needs after 1945, gave the politically weak area a boost it never would have received otherwise. A number of defense highway acts had been passed during World War II, and these were broadened afterward during the Cold War and then the Korean War. As a result, the Department of Defense built more than eight hundred miles of roads in the Four Corners region during the early 1950s as part of the Atomic Energy Commission's program to provide access roads to mines and mills. These were not just gravel roads to some isolated spot where uranium had been discovered; they were, in some cases, major highways. Highway 160, which led to the

park's entrance in the stretch between Durango and Cortez, found favor because it ran to the uranium smelter in Durango. In New Mexico, Highway 44 from Farmington to Albuquerque was improved for similar reasons. These kinds of roads and highways provided needed links to the national highway system and revolutionized the regional economy.

New plans continued to flow freely from Washington. Whereas U.S. Route 66 through Gallup had once been the focus of travel (and song), by the second term of the Eisenhower administration the federally funded interstate highway system had begun to steal some of the attention.[7] Denver—and Colorado as a whole—would benefit mightily from this program. Although none of the interstates came near to Mesa Verde, they brought the visitor to Colorado and within easy traveling distance of the park. The Four Corners finally had been joined by highway ties to the rest of the United States, except directly to the west. That possibility, too, was a subject of serious discussion, if not immediate action.

The adventuresome now flew where once they had ridden or driven. Only a generation before, Will Rogers had virtually pioneered private flights into southwestern Colorado; now commercial flights landed regularly at both Durango and Cortez. From there, a short car or bus trip brought Mesa Verde within easy reach. Most Americans, however, had not yet become enamored of air travel, so most of them continued to drive their cars over mountain and desert to reach the park. Railroad travel, no longer feasible, ceased. The unprofitable Rio Grande Southern had been abandoned and its tracks torn up by the parent Denver & Rio Grande Western. The D&RGW still ran trains into Durango, but they would not last much longer. Passenger traffic had dwindled to nothing,

and freight barely produced enough revenue to justify itself.

Park administrators had a hard time matching the outside road improvements, money being their major stumbling block. W. Ward Yeager, acting superintendent before Rose, expressed what many of his predecessors had thought and what many of his successors would echo, "However it is not in error to say that road construction or major maintenance has continued to some degree from June 1911 to today, 36 years of struggle with unstable foundations and ever improving road standards." He might have gone on to add that more money had probably been spent on roads and road maintenance in Mesa Verde than on any other single item, including archaeology.

The major breakthrough in highway improvement came in 1957 with the elimination of what the *Denver Post* described as "the hair-raising 'knife-edge' road so notorious among

tourists." The shorter and safer route to Chapin Mesa that replaced it included what was, at the time, the longest highway tunnel in the state.[8] That road project was claimed as part of the Mission 66 Program but actually preceded it. Technically, funds had been appropriated for the road before Congress launched Mission 66.

The Mission 66 program was a dream come true for the National Park Service and benefited the whole country. The service's director, Conrad Wirth, described it as a park "renaissance." The National Park Service designed Mission 66 in response to funding shortages since the start of the war, increased visitation, and people coming by car who wanted new facilities adapted to their needs. The goal of Mission 66 was to overcome years of neglect and to revitalize deteriorating park facilities. Wirth pulled no punches when he warned readers in a *Reader's Digest* article (January, 1955) that their visit to a park "is likely to be fraught with discomfort, disappointment, even danger. . . . It is not possible to provide essential services."[9] The program was to be run for ten years and be completed by the fiftieth anniversary of the National Park Service in 1966.

For Mesa Verde, Mission 66 would be one of two programs that would significantly change the park in the next decade, the other being the Wetherill Mesa Project. Mesa Verde had endured some difficult times. Summer days found the Spruce Tree House and museum area overcrowded, though never as much so there as in other, more popular, parks. The traditional plan of centralizing all activities on Chapin Mesa came under fire as "the greatest single threat to the integrity of the Park and to visitor enjoyment." The idea had been fine for an era of more limited and leisurely use, but it would not do for the 1950s. Nusbaum had been right

twenty years before when he issued a warning on the subject. Mesa Verde, already a small park, shrank considerably when it was measured in terms of space suitable for visitor development. Something had to be done.

Plans for Mission 66 moved rapidly at Mesa Verde and reflected the concept as it was promoted throughout the whole park system. The visitor service program was to be updated to enhance the understanding and appreciation of the park's "unique attractions"; new archaeological areas were to be opened as exhibits. The lodge, cabins, and campground would be relocated, and adequate and appropriate staff and facilities would be provided for park management, protection, and maintenance. All these things were to be accomplished while doing "business as usual" each season; the integration would be "breath taking," if it could be accomplished smoothly. This ambitious

program assumed that the end result would be the maximum constructive and wholesome use of Mesa Verde's prehistoric and scenic resources.

The program sounded good in theory, and it would eventually prove beneficial in practice, but it jumped off to a bad start. Colorado Senator Gordon Allott became ill humored over what he charged was the so-called secrecy of planning, a "demonstration of arrogant bureaucratic power." He protested the plans to relocate the lodging and camping facilities and the one to convert Spruce Tree point into an archaeological center. "The individuals responsible for this cockeyed plan are the very ones who have kept the park from being properly developed," he bitterly complained. The senator was supported by some local people, including Ansel Hall, who thought the basic idea sound but the secrecy untenable. Hall particularly opposed

The horseback trip on the Spruce Canyon trail, long a popular attraction.

Courtesy: Mesa Verde National Park

moving the lodge to Navajo Hill and successfully fought that plan until his death in 1962. To him, "the public was better served at Spruce Tree."

"Cockeyed" the plan was not, no matter what one's opinion of the secrecy of the planning process might be. Oscar Carlson, superintendent from 1952 through 1958, endorsed it and waited for the necessary funds to arrive. He would be gone, as would the decade, before the program entered into full swing at Mesa Verde. The delay caused dismay, and Chester Thomas, the new superintendent in 1959, a tall, white-haired, pensive-appearing man, felt the need to encourage his staff in December, 1959, after a trip to Washington. The project's director said reassuringly, "I urge all of you, especially those that have not received any substantial help as yet, to have faith in MISSION 66 and be optimistic. Optimism is the best cure I know of for hard knocks."[10] Mesa

Verde personnel, therefore, awaited the 1960s with as much optimism as they could muster.

The renewal of major archaeological work, to be symbolized by the Wetherill Mesa Project, generated more excitement on the local level. Where once the great southwestern archaeologists—Fewkes, Kidder, Nusbaum, and Morris—had dug and collected, a long season of relative quiet had settled in. Mesa Verde's benchmark excavations and reports had been completed years before, and the park had quietly faded from its leading position as a source of ongoing prehistoric excavation. Unlike the majority of the Anasazi sites, Mesa Verde had a dual role to play in public visitation and in education and scholarly investigation. The former function was always paramount with the government, the latter an adjunct to be nourished when funds and staff became available.

Archaeological studies had never

actually ended; they had just been refocused. A systematic survey of prehistoric resources that was started in the mid-1930s continued into the 1970s and was eventually to identify some four thousand sites within the park. After World War II, a series of excavations of mesa-top and talus-slope village sites was conducted to find out more about the pre-cliff-dweller era. Deric O'Bryan (after the Nusbaums' divorce, he took his mother's maiden name) returned to the scenes of his youth to excavate a series of mesa-top ruins.

In 1953, the University of Colorado launched the first of four yearly six-week summer sessions of field research, a program that coupled research with training students in field methods. Professor Robert Lister remembered it well: "We lived in the school house and old CCC foreman's barracks in the Utility area. Florence [his wife] cooked for 30 students (and a few

The National Park Service, joined by the National Geographic Society, was already planning the Wetherill Mesa Archaeological Project when this September, 1958, tour of Mug House took place.

Courtesy: Mesa Verde National Park

seasonal rangers who couldn't stand their own cooking), and studied the pottery recovered." They cleared three ruins from 1953 through 1956.[11]

Now, in the 1950s, with new scientific methods and research techniques, it seemed appropriate that a full-scale, intensive multidisciplinary research program be launched. The goal would be to learn as much as possible about the inhabitants and their environment and to bring into focus as sharply as possible Mesa Verde life that had only been hinted at by earlier work. The ultimate benefit would accrue to the visiting public.

Archaeology alone would not be served. The overcrowding of popular cliff dwellings during the peak summer tourist season cried for relief. Chapin Mesa, less than 10 percent of the park's area, attracted almost all of the tourist traffic. This pressure would be alleviated if a series of ruins exhibits to rival the famous triumvirate of Spruce Tree, Cliff Palace, and Balcony House could be excavated, stabilized, and opened to view somewhere else in the park.

The Wetherill Mesa Project was designed with these two goals in mind —research and new exhibits. The selection of Wetherill Mesa on the park's western boundary came about naturally because of its outstanding cave sites and small pueblos on the mesa. It also could be tied nicely into the planned new visitor center on Navajo Hill, part of the Mission 66 Project.[12]

Mesa Verde benefited from more than Mission 66, because the National Geographic Society took an interest in the Wetherill Mesa Project. Four generous grants of fifty thousand dollars each, which began in 1958, allowed research not supported by federal funds, such as that in human osteology and in areas outside the park—for instance, the famous Nordenskiold collection.

The project got under way in the fall of 1958. The first season brought the excavation of Long House and the beginning of an archaeological sites survey. A visitor caught the excitement and sense of adventure:

> Everywhere there was tense, purposeful activity. No one could be sure what the next spadeful of earth would uncover; what these debris-filled rooms would tell us of the fate of their vanished builders. . . . Meantime, the vast canyons will continue to echo the sounds of the 20th-century science at work as the past yields its secrets to modern techniques, and an almost lost way of life emerges from the shadows.

By the end of the second season eight hundred sites had been found within ten square miles. Laboratory work began at the same time to study the results of the ongoing field work.[13] Not for over a generation had there been so much archaeological excitement at

Mesa Verde. Never before had there been such a large-scale, well-funded, scientific project.

Amid the planning and projects, park season after park season rolled by. The popularity of Mesa Verde and the use of its facilities increased almost daily, it seemed. Visitors were coming now in larger numbers from all over the country, a change noticeable even in the last war year of 1945. Colorado visitor totals stayed far out in front, but California moved into the number two position, followed by New Mexico and Texas. When the 1952 season ended, California had cut sharply into Colorado's lead, followed by Texas, New Mexico, and Illinois. The nearby Four Corners states no longer dominated; better highways and higher incomes had put America's middle class into the car and on the road.

Tourists drove extra miles to see the park, encouraged by articles such as the one that appeared in the travel sec-

tion of the *New York Times*, July 2, 1950. The writer soothed the fears of timid travelers by assuring them that even those unaccustomed to driving in canyon country would be perfectly safe if they observed the 35 m.p.h. speed limit, took the caution signs literally, and kept their cars in gear on the downgrade! The article praised the museum, the "erudite" park rangers, the campfire talks, Spruce Tree Lodge, the horseback tours, and the Navajo dances. Something would surely appeal to every visitor. It went on to gush over the beautiful scenery of wildflowers, canyons, and piñon and juniper forests. Those motorists jaded by touring the Rockies would find that "after experiencing eye fatigue from gaping at peaks, gorges, waterfalls, glaciers and other natural spectacles, there is welcome mental stimulation in studying the ruins of Mesa Verde." The *Kansas City Times* (June 22, 1956), saluting Mesa Verde's golden anni-

versary, recommended that its readers pause in their Rocky Mountain tour for a chance to "study civilization of yesterday, and enjoy the modern overnight accommodations."

The thousands who came (the millionth visitor since the park's establishment arrived sometime in the early summer of 1953) found a park in which the Mesa Verde Company had steadily upgraded its concessions to include new cottages, the remodeling of the lodge, better buses for expanded sightseeing, and even a Kids Korral for child care. Ansel Hall strongly believed "the visitor should have a quality experience in the park." As much as possible, he energetically wove together the park's interpretive program with his concession business. This alliance, Hall believed, would strengthen the visitor's experience. He also promoted Mesa Verde with enthusiasm. June Hall remembered one method that her husband used to do that:

Mesa Verde's popularity had produced a crush of visitors by the mid-1950s. Spruce Tree House could hardly handle any more people.
Courtesy: Mesa Verde National Park

He wrote little information folders, all the advance information people needed. He would go around and distribute those things within a radius of a hundred to a hundred and fifty miles, so that people as they came in this direction would find these circulars in motels, service stations and places like that. This was one of the best ways of publicity.

Hall believed that the concessionaire should promote the park, just as any other businessman would promote his business.

In the mid-1950s, the company also developed the Point Lookout Lodge complex outside the entrance as an alternative to staying in the park. After the war years, when they had gone into the red by almost $33,000, the Halls had finally turned a profit in the early 1950s. But not everything came up roses for them. Negotiations for a new concession contract dragged on for years, probably explaining in part why Ansel became so upset over the alleged secrecy of Mission 66. Causing more anger was the government's plan to cancel out the company's long-range improvement plans. Further hassles ensued when the company had to approach the National Park Service to ask for new rates in the face of steadily increasing expenses. June Hall presented their side of the story: "We were in sort of an adversary position. They were always holding us down in our rates, trying to make us comparable to the local prices, while our customers didn't come from there." She was confident that their customers would accept higher rates.[14]

That assumption was questionable. There were always complaints from disgruntled visitors about high costs, lack of accommodations, and other irritants. Some of them went directly to the company; others took their complaints to the National Park Service, where they sometimes became a matter of discussion at staff meetings.[15] The staff also discussed the pros and cons of year-round operation (no decision was reached) and the closing of the Mesa Verde school. It was decided not to abandon the school, because parents wanted to keep their elementary-age children near home to avoid a long bus ride, during which one ranger/driver remembered that his riders "could think of ways to cut up." The superintendent recommended in 1949 that his staff members work to improve their writing skills and was pleased when they got better. Jean Pinkley, the outstanding woman ranger/park archaeologist of her era and a prominent southwestern archaeologist in her own right, planned to improve upon her writing by researching and then writing a history of Mesa Verde. For unspecified reasons, and "much to my regret," she dropped the project.[16]

Vandalism continued to plague the

Ansel Hall and Amy Andrews greet Frontier Airline hostesses at the Spruce Tree Lodge in 1953. Frontier's advertising helped to promote Mesa Verde, as the poster indicates.
Courtesy: William Winkler

park, even after years of public education to encourage preservation of the archaeological record. The exciting possibility of finding an ancient artifact proved too tempting for some Americans, including a Dayton, Ohio, teacher, his wife, and their children, who were caught digging. The father attempted to justify their actions by pleading that they had dug only in a cave and had not disturbed anything that park rangers would not have disturbed anyway! That excuse failed to prevent their being fined twenty-five dollars.[17] If teachers, of all people, could not follow the rules, it is understandable that this problem persisted from 1906 through generations of visitors.

Life for the staff had not changed much over the years. Jeannie Lee Jim, a Navajo whose father worked at restoring ruins and a "lot on the Knife Edge road," remembered, "It was a lot of fun growing up at Mesa Verde." She went to the dances to watch her father and his friends; sometimes the dancers collected as much as fifty dollars. For these Navajos, life at Mesa Verde was better than it would have been back on the usually economically depressed reservation.

The Mesa Verde "family" included everyone from the seasonals to the superintendent. They lived and worked together within the confines of the park. This togetherness occasionally bred problems; as one person recalled, "you lived too close to each other in the winter time, in my view in retrospect." Putting personal conflicts aside, the employees represented the best that the National Park Service had to offer, none more so than the often crusty, "long, tall" Jean Pinkley, with her dedication and love for Mesa Verde. She was the kind of long-time park service employee who just "gave and gave and gave." Like Don Watson and all those dedicated people who presented campfire programs on their days off, she worked literally night and day.

She used to collect wildflowers [again, on her day off] for the Natural History museum, where she labeled them. She collected wildflower seeds and, after the new road was put in at the fire tower lookout, she personally and tenderly scattered and planted and urged all the wildflower seeds in that disturbed area.

She loved being a ranger. When it was her turn to do campfire, I would never miss it. . . . She had a way of telling campfire circle stories that were just wonderful.

Occasionally, the younger members of the "family" tested the patience of their more reserved elders. In 1946, their youthful exuberance led them to hold an evening party in one of the Spruce Tree House kivas. Everything was going according to plan as they sat down to "play cards and listen to Glen Miller music." A broken tree branch with a coat draped over it covered the kiva entrance to prevent a tell-tale glow of light from giving the youngsters' presence away. To double security, a lookout had been posted near the trail to warn of anyone's approach. Unfortunately for the group's best-laid plans, the lookout focused more attention on his date than on shadows moving down the trail. A ranger detachment, led by Jean Pinkley, slipped past the watch and surprised the shocked gathering.

The stern words, "It is my duty to advise you that you are under arrest," were the first ones the mischievous youths heard. They trooped out, eventually to be confronted by mortified parents and to face a solemn appearance before a federal magistrate. Each participant was fined five dollars. In later, more relaxed, times the survivors dubbed themselves the "Kiva Bridge Club." [18]

All work, with no relaxation, did not characterize all of the employees' waking hours. There was the lodge, the meeting place for park service personnel ("their home away from home"), and the little Sipapu Bar, where they had "a lot of fellowship." The schoolhouse, following that old frontier tradition, served as the center of family parties and programs.

Ranger Kenny Ross remembered the shopping trips to Cortez, Mancos, and Durango, especially the winter weekends when Mesa Verde people would gather at the Strater Hotel in Durango and "have a lot of fun, sometimes almost destructive fun." Summer left little time for anything other than work; winter at the park brought homemade amusements, including parties, barbecues, and "lots of beer." [19] For these people, Mesa Verde was not simply a national park to visit and then leave for yet another place— it was a home and a livelihood—and perhaps a life-long love affair with the canyons and mesas. They gave it substance and flavor in the grand tradition of the Wetherills, Kelly, and Nusbaum.

CHAPTER TEN

"A Solid Mass of Milling Humanity"

The 1960s started out as had no other decade in the history of Mesa Verde. The Wetherill Mesa Project was well under way, and Mission 66 promised to bring about needed improvements. Exciting times, these, as the park fairly buzzed with activity.

The peak of activity at Wetherill came in 1961, with four field crews working at various sites and a laboratory team cleaning and cataloguing items recovered from the digs. A steady stream of participating scientists from other agencies and institutions visited the project to contribute their expertise and to tour "the largest archaeological program carried out" at Mesa Verde,

one that "ranks with the most extensive ever performed in the United States."

Al Lancaster, who had worked at Mesa Verde since the early 1930s, having been one of the earliest members of the stabilization crew, recalled some resentment of the Wetherill Mesa group by the park people, which was ultimately resolved. Lancaster was "in charge of excavation and stabilization of Mug House and Long House. I enjoyed it all." So did archaeologist Robert Lister, who served on an advisory committee to the project, which met several times with the National Geographic Society research committee. Lister later said, "I recall the NGS

photographers bringing in a group of airline stewardesses to pose among the ruins and also how well the NGS provided for their committee members—hotels, food and drink, rides in special cars on the narrow gauge railroad, etc."[1] Lister, whose career at Mesa Verde spanned several decades, remembered, with some amusement, one unnamed superintendent who kept referring to the ruins as "fossils"!

The fifth and final season of field work in 1963 found a reduced crew making a few last test excavations and stabilizing endangered sections of four large cliff dwellings, which would be viewed from vantage points

The days of primitive archae-ology had long disappeared when the Wetherill Mesa Project began. A sand-stone slab threat-ened Mug House, but a hard-rock miner, cribbing, and blasting saved it.
Courtesy: Richard Ellis

on the cliff edge. Laboratory and paper work continued into 1965, when the project's field work and research were completed at a cost of over $1 million. Three cliff dwellings had been cleared and eight other ruins had been excavated to depict the full sequence of Mesa Verde culture. A second section of the park was now ready for visitors, as soon as a transportation system could be devised.[2] All in all, it proved to be an outstanding program, one that benefited scholar and visitor alike.

Archaeologist Alden Hayes captured the spirit of the project and spoke for others, when he wrote:

Those of us who were privileged to take an active part in the exploration of Wetherill Mesa devoutly hope that each visitor in the future, who looks down at the sightless windows of Double House from a rock ledge or who rounds the bend in the cliff to set foot in Long House, will experience some of the same thrill of discovery that was ours.[3]

After the completion of the Wetherill work, the University of Colorado again had crews in the field, under Lister's direction and with the skilled assistance of Lancaster and some of the experienced Navajos. It had been a busy period in the park. Eventually, the public would gain further understanding under less crowded conditions from all this effort.

This multidisciplinary research program added immeasurably to the knowledge of Mesa Verde prehistory and placed Mesa Verde back in the forefront of southwestern archaeology's current developments. The fortunate circumstance of available money coincided with park needs as never before or since. The park, the visitor, and the scholar benefited from the Wetherill Mesa Project; its impact is still being felt twenty years later.

The opening of a new area could come none too soon—crowds literally overran the park during the peak days of the summer season. Every room at the lodge and all campsites were occupied nearly every evening in 1963, and an estimated 200 to 300 cars were turned away. And conditions got worse. By July, 1965, Superintendent Chester Thomas pointed out the obvious: Any cliff dwelling trip of over forty people was considered a "potentially dangerous one both from the standpoint of the damage to the ruin and the risk of human life from crowding and joggling" in the confines of the cave site. That month, 619 groups had toured Cliff Palace, of which 26 percent fell into the acceptable size range, 12 percent were barely manageable, and 62 percent were unmanageable parties that included up to 210 individuals. "There were times when people were strung from the top of the in-going stairway to the top of the exit ladders, a solid mass of milling humanity."

Thomas went on to note that in July, 1965, for the first time in the history of the park, a month's visitation figures exceeded 100,000.[4] That number by itself represented a staggering total, but it becomes even more startling when one realizes that the cumulative total of Mesa Verde visitors had not topped that figure until sometime early in the 1930 season, twenty-four years after creation of the park.

Mesa Verde's popularity and the throngs of "milling humanity" threatened ruination of the tourists' visit and serious damage to the cliff dwellings, even with the ongoing maintenance and stabilization programs. One description of a trip into Cliff Palace in mid-decade went this way: The cave acted as a sounding board for "scuffling feet, wails of crying kids, the rangers' voice; bedlam is the rule of the day all summer long." With the rangers forced to "yell above the racket . . . interpretation at this site is rapidly becoming a farce." Reform had to come and it did, with a ticketing system that limited the number of visitors to Cliff Palace and Balcony House.

Self-guided tours of Spruce Tree House were tried, without success, because few people "paid any attention to the number of stations or referred to the guidebooks." Superintendent Thomas concluded that self-guided tours would not be used in the ruins unless he were forced into it.[5]

Mission 66 continued to promise some relief from the crush of visitors. As the years sped toward the end of the project, discussions moved slowly concerning new campgrounds and a lodge away from Spruce Tree Point. The surging crowds of the 1960s added urgency to the deliberations. One stumbling block finally was removed—a new concessionaire contract was signed in 1964, after on-and-off negotiations over the course of thirteen years. Ansel Hall did not live long enough to see the conclusion; the company remained under family ownership, but the new management did not hold Ansel's strong objections to moving the lodge.

There were some complaints about allowing the continuation of a monopoly in the park. Circumstances in the national parks in general, however, were not conducive to effective competition. Eager tourists, busy running hither and yon, did not have the opportunity or the desire to study and support competitive enterprises. From the point of view of the National Park Service, a regulated monopoly appeared "preferable" to competition in park concessions; one concessionaire seemed easier to keep tabs on than several.[6] Competition outside the park gave the visitor a choice in lodging, and in Mesa Verde's case particularly, nearby campgrounds were able to relieve some of the camping pressure inside the park by the early 1970s.

The Mesa Verde Company and the National Park Service moved ahead toward planning and developing new facilities. The final decision placed the lodge on Navajo Hill and the campground at the upper end of Morefield Canyon. Bill Winkler, commercial manager for the company, told how the final lodge site was chosen:

The day it was selected, I remember walking through the sagebrush on that windswept hilltop, with the regional director of the Park Service. He had a walking stick with him, and he plopped it in the ground with a big thump and said, "Let it be there." That's how they picked the site. . . . He was angry as to how hard it had been to get to this point [in the negotiations]. It hampered his vision as to what the people needed. Some of his staff could see that it was going to be a real challenge to develop a good visitor experience out of this site he had selected. I remember to this day his comment, "Let them look at the oakbrush." I think the architectural firm selected was very sensitive to the needs and came up with the best.

Construction on the Far View Lodge and service station began in late 1965, and rooms were ready for occupancy by the following season. Only one small problem remained: Guests had to take their meals at the old Spruce Tree Lodge, some six miles to the south. Construction at the Morefield Campground, meanwhile, moved forward. Finally, at the end of the 1967 season, all facilities at Spruce Tree Point were turned over to the federal government.

Far View, by then, had a restaurant and a cafeteria, as well as other concessions. The former hospital, which had evolved into a first-aid station as times changed and transportation improved, evolved one more time into a remodeled food service facility for visitors to the museum and Spruce Tree House.

The Far View Lodge, sitting amid the oakbrush on that windswept hill, overcame its unpromising location, thanks to the architects and to the Winklers' dedication. The magnificent sweeping views to the south and west contributed their share to the lodgers' enjoyment of the site. Discussing those times, Bill and Merrie Winkler explained:

. . . a hotel or inn is a very personal place. You either relate to it or you don't. What we wanted was that lodge to leave an impression on the

Navajo Hill, the Visitors' Center (foreground), and the Far View Lodge (background) are locked in by a winter's day.
Courtesy: Mesa Verde National Park

visitor; I guess that's the best way I can express it. The visitor came, saw the lodge, would stay in the rooms, eat at the lodge, then they would come away and say, "I will never forget Mesa Verde." A lot of motel rooms look alike; we wanted people to come away with a different feeling, especially with that lodge. We really poured ourselves into that lodge, wanted that to be a super interpretive experience.[7]

The new generation of visitors would have to judge for themselves the success of the Winklers' dreams and efforts.

The long-felt need to relieve crowding at Spruce Tree Point had been met, at least partly. At the same time, plans were under way for a new visitors' center on Navajo Hill and for the organization of tours through the Wetherill Mesa sites. All a part of— or a spin-off of—Mission 66, some of those plans would come to fruition long after that project had become history. Like Rocky Mountain National Park, which received similar help on a grander scale, Mesa Verde was better prepared for the tourist crunch of the seventies.

So much progress had its price, even if it was only an emotional one. Gil Wenger, chief park archaeologist, remembered that "many older folks commented that they hated to see it [the lodge] go"; it had been a delightful place in earlier years.[8] Memories alone remained by the beginning of the new decade, as the National Park Service removed buildings and began "landscaping."

Memories were also the stuff of the Wetherill-Mason family reunion in the park in June, 1965. For a brief moment, the park turned back the clock to honor the family that, seventy-six years before, had started it all. It was just like old times, even to the reinflaming of some long-simmering arguments.

Except for that continuing debate over whether Richard or Al had first seen Cliff Palace, the reunion proved to be a rousing success. The "Al" faction carried on a running feud with the National Park Service, much to Jean Pinkley's disgust, over what Al's supporters believed were unfounded pothunting accusations made against the Wetherills.[9] The feud amounted to a tempest on a potsherd, but it managed to stir up feelings long thought to be dead.

Pinkley also became angry, and justifiably so, with the Rocky Mountain AAA over its 1964–65 issue of "Where to Vacation in Colorado." The motor club described the Manitou cliff dwellings as an "archeological preserve dating from approximately 1019 A.D." The AAA rubbed a raw nerve with that item; the park staff had already suffered nearly sixty years' worth of aggravation from the impostor. This latest description brought a sharp retort from Pinkley: "Not only are they fakes, poorly constructed fakes at that, but the self-guiding panel exhibits in place are full of mis-information, some of which is actually ludicrous." She rated it as no better than a "tourist-trap," whose reproductions "are not an archeological *preserve*." [10]

On a more positive note, the Navajo Trail (Highway 160) was finally completed across the Navajo Reservation in Arizona. The *Denver Post*, September 17, 1962, described it as "a vital east-west connecting link between Mesa Verde and the Grand Canyon." As the shortest, most scenic, "all-weather route" between Los Angeles and Kansas City, Highway 160 generated new tourism possibilities for Mesa Verde.

For Cortez, the new highway provided the final link in its tourist chain; at last, the city was tied directly to the Arizona and California tourist mar-ket. Now Cortez emerged as a serious threat to the long-time dominance of Mesa Verde tourism by Durango. Highway 160, southwestern Colorado's main artery, stretched between the two towns, and each planned to domi-nate that gateway to the park. Cortez grew by two-and-one-half times, and Durango topped ten thousand in popu-lation by 1960. The conversion in the 1960s of the narrow-gauge railroad from Durango to Silverton to a tourist attraction, providing a round-trip train ride, hinted at a nearly unbeatable bonanza for future tourism. Old-timer and banker Neil Camp accurately prophesied that the railroad "may be as important to Southwest Colo-rado as the establishment of Mesa Verde National Park." [11] Durango also acquired a ski area when Purgatory Resort opened twenty-five miles north of town, but this only slightly affected park visitation. Most people did not think of Mesa Verde in the winter, despite its own special charms at that season of the year.

The two rival towns occasionally joined in a common promotion, but more often their relationship remained at the dog-eat-dog level of the nine-teenth century. Each sought to prevent the other from gaining an advantage. The National Park Service and the Mesa Verde Company were able to promote without the obvious bias and prejudice often seen in the efforts of Cortez and Durango. Other firms joined with them in special promo-tions; one example was Frontier Air-lines, which did business in the Four Corners region. All the publicity paid off handsomely in the long run, as tour-ism boomed in southwestern Colorado.

The road system outside the park was now in place and needed only maintenance and repair to keep the traffic flowing. Inside the park, slides, buckling, and road damage continued to undermine crucial parts of the roadway, which was underlain by the unstable Mancos shale. Money, repairs, and plans all failed to overcome the problems; drivers still had to slow down to pass work crews and dodge chuckholes. Traffic delays irritated impatient travelers, some of whom simply turned around and left. Patience was a prerequisite for enduring the struggle to improve park roads.

Superintendent Chester Thomas, an experienced administrator who had dealt with many of the same problems at Zion National Park, worked all the while to build bridges of cooperation to the neighboring communities. He encouraged his employees to "become good neighbors," to join civic clubs, library and hospital boards; to work with the Scouts; and simply to be involved wherever the opportunity arose. Park wives, he believed, often did more

along these lines than their husbands. He understood the generations-old love/hate relationship between the West and the federal government, and he endeavored to reconcile it: "Mesa Verde National Park and a large number of our parks and monuments are in or near small communities where the people tend to be conservative and to hold the general attitude that Federal activities are suspect. Quite often as representatives of the Federal Government, employees are also suspect." He painted a fair picture of Mancos and Cortez and, to a lesser degree, of Durango. He pointed out that the towns needed the jobs and money that the federal agencies provided, but they did not have to like the purveyor or its employees. This distrust, or jealousy perhaps, would have been perfectly understandable to the Wetherills and their neighbors of the 1880s.

Thomas, though, did not stop his

reconciliation efforts there. He was fully aware that attitudes worked like a two-way street and that government employees could make impressions that reinforced preconceived opinions. "By the same token, small communities are suspect by our employees," who saw their life centered in the park: "To hell with the community and what people outside may think." This kind of antagonism boded ill for the park, Thomas warned, "We as individuals, our institutions, our country and our bureaus, prosper largely as the image we present to the public is good or bad."[12] Thomas hit the mark on all counts, but his education efforts fell on hard times in the 1960s and early 1970s. The Vietnam War and the Watergate misadventures dragged public confidence in the government down to nearly all-time lows.

Mesa Verde could even be troubled by a seemingly harmless government decision, such as the one that allowed the states to adopt daylight saving time. In 1965 Colorado went along with the plan, but its three neighboring states (Arizona, New Mexico, and Utah) did not. The park staff anticipated problems but did not realize their magnitude until June. The campfire talk lost its flavor in daylight, so it had to be delayed until 9:00 P.M., which made an intolerably long day for the speakers, some of whom had gone to work at 7:00 A.M.

Employees started work very early, because people began arriving in the park at all hours. Early arrivals were not attracted to the early trips into the ruins, which were poorly attended and were eventually dropped in favor of late afternoon ones. Traditional meal times had no meaning, thrown completely out of kilter as they were by hungry tourists. Some of them ate breakfast while others nibbled their lunch. Campers started to arrive later in the day in order to take advantage of the extended driving hours. The superintendent confessed, "no one could imagine the difficulty the camping situation would create." [13] Despite Jean Pinkley's fears that all of these disruptions would put an end to the Interpretive Division, everyone adjusted and the park survived.

The federal government unintentionally created other problems, too. When supersonic planes began to fly over the park, creating their sonic booms, they seemed harmless enough. Not until 1966 did the frequency of flights (almost daily by December) produce enough thundering vibrations to threaten the cliff dwellings. Protests went immediately to the National Park Service and to the Federal Aviation Administration: "We are now faced, however, with a new threat to the continued preservation of the ruins —the ground jarring, shockwave effect of the 'sonic boom,' . . . they do present a potential threat to the structural stability of the fragile, original prehistoric walls." Special devices to record pressure sensitivity were installed in several ruins. Then, at last, a strongly worded communiqué to the Air Force recommended that its flight patterns be moved west of Mesa Verde to the canyon country. [14] When that was accomplished, the threat receded.

Even though the modern world kept closing in on Mesa Verde in the most unexpected ways, some of the pressures of the 1960s looked familiar. Jesse Nusbaum would have empathized with Meredith Guillet, superintendent in the late 1960s, who complained about the overtime it took to gather statistics for government reports. Washington promised reimbursement, a gesture that ignored the point Guillet was trying to make. Complaints about excessive paper work did not relieve the burden of the rapidly multiplying required reports and the lost time that could better be utilized for something more worthwhile. The National Park Service had difficulty finding qualified seasonal rangers, and the Mesa Verde Company had a hard time retaining its staff until after Labor Day; neither problem was new. Some employees' attitudes shocked even the old hands, however. Roger Hall complained about employees who agreed to stay and then went back on their word: "They don't even feel it is necessary to offer an explanation—it is the nature of the times."

Tourists and employees were no less accident prone than in earlier days. The hordes of tourists and the high level of activity in July and August, the peak months of each season, generated most of the mishaps. In August, 1965, for example, 258 persons required some "form of first aid," the number being almost evenly divided between visitors and staff. Two years later, the same months brought reported injuries of

turned ankles, wrenched knees, and one head-first fall into a kiva.[15] Some people seemed to be accidents looking for a place to happen.

All previous superintendents would have recognized the continuing plague of vandalism. In April, 1961, in what appeared to be a major cleanup of unresolved cases, letters were mailed to people from as far away as Massachusetts and California (the list of recipients was three pages long). The letters all opened with "It has recently come to our attention that your name and address are inscribed on government owned structures in Mesa Verde." After politely requesting that the individual return and remove the offending inscription or arrange through the chief park ranger to pay for someone else to do it, the letter flashed the iron fist. A fine of not more than five hundred dollars or six months of imprisonment awaited those who failed to respond. Probably the most shocked

and embarrassed of the miscreants were several adults whose names had been left by some of the boys whom they had chaperoned on a tour of the park![16] Fortunately, those who had the urge to leave a marker to their memory constituted only a very small percentage of the visiting public. Slowly and painfully over the years, Americans had become more aware of their individual responsibilities as stewards of their national parks.

Concerns could go both ways—the public had some complaints of their own about developments in the park. Objections quickly surfaced to a proposed reduction of the deer herd in the park in 1966, after the number of deer had outgrown the available food supply. Some of the more emotional protesters saw the plan as a plot to kill the lovable "Bambi" of childhood memories. Only after the superintendent made many appearances and answered reporters' questions from as far away as Seattle did the tempest subside and the reduction take place. Even the state of Colorado jumped into the fray briefly with the cry, "The State owns all game." Colorado might think that, but the question has never been decided in court. From Mesa Verde's viewpoint, these are "Federal deer." The wildlife in the park more than held its own and included mountain lions and bobcats. Abert squirrels had to be reintroduced to supplement the dwindling populations, as did the Gunnison's prairie dogs.[17] Those frisky little fellows gave fits to the staff when they refused to stay in the areas assigned to them!

Friction between the National Park Service and the Ute Mountain Utes remained unresolved decade after decade. Some of the park complaints were old ones. Sheep grazing and poaching were virtually impossible to prevent. The Ute section of Mesa Verde appeared to be valuable as domestic sheep pasture, but it proved unsuited to continuous utilization, which led to erosion. The sheep, not recognizing man-made boundaries, moved contentedly onto park land to graze. Discussions about effecting a land swap failed when no suitable government land could be found.

The Utes had their own grievances, making negotiations that much more difficult. They claimed that the park employed Navajos on labor projects to the exclusion of Utes. These two tribes also disputed part of the land that the Utes believed they had been awarded in the 1911 and 1913 exchanges for part of Mesa Verde. The Navajos eventually prevailed, and the Utes received other land and financial compensation. Unhappy over this turn of events, the Utes blamed the government, meaning Mesa Verde, which inherited a further legacy of mistrust.

In 1947, the Utes had taken their claims to court, suing for payment for millions of acres of land in Colorado and Utah. Part of this case involved the Southern Utes and that ill-starred 1911 land exchange. In a precedent-setting 1952 decision, the Court of Claims had awarded the Utes $32 million, which was divided among the various bands. This, the first major Indian victory, opened the door to a series of later suits.

Other Mesa Verde issues continued to fester. Discussions involving land exchanges or sales to acquire archaeological sites or a better roadway went on sporadically. Informal negotiations in 1957 to arrange a possible exchange for the rich archaeological area south of Chapin Mesa had been indefinitely postponed with the discovery of potential oil and natural gas sites. No progress was being made, and the atmosphere of mistrust and failure did not improve. Superintendent Thomas's request that "all members of the Park family take every available opportunity to promote good relations with the Utes" came too late. Platitudes, as well intentioned as they might have been, would not heal deeply ingrained animosities.

Superintendent Meredith Guillet, who came from an old Montezuma County family that traded with the Utes and Navajos, had first worked in the park in 1930 and then returned with the C.C.C. Now he was brought back, in 1966, to help resolve some long-festering Ute problems. With skills born of experience and cultural understanding, Guillet moved to work with the park's neighbors. All his patience and tact were required for the job. He and the National Park Service cooperated with the Utes on a plan to develop the Indians' archaeological sites directly south of Mesa Verde. Out of the studies and discussions, which began in the mid-1960s, came the Ute Mountain Tribal Park. The superintendent hoped it would take some of the visitation pressure off of Mesa Verde and provide jobs and tourist income for the tribe, which badly needed both.

But there were other complications. Part of the loop road to Cliff Palace crossed Ute land, and failed negotiations for a road to Wetherill Mesa had caused hurt feelings, particularly regarding Chief Jack House, who had been tactlessly pictured at a press conference as living rather primitively in a hut. The superintendent worked hard to overcome past animosities, and he eventually soothed feelings. Guillet, who knew Jack House, "got along good with him and we got everything settled. We got boundary lines set and everything." For the moment, the tension seemed to relax. Looking back over his superintendency, Guillet considered "good rapport with the Ute Tribe" as one of his major accomplishments.[18]

In the midst of things old and new, in 1965 Mesa Verde for the first time maintained a formal winter schedule of tours. Before then, tours to Spruce Tree House had been conducted on an irregular basis (at least as early as 1960, when it was suggested that the trail be shoveled free of snow). Now there would be two tours a day. The new policy was publicized in neighboring communities, and 201 visitors came that December of 1965.[19] The potential popularity of winter was demonstrated the next December, when nearly twenty-five hundred people arrived; however, the same month in 1967 showed the inherent pitfalls; the number of visitors was cut over 60 percent by a record snowfall.

The next year, Mesa Verde received automatic nomination for the National Register of Historic Places by virtue of its previous designation as a National Landmark. The new status, of course, helped to promote the park and give it additional prestige, which perhaps at this late date was hardly needed.

Mesa Verde, by the end of the 1960s, had emerged as a major tourist attraction and economic benefit to the Four Corners region. Most tourists, it was hoped, agreed in principle with the comments of one of their contemporaries from St. Joseph, Missouri: "I was impressed at the manner in which you people conduct this operation. I am sure that foreign visitors as well as American citizens are very proud of what is being preserved for us to look at and study." The National Park Service could take pride in its accomplishments. The 1960s had generated much progress and ground work had been laid for future developments.

Over half a million visitors entered the park in 1969, a new record and a significant indication that Mesa Verde had come of age. How to handle these numbers, this "solid mass of milling humanity," while maintaining a pleasant learning environment would be a major challenge for the next decade.

CHAPTER ELEVEN

The Best of Times, the Worst of Times

The record numbers of visitors predicted for the 1970s began to arrive as the decade opened. And during 1976, the bicentennial year of the United States of America, an all-time high of 676,935 people visited the park, where two hundred years did not even begin to reach back to the point at which the Anasazi era ended. That surge was followed by a slide, which would not be reversed until 1980. A previous decline in 1973–74 and the one in the late 1970s were both caused when a threatened gasoline shortage created by the international oil crisis produced unprecedented higher prices at the pump. The alarmed public stayed nearer home. Rocky Mountain National Park suffered the same fate, although it still far outdistanced Mesa Verde in popularity, topping 3 million visitors in 1978.

Despite the boom-and-bust aspects of the 1970s, Colorado benefited mightily from the magnetic attraction that both of these parks held for the traveling American. As Colorado benefited, so did other states. Commenting on the impact of the national park system to local economies, Director George Hartzog noted that $7.8 billion had been spent by visitors on their way to and in the vicinity of all parks in 1970. He recommended to his superintendents that they keep that salient fact in mind, warning them at the same time not to sacrifice basic park values for short-term tourist gains. Such tactics would surely "kill the goose that lays the golden eggs."[1] The planning and work that went on at Mesa Verde in the 1960s had been designed to resolve that dilemma before the park was forced to pay a fatal price for its growing popularity.

A survey in the 1970s showed that the typical visitor's experience consisted of a self-guided tour of a cliff dwelling, "supplemented by a walk through the museum," and an hour and a half drive along the ruins loop.

Self-guided tours had returned to favor because of the excessive amount of time and the number of rangers required to run continuous guided tours in all the ruins. The typical tourists came, saw, and hurried on to another spot. The typical family spent about six rushed hours in the park from entry to exit.

One innovation to keep crowds and traffic under control was tried: the distribution of tickets for specified times to tour Cliff Palace and Balcony House. Spruce Tree House stayed on a self-guided basis, with rangers always patrolling the ruin to supervise and to answer questions. Ticketed times alleviated some of the standing in line and the tiresome waiting and allowed a maximum number of visitors to explore the sites.

More relief came in 1973, when most of Wetherill Mesa was finally opened for visitation. Money shortages and an unfavorable political climate, brought on by the Vietnam War, had kept the project in limbo for years. Proposals had been "hashed over and over" about what to do and how to do it with the least possible damage to the fragile ruins. Uncontrolled visits seemed to be out of the question, and the government did not have the funds to carry out the ambitious original plans. When some money finally became available, the road to the mesa was built. Then came the energy crisis of 1973 and, with it, popular enthusiasm for conserving gasoline. The Mesa Verde Company capitalized on those circumstances to purchase a mini-train to transport visitors around the Wetherill Mesa sites, after a bus had brought the passengers there from the new Far View complex.[2] Reviewing those years, Ron Switzer, superintendent in the 1970s, emphasized that they required "real pioneering." He pointed out that the mini-trains were the first alternative transportation system in the National Park Service, "outside of the Mall in Washington." He and his staff planned stabilization projects, shaded waiting areas, guided tours, and built shelters over the fragile surfaces of ruins sites and trails. "I can tell you that hanging paved trails on the edges of the mesas is quite a difficult engineering feat, but we did it, mostly with day labor and materials and a couple of very good trail foremen." Switzer complimented his staff for their efforts: "We had some marvelous dedicated people on the staff with some rather unique and amazing skills."[3] Insufficient funds meant it would be 1987 before all the projects and plans begun during his administration would come to fruition.

The first visitors toured Long House; later in that summer of 1973 other sites were opened. Wetherill Mesa and the Far View Visitor Center were able to take some of the pressure off of Chapin

Mesa. For the first time in the park's history, there was an easily reachable alternative to the popular attractions of Chapin.

Year after year, the park headquarters were flooded with "literally hundreds of requests" for information. And they came not just from Americans—foreign visitors showed ever-increasing interest in the park, too. Those who arrived were given handouts in German, French, Japanese, and Spanish. These helped the education program, but by the end of the decade, serious consideration was being given to hiring seasonal interpreters who spoke one or more of those languages. Over the years, Mesa Verde had gained a worldwide reputation that rivaled Yellowstone's among the national parks in the United States.[4]

The steady upsurge in numbers forced the National Park Service into planning once more for the future and,

to a lesser degree, into reevaluating the purpose of Mesa Verde. The non-renewable Anasazi sites imposed strict limitations on the potential for park utilization. The use, management, and protection of the park had to be continuously evaluated as its popularity threatened its existence. A 1979 management plan specified the numbers of visitors that could be handled without seriously endangering the "unique experience for which Mesa Verde has been famous."

It was decided that no more than nine hundred visitors per hour should be allowed through the park entrance in order to avoid degrading the visitors' experience. To achieve that goal would require putting a limit on visitors at the peak of the summer season, a possibility that received some consideration before it was discarded. The limit on visitors per hour was eventually rescinded.

As alternatives to limiting numbers, the 1979 report recommended extending the visitor day, scheduling additional guided tours, opening more cliff dwellings to the public. All these modifications would require more staff and more funding, neither of which the National Park Service could supply. In a reiteration of some of the ideas that had been discussed but never implemented during Mission 66, it was recommended that park headquarters be relocated to the entrance and that some of the permanent staff be moved off the mesa. To meet the changing interests of the public, it was proposed that the foot and bike trail system on Chapin Mesa be expanded and that an effort be made to acquaint visitors with the "numerous recreational and educational opportunities" available within the park and the surrounding region.[5]

Those kinds of possibilities within

the park were limited. Unlike Rocky Mountain or Yellowstone, where a variety of scenery and experiences lay in wait for the adventuresome, most of Mesa Verde remained off limits to the visitor. As a September, 1973, article in the *Los Angeles Times* reminded its readers, this was the only national park in the nation where visitors found themselves not "free to hike at will through the back country."

Despite the obvious need to expand tours and park facilities, the bold and intense Ronald Switzer, one of the youngest and more controversial of the park's superintendents, was restrained by economic considerations and forced to cut back. "The park was underfunded," in his opinion, but Switzer pushed ahead with fine-tuning the park's management system, which included reorganization. "Sometimes you don't make friends when you do that kind of thing, but it took some of the unmet needs and responsibilities

and put them where they belonged," the aggressive superintendent admitted. "All in all it was great adventure and a very serious management challenge." When evaluating Switzer's administration, several park contemporaries concluded that "he did a good job."[6]

The rising cost of gasoline and other forms of energy forced the National Park Service to economize to stay within budgeted allotments. The first real impact of the crisis came in 1973–74, for the park as well as for the visitor. The cost of gasoline, which soared to over a dollar a gallon, sliced alarmingly into both the park's and the travelers' budgets. A casualty of the cutbacks came in the winter of 1975–76—all the campgrounds were closed, thereby ending the era of winter camping in the Chapin Mesa picnic area (Morefield Campground had never been open in the off-season). A press release explained that "increasing reductions" of budget and of personnel

ceilings had left the park unable to expend the money on personnel to maintain winter camping.[7]

The National Park Service adjusted to the changing times, and so did the Mesa Verde Company. The company rolled strongly and profitably into the 1970s, featuring its new Far View complex, but changes were coming in the concessions business throughout the park system. Bill Winkler, Ansel Hall's son-in-law and now president of the company, explained why:

The big companies started to come in. There was great thrust for control among concessionaires. The rules and regulations became almost worse, and they worked in a way I don't think the National Park Service even suspected. These big companies, with political power— they worked with senators throughout the country—they could handle the government. But a private concessionaire individual could not always deal with the government successfully.

To complicate matters, the new generation of Hall children "had greener fields to go plow, they didn't want to be park concessionaires." As Bill expressed it, "there were no replacements coming up. . . . I felt compelled to get dividends out to the family, and the National Park Service still needed a couple of million dollars' worth of development." Some other members of the family, weary of the expenses and the struggles, favored selling out. Pressure built on the Winklers to end the Hall generation at Mesa Verde. Bill himself was reaching the stage of "burn out." "I'm convinced you make contributions until you've given all you can and beyond that there is a flattening of the growth curve. I guess we had reached that flattening."

After analyzing the possibilities, Bill decided to sell and started to negotiate with ARA, a Philadelphia-based company. ARA had purchased the Virginia Skyline Company from a friend of his, and Winkler liked their established record in Shenandoah National Park. Following a lengthy process that went all the way to Washington, the National Park Service approved the sale to ARA, at the same time expressing some reservations about the demise of the family operation and the arrival of corporate control. Implications for the future could not be allowed to deter the required action, and the sale was completed in 1976, ending nearly forty years of Hall management.[8]

The Mesa Verde Company actually had little choice but to sell out; the times, government policy, and family and business considerations weighed heavily against its continuing. Although the average visitor who came to the park in the spring of 1977 would not have noticed the change in management, the withdrawal of the Mesa Verde Company signified the end of an era that went back to the very first days of the Mesa Verde concessions. The trend toward consolidation and corporation control, which had been going on in American business for years, had finally caught up with the park. Without question this change took the personal factor, the individual touch, out of Mesa Verde, as it had done at Yellowstone and Rocky Mountain national parks. At Rocky Mountain, the government purchased private land holdings within the park in order to remove the buildings and restore the sites to their natural state.

One change the repeat visitor might have noticed by mid-decade was that two long-time favorite activities had disappeared. Since the days of the Wetherills and C. B. Kelly, horseback riding had been available for those tourists who wanted to examine some of the outlying ruins. It was no more.

On crowded summer nights, the new Morefield Campground became the second largest community in Montezuma County.
Courtesy: William Winkler

First, the horses were removed from the museum area to the Morefield Campground, where they could be ridden around a couple of trails, hardly a memorable adventure. When that contract ran out, the government ended the concession, saying quite truthfully that it was "more recreational than interpretive." The way the cancellation was handled shocked some people, including the Winklers, who had no financial interest in the horseback riding concession. Ansel Hall had long ago sold it, realizing it took special people to run it. "It was a terrible thing. The government just zeroed in on him [Emmett Koppenhafer] and got him out. I had always heard this could happen if the government wanted to get rid of you."[9]

The ever-popular Navajo dances ended, too. The Navajos were not of the Pueblo culture, it was argued, and therefore their dancing "was not authentic" within the Anasazi tradition. So that favorite of the evening campfire, which dated back to the 1920s, also vanished. The campfire talks themselves migrated to the Morefield Campground, where a new and larger amphitheater awaited them. Finally, after more than fifty years, the annual planting of a cornfield was discontinued.

Most of these changes went unnoticed, except by old-timers. But new visitors were not reluctant to complain about procedures that irritated them. One family objected to being told that the narrow roads meant they had to leave their trailer outside the park and remove their wide-vision mirrors from the side of their car. Unwilling to tolerate such inconvenience, they left, grumbling all the while about the silly rules. Safety rules on narrow roads were made to be ignored by many, who saw them as deterrents to their fun. A father complained that the ARA Company would not redeem aluminum cans

for five cents, destroying his children's impression that "ecology pays off."

Some of the old familiar complaints resurfaced, as they always seemed to do seasonally. High prices—seventy cents for a can of soda—appeared exorbitant to a Massachusetts couple. An Arizona man became irate when he found several cliff dwellings closed because of bad weather during April, 1977. He complained that he had received no notice of this and had therefore paid the two-dollar entry fee without being "able to utilize the park adequately." A charge of false advertising came to park headquarters from a California man who had read a sign at the Durango train depot saying that reservations were needed to stay overnight in the park. He promptly called, only to find out that they were not; his complaint was that he was out $1.50 in phone charges.[10] American tourists are fascinating creatures; some seem never to be satisfied.

Content or complaining, tourists made an economic impact on nearby communities. Cortez, for the first full decade, basked in the glory of being a gateway to Mesa Verde; paved highways now stretched from it in all directions. Its income from tourists had grown, and jobs had expanded as more tourist-related businesses sprouted. Like neighboring Durango, however, Cortez found that tourism provided mixed seasonal blessings. During the off season, employment suffered and income slumped. The tourist-based economy was subject to yearly highs and lows.

Meanwhile, a subtle change was evolving in Durango's love affair with Mesa Verde. Where once the park had been the major attraction, along with the mountain scenery, now the community had a famous narrow-gauge railroad in its front yard, an expanding ski area in its back yard, and Lemon and Vallecito reservoirs nearby. Mesa Verde sat fifty miles from town and had to be shared with a rival.[11] Ever so quietly, promotion shifted toward the attractions nearer to home, which required no sharing of profits or publicity. Mesa Verde was never ignored—it just received lower billing, where once it had been the feature attraction. The shift went largely unnoticed and followed no preconceived plan by any individual or group. Good business practice dictated that the newer, home-based attractions be promoted more vigorously. The park would always be there to draw tourists and contribute its share to the economy without much advertising on Durango's part.

Amid the changes, Mesa Verde evolved, looking both toward the past and to the future for guideposts. Over the years, the number of people employed in the park had steadily increased. In the bicentennial year there were 39 permanent positions and 122 seasonals, most of which involved maintenance and interpretation. In honor of the national celebration, the park installed bicentennial symbols on all the buildings, flew the official flag, and sponsored programs and films, as did other parks. Of special interest were the exhibits constructed by the museum staff to inform visitors of the relationship between the prehistoric inhabitants and the nation's birth. One of them depicted the Dominguez-Escalante expedition, which had passed near the area during some unusually cool and damp August days two hundred years before. Events so recent as that, in relation to Mesa Verde, hardly deserved more than passing mention in what Alfred, Lord Tennyson, called "the eternal landscape of the past."

Something that emerged in the 1970s and signified a reawakening of national interest in the country's history was a growing awareness of the park's history and of its historic structures, as opposed to the prehistoric culture that had always attracted the lion's share of attention. Spruce Tree Point came in for special mention, and Jesse Nusbaum's plans and building efforts earned praise for being "sensitively and knowledgeably designed" to fit into the "setting and history without jarring visitors from their communion with the past." The people who dominated the park story, not just the buildings, merited scholars' attention. The Wetherills' contributions, especially Richard's, underwent a historical metamorphosis. Where once the family had been castigated as "pothunters," now the role of the family in drawing attention to the ancient culture and its ruins, and their pioneering efforts to preserve the relics, became subjects of approbation. The long-overdue recognition was accorded none too soon, in the opinion of family descendants.

An older park tradition was also revitalized about this time. Indian weavers, and occasionally potters, who had once displayed their skills for visitors, now put on "living history" demonstrations. And, finally, an oral history program to interview old-timers who had played roles in the Mesa Verde story was planned in 1979 and started the next year.[12]

The Mesa Verde Museum Association, founded in 1930, took on more projects throughout the 1970s than it ever had before. It published pamphlets and books, both in the historical and prehistorical fields, and donated money to the park to purchase interpretive items not available through regular government channels. The library continued to expand its book holdings within the limits that its budget allowed, thus enhancing the research opportunities for scholars.

Every improvement held the potential for enriching the visitors' experience, an ever so important criterion. A 1979 study emphasized that Mesa Verde relied on effective interpretation, "perhaps more than any other national park." The best way for people of today to acquire empathy for the Anasazi was to spend time at the ruins and in the park, the report concluded. The park, created to preserve antiquities, now offered a broader opportunity to savor the land, the environment, and the remains. Through matured interpretation, a deeper appreciation of Anasazi life could be acquired. To Mesa Verde's detriment, heavy tourist pressure, travelers' time limitations, the fragile nature of the dwellings, and their restricted capacity precluded most opportunities for in-depth personal exploration. The inevitable shallow exposure called for "effective interpretation" to fill the gap. As the popular and perceptive ranger Don Watson had written, the ruins were the "least important part. Cliff Palace is really built of the hopes and desires, the joys and sorrows of an industrious peo-ple. It is not a cold empty city, for it is still warm with the emotion of its builders."[13] To make these Anasazi and their culture come alive had always been a challenge to and a goal of the National Park Service. Each decade, with its new interpretive resources, and each archaeological dig, with its new discoveries, helped bring this goal a little nearer to realization.

One of the most popular methods of achieving educational enlighten-ment continued to be that long-time favorite, the campfire program, which was held nightly from late May into September. Popularity and tradition did not mean stagnation, and new ideas constantly enhanced the presentations. For instance, the twenty-two thou-sand people, give or take a few, who witnessed the programs in 1976 were surrounded by taped music and sounds that accompanied the slide shows.

Interpretation never came easily, explained Gil Wenger, who worked

Kelly's cabin
was a memory
for only a few
old-timers by the
1970s. Compared
to the cabin, this
Denver-area fam-
ily's campsite in
Morefield Camp-
ground could
be described as
luxurious.
Courtesy: Mesa Verde
National Park

with the interpretive services throughout the decade. First, personnel had to be selected who were knowledgeable interpreters and enthusiastic speakers; fortunately, he said, "we had more real good ones than we had bad." Developing "good interpretive literature" took special skills and a feel for the nature of the park and the public. During the complex daily routine, rangers moved from one site to another to spell each other and to present their talks and answer questions. Absolute punctuality was required, a goal sometimes difficult to achieve with the "poorly operating GSA cars from the Farmington motor pool." Another unexpected problem surfaced: "Some of these [vehicles] were so old they still had clutches in them and we had to train young adults how to drive with clutches."

Gil Wenger enjoyed everything about the park, even the tribulations that went along with the job. "I believed in my job of serving the public," he reminisced, and in the long-established tradition of Mesa Verde, he put in many hours of unpaid overtime. Working with youngsters especially delighted Wenger; like others before him, he went to schools, "both near and far," to relate the story of the park and its people.[14] Jesse Nusbaum would have empathized when Wenger commented that he often "caught heck for being out with them [public] instead of pushing paper."

The discerning public took pleasure in the improvements that were being made, though they were largely unaware of the arduous efforts that went into them. Pageantry in the grand tradition of Virginia McClurg and Aileen Nusbaum had commanded instant attention and appreciation. Wenger and his interpretive staff put about three hundred *luminarias* (candles in paper sacks) in Cliff Palace to illuminate the ruin one evening in August, 1979, while some of the Navajo staff chanted tribal songs. This lovely innovation gained instant popularity and was repeated for several years, into the 1980s.

The staff also worked with the Ute Mountain Utes to train them in ruins stabilization and to help them to develop an interpretive program for their tribal park directly south of Mesa Verde. Not all the significant ruins fell within the park's boundaries, and the Utes moved determinedly to preserve theirs, as well as to tap the potential tourist trade. Their isolated reservation stood in need of an economic boost. Although the Ute education program was the most extensive, the Zunis, Crows, and Apaches also came to observe and to receive training. The heritage of Mesa Verde was being passed on to future generations.

While that positive tradition was being furthered, the past was also willing its never-ending road problems to the present. Superintendent Switzer reported during a June, 1973, staff meeting that slides plagued the roads and trails. Continual road patching made it seem that as soon as "one section is repaired, another breaks up." The expense and frustration of the one-sided struggle seldom abated, always appearing on the superintendent's agenda. To make matters worse that same year, the new Wetherill Mesa road began to "cause some problems."[15] There appeared to be no end and no solution to road difficulties.

All these nagging nuisances proved to be mere preliminaries to the main event. After an excessively wet fall in 1978, two slides, on April 27 and 29, 1979, buried the road on the east side of Point Lookout and closed the park for a month. The second slide, termed "massive," deposited an estimated 150,000 cubic yards of rock and mud. The disaster ignited an equally massive effort to remove the debris

and, if possible, to stabilize the road permanently. The staff promptly fired up its public relations machine by several degrees and attempted to blunt the adverse publicity. Daily reports about road conditions were issued to press, television, and radio, and all three major television networks taped feature stories at the site. Park rangers met visitors below the slide and "satisfied many frustrated persons who could not enter the park with pleasant discussions and sympathetic responses." An apprehensive local tourist industry fretted and stewed, predicting losses up to a million dollars. The last days of Switzer's superintendency were troubled by controversy generated by the slide.

Any delight in the Mesa Verde disaster came from the school children of park families, who were convinced that they would not be able to connect with the Mancos school bus. The park school had finally closed over a

decade before, with all grades now being bused. The children's joy proved short-lived, as foot trails were constructed around the slide to allow them to meet their transportation to and from school. After an expenditure of $736,500 for repairs, the road and the park were finally reopened to the public on May 30, 1979.[16] The cost over the years to stabilize the shifting Mancos shale and the continuing expense of maintaining that stretch of road far exceeded the money spent on the entire Wetherill Mesa Project, far and away the park's most elaborate archaeological endeavor.

Fires, too, continued to harass Mesa Verde, as they had for years. The average number from 1926 through 1979 had been ten a year; the thirty fires in 1972 set a record. Included in that number were a 2,680-acre burn on Moccasin Mesa and a 700-acre blaze on Wetherill Mesa. The "unique flammability of Mesa Verde pinyon-juniper forests" always posed a threat to the park and its visitors. When the mesa became dangerously dry, campfires and smoking were prohibited.[17] Fire fighting equipment, including a helicopter, and trained staff stood ready for the call they hoped would not come.

As if slipping roads and rampaging fires were not discouraging enough, airborne pollution also threatened Mesa Verde. This plague posed two threats: a smoky haze that despoiled the once pristine vistas, always one of the park's greatest charms, and the potential erosion of the ancient structures by the acids in the pollution. By 1979, the park was involved in several programs to monitor air quality and visibility.[18] The great threat came not from within the park, but from the coal-fired Four Corners and San Juan power plants. Smoke from these plants created a haze over the once strikingly clear view to the south toward Shiprock. To a lesser degree, pollution came from coal-, wood-, and oil-burning stoves and fireplaces; use of cars also contributed to the problem.

Once it had seemed less threatening to build giant power plants in lightly populated areas, where industrial smoke, settling over fewer voters, would not become so politically volatile an issue. Likewise, as Americans tried to save on heating bills, they reverted to some of the more primitive heating methods of their pioneering forebears. Unintentionally, in both cases, they polluted the Four Corners atmosphere, threatening their environmental heritage there and elsewhere throughout the country. Such was the cost of modern life on Mesa Verde.

The 1980s

At some point in a narrative that moves toward the present, the account ceases to be history and evolves into a chronicle of current events. We have reached this point. It could be justifiably argued that the elusive date occurred several decades ago, that date after which events have not been filtered through enough time to gain the objectivity essential to an evaluation of their relationships and their relative significance. But the Mesa Verde saga does not stop at some point to wait for a historian's evaluation—it stretches on into an unknown future.

Our philosophical musings may seem trivial when weighed against the Anasazi epic. Why should we in the twentieth century presume to be the arbiters of historical chronology? A valid claim could be made that the history of Mesa Verde ended with the Anasazi habitation and that everything since then falls into the category of current events.

Nonetheless, "With weeping and with laughter, Still is the story told," in the words of the nineteenth-century English poet Thomas Macaulay. Inquisitive visitors continue to come and wonder at the silent shadows of a vanished people. After the disastrous slides and the gasoline shortages of 1979, visitation rebounded strongly in 1980, a trend noticeable in many western parks in the 1980s. A visitor-origin survey conducted in late July 1980, provided interesting information about where tourists came from. (License plates no longer gave reliable information, since so many cars are rented in Colorado.) Colorado retained its number one ranking, with 15.6 percent of the visitor total. Texas, California, and Arizona followed the host state. Neighboring New Mexico was in fifth place, after West Germany. Confirming the trend over the past twenty years, 11.8 percent of the visitors came from foreign countries, mostly European. Because of a favorable exchange rate for the German mark, West Germany led the foreign contingent with 3.9 percent of the total. Thirty-one foreign countries (the most distant was Australia) were represented. Park visitation had become truly global. To accommodate this international interest, the park staff continued to distribute handouts in German, Japanese, French, and Spanish.[1]

Bilingual rangers were much harder to come by than foreign visitors. The problem was not all linguistic. As Superintendent Robert Heyder, a California-born, twenty-five-year veteran of the National Park Service, points out: "A lot of times they may be linguistically fluent in conversation, but not especially fluent in archaeology." Fortunately, most Europeans who come to the United States possess at least a passable understanding of English. Nonetheless, recruitment of multilingual rangers remains a challenge for the National Park Service; the foreign visitor has embraced the United States' national parks with great enthusiasm.

The things that tourists considered to be "extremely important" to them during their Mesa Verde visit were evaluated by a survey in 1983. Park cleanliness led the list, followed by information about the park, "clean, clear air," self-guided tours, and overlook sites to view the ruins from the canyon rim. The priorities expected by the park's administrators, such as museum displays, interpretive signs, and park rangers/interpreters, trailed well behind the leaders. The public also attached great importance to the opportunity to see a variety of flowers, trees, birds, and animals. The public was also well aware of the pollution haze that sometimes hung over Mesa Verde, and they strongly voiced the opinion that it detracted from their overall enjoyment of the park.[2]

Except for a dip in 1984, visitor totals have continued to rebound; they reached 658,000 in 1986, still 18,000 behind the park's all-time best year of 1976. To make the public accommodations more comfortable, ARA has remodeled and added to its Far View complex, even to the point of installing a television set in the ever-popular Sipapu Lounge, so that visitors can enjoy a relaxing drink without missing their favorite programs. The accoutrements of twentieth-century life continue to invade Mesa Verde relentlessly.

In a new six-year experimental program, in 1986 ARA took over operation of the Morefield Campground from the National Park Service, which continues to provide major upkeep and law enforcement. The popular campground, with 477 individual and 17 group spaces, is the third largest in the park system.

ARA, along with the National Park Service, has come in for its share of criticism over the years, particularly

Chief Park Ar-chaeologist Gil Wenger (left), Superintendent Robert Heyder (right), and a delegation of Chinese visitors prove that Mesa Verde had become an international attraction by the 1980s.

Courtesy: Mesa Verde National Park

from people who thought that it had failed to maintain the concessionaire spirit or the publicity efforts of the old Mesa Verde Company. ARA lost the exclusive right to provide public transportation within the park in 1983, but in all other ways has maintained the operations as before. Even with some problems, the concessionaires' record of accomplishments at Mesa Verde continues to be very good; compared to Yellowstone, where constant troubles led to the firing of one company, the record here has been exemplary.[3] Mesa Verde had been fortunate in the postwar years. The foundation laid by Ansel Hall had held solid and been modified as necessary; both the park and the visitor benefited enormously.

The never-ending battle to preserve the ruins and ensure that the public would always have something worthy to see has rolled on year after year. An important milestone in this on-going effort passed almost unnoticed in 1984, the fiftieth anniversary of a permanent ruins stabilization program. From April through November, the staff carried out crucial maintenance/stabilization projects. Most visitors fail to realize that anything that has been exposed, excavated, or stabilized requires "a lot of maintenance each year, particularly the mesa top ruins." An innovation in preservation was tried—placing temporary covers over the mesa-top ruins to protect them during the winter season. The effort proved to be expensive; $3.2 million was spent in 1986 for nylon "curtains tinted in sandstone color" to help protect ten of the park's most delicate kivas and pit-houses, obviously the most susceptible to erosion.[4] Those sites were normally closed during the off-season, so visitors would not feel cheated by being unable to see them on their winter tour.

Of course, stabilization is more than just maintenance for the "wear and tear" of the cliff dwellings and mesa sites that the public actually visits. Chief Park Archaeologist Jack Smith has devised a continuing program for the important back country ruins. Although limited by funding and logistics, "we've built up quite a record of stabilization in remote areas." The project involves checking the "state of the ruin" for signs of vandalism and developing a work plan. Smith's crew has a decided transportation advantage over its predecessors:

The big problem is getting to the places, not only the people, but water, tools, stabilization supplies, etc. We have been very lucky. There has been a helicopter available to us all the years this back country program has been going on. It is stationed here for fire fighting duties, and we fit ourselves in during the free time. . . . That way we can do this work in ruins that would virtually be impossible if we had to go on foot.

It is almost prohibitive the old way; now we can fly in and out in a few minutes.[5]

Inroads from the modern world thus have their positive side.

Regrettably, Wetherill Mesa has never won public favor. Even in its best years, it has attracted just over 10 percent of the visitor total. Perhaps the popularity of the museum and the better-known ruins overwhelmed it; more likely, the concept of a bus visit never caught on. The opportunity to visit Wetherill Mesa lay near the bottom of the 1983 list of attributes that visitors named as essential to a successful experience. The individual freedom and ease of access found on Chapin Mesa defeated the best-laid plans for the more regulated Wetherill Mesa tour.

The unexpected underutilization of Wetherill Mesa stimulated plans for change. It came with the 1987 season, when, for the first time, visitors were permitted to drive private cars to Wetherill Mesa. From the parking lot, the shuttle still carried tourists to the ruins. Easier to overcome than visitor disinterest were the recurring swarms of yellow jacket wasps, which threatened the public at Step House and in the Wetherill Mesa snack bar.[6] They could not be classified as part of the wildlife that visitors wanted to experience first hand.

In contrast with the low rating of the bus tour, "clean, crisp air" ranked near the top of the list of attractions, and the Park Service has worked diligently to maintain it. Of equal importance, it has attempted to get back what it had lost. At times the effort seems an all-consuming, expensive, and very discouraging struggle toward an elusive goal. Testing for acid rain (which has already showered the park),

monitoring of air quality, and visual observations have continued unabated during the 1980s, with more complex equipment; each season of investigation has produced a larger data base from which to work. Down the road, if the present trend persists, there will quite likely be major litigation, because the park is enjoined by federal law to prosecute violators of the federal air standards. Assessing his tenure at Mesa Verde, Heyder says, "I think that [air quality] is one of the big things I have been involved in in my career here." The issue can only grow larger for Superintendent Heyder and his successors.

The park staff is fighting to preserve one of the great heritages of Mesa Verde: the stunning, sweeping panoramas of mountain, valley, and desert that present themselves to view around nearly every corner as one climbs the mesa or drives along the rim. The very first explorers had commented on the pristine vistas, and the government record goes back to 1905–06, as part of the testimony on the park bill. A 1906 report concluded that the trail running into Mesa Verde "is one of the grandest and most extensive views in the country." Now, after all these years, such intangible treasures are threatened, and all Americans will lose if the shortsightedness of the present is allowed to cloud the environment and to dictate the future. The inability to control the threat of human beings to this priceless treasure speaks sadly of current priorities, as the boundaries between parks and civilization are narrowed.

The park's own contribution to pollution was the easiest to solve of the crimes against nature. Use of solar water heaters conserved energy and helped to improve air quality. Wherever possible, the use of electricity and fossil fuels was curtailed, an innovation that saved money and eliminated some of the engine exhaust and smoke.[7]

Mesa Verde, though it honors the past, nevertheless moves with the tide of present and future. The "computer age" arrived in 1984, and the next year a computer programmer was hired. Mesa Verde held out enormous computer possibilities. With its 4,009 ruins and its artifacts, library, documents, and photographs all crying to be catalogued and programmed, the park was a prime candidate for use of computers. The researcher and the archaeologist of the future will find their tasks simplified once the conversion is completed.

Progress has also been made in hiring women and minorities, particularly among the seasonal employees. Originally, Navajos furnished 90 percent of the work force, but that practice changed decades ago, and hiring patterns became oriented toward white, Anglo-Saxon males. Now a concerted effort is being made to change those patterns. For example, department heads have visited colleges to recruit women and minorities, and Beverly Cunningham was appointed federal women's coordinator. Efforts, including Braille park folders and wheelchair ramps, have also been made to improve the park's accessibility to the handicapped. Some of nature's barriers, however, have proved nearly insurmountable in attempting to allow full access to all the park's attractions by the handicapped.

The neighboring Utes have not fared so well. The legacy of Indian mistrust and government exasperation has continued in the 1980s. The loop road on Chapin Mesa, which crossed reservation land as a result of surveying errors, incited clashes between the two factions, including ones involving roadside advertising and an attempt to

One of the pleasures for the Mesa Verde staff is cross-country skiing in some of the region's most beautiful country.
Courtesy: Mesa Verde National Park

collect tolls. By mid-decade, the two were confronting each other over road location, water, and sewage connections to this small parcel of land on Soda Point, which the Utes had ideas of developing. The ultimate decision may have to be made in court.

For the Utes, developments that included helicopter rides and snowcone stands were intended to create jobs and bring in revenue for a reservation suffering from 60 percent unemployment. A displeased National Park Service considered the Indians' enterprises "an undignified intrusion on the peace of Mesa Verde National Park." Negotiations, once again, seem to be tangled in a web of misunderstanding and cultural differences.[8] After eighty years, these two antagonists hardly appear to be any closer to reaching a compromise than they ever were.

With some things new and some things old, activities of the park go on. Park staff (comprising forty-eight permanent and seventy-six seasonals in 1986) still complain about too numerous and over-long meetings and training sessions; one on self-development, entitled "What I Think, Is Why It Is," drew yawns. The ski slope of yesteryear has disappeared, but the tennis court has held on to its status as a popular attraction on a warm summer evening. Its rival now is volleyball, one of the newly popular activities for young America. Jogging and bicycling claim adherents: Who could ask for more beautiful country in which to exercise? Yet recreational options for the staff remain limited; even with better roads, the nearest town is still forty-five minutes away, and most of the back country is off limits.

A sign of the intrusion of the modern world came in the beautifully produced 1984 guide, which warned that "park visitors can be the target of professional thieves." Among the recommendations were to lock cars and to take "valuables with you or leave them in a secure place." Some rules, of course, never changed; parents were sternly warned to keep their children away from canyon rims and to caution the youngsters not to throw rocks or objects into canyons. Reiterating an old theme, park visitors were admonished to consider the varied altitudes of the park before they set off on hikes or climbed down into ruins.

To enrich the public's appreciation of the park, the Mesa Verde Museum Association has maintained its dedicated work in the interpretive area and in its remarkable little bookstore in the museum. The Association estimated in 1985 that it had reached over 800,000 persons through its publications and sales.[9] The discerning visitor was being well served by this group and by the museum, both of which continued in the tradition Jesse Nusbaum had established for them over forty years before.

A particularly busy time for the Association and for the park came in September, 1984, when Mesa Verde served as host to the First World Conference on Cultural Parks. Mesa Verde had been designated a World Heritage Cultural Site by UNESCO just six years earlier. The park was recognized for meeting all the criteria for inclusion: outstanding universal anthropological, ethnological, historical, and aesthetic values. It was the only site in the United States to be so honored. This recognition by the international community has helped to expand interest in the park and no doubt has served as an impetus to increased foreign visitation.

Planning for the conference began in the early 1980s and went "down to the wire as far as conference planning goes." The theme—preservation and use of cultural treasures—appropriately honored the man to whom the conference was dedicated, Gustaf Nordenskiold.[10] Those who attended caught the global vision of the need for care and management of the world's priceless cultural resources.

Special events were staged to increase the visibility of Mesa Verde's cultural attractions. At one of them, an Indian arts and crafts festival, the artists had the opportunity to sell their works and the public had the opportunity to experience the native culture. This idea, slightly modified, was extended into 1987 with a permanent art gallery at Spruce Tree Point. The Telluride Chamber Players, who have appeared in concert in the "magnificent setting" of the Spruce Tree Amphitheater, have added the new dimension of classical music.[11] Mesa Verde's cultural mission is advancing along a wider front than ever before; Virginia McClurg would approve.

All these events have helped to attract more tourists, delighting local merchants and neighboring communities. Durango, though, has failed to exploit its position to the extent that it had done in the past. The trend appearing in the 1970s became obvious in the 1980s, as the promotion of local attractions pushed Mesa Verde into a secondary position. Durango merchant Jackson Clark explained:

> I don't think that people in Durango have any conception that they have a rare prehistoric national treasure there. I think if you go up and down the street and you ask people in service stations, garages, motels, and restaurants what's there to see at Mesa Verde, most of them will tell you, "I've never been there." I heard a clerk at the Strater Hotel say one time, "Oh, you don't want to go over there, just a bunch of dead Indians . . . a bunch of broken down houses; they have no significance." I think that's the thing.[12]

The substance of this trend to downplay Mesa Verde cannot be denied.

Virginia McClurg would have been pleased with the variety of cultural events now available to visitors. This performance is by the Telluride (Colorado) String Ensemble.

Courtesy: Mesa Verde National Park

However, by the mid-1980s, a major reason for it lay in the more sophisticated tourist analysis and promotional efforts by Durango, not in a calculated effort to snub Mesa Verde. With limited funds, the Durango Chamber/Resort Association targeted certain groups with specific appeals. Mesa Verde led the list for international groups, because they were "high on parks." The majority of the city's promotion was directed toward the national market, where Americans' love affair with the narrow-gauge steam engine made the train between Durango and Silverton the number-one attraction; skiing took first place in the winter. The Association did work closely with ARA to advertise Mesa Verde National Park as part of the total package.[13]

Superintendent Heyder has tried to bridge the miles and create more cooperation between the park and Durango. Too often, however, he and others have run up against the generations-old rivalry between Cortez and Durango. The prevailing conception seems to be that the park belongs to Cortez and the train to Durango, albeit, as Heyder pointed out, "I don't think the park really belongs to any town, it is a national park." Rivalry and competition, instead of cooperation, still characterize the relationship between the two communities, and they rarely collaborate on promoting Mesa Verde, which unquestionably brings tourists and profits to both communities.

Heyder has also pinpointed another problem that has long troubled southwestern Coloradans—the lack of support from the more populous eastern slope of Colorado beyond the Continental Divide:

This area seems, kind of regrettably, almost a stepchild of the eastern slope. . . . You read the Denver papers and there is very little about this corner of the state. . . . I wouldn't go so far as to say they are not interested in this part of the state, but there are times that make you wonder.[14]

The parsimonious coverage given the park in the 1980s by the *Denver Post*, the "voice of the Rocky Mountain Empire," as it calls itself, gives credence to the allegation.

Southwestern Colorado's feeling of isolation reflects not only its true physical isolation but also its lack of political power, a dash of parochialism, and a weak financial base, laced with a certain amount of urban jealousy. The debate began to intensify in the mid-twentieth century, when the development of natural resources, particularly water, and a fair sharing of state revenues became topics of critical importance. Colorado's Front Range urban corridor, stretching from Fort

Collins to Pueblo, holds 80 percent of the state's population and controls its political and economic heart. Real or fancied slights of the Western Slope are perhaps unintentional, and city dwellers are often unaware of their impact on rural southwestern Coloradans. Regardless, the impression of neglect has created antagonistic thoughts and reactions. Denver, the symbol as much as the cause of all the animosity, seems aloof and patronizing to its country cousin, the distant corner of Colorado. Some of the surrounding Four Corners states have been much more forthright and aggressive in advertising the attractions of this area than the home state has been. "I think it is sad, I think they [Denver and the state] have a hell of a lot to offer to promote Mesa Verde tourism." [15] Nothing has as yet been able to reconcile Durango and Cortez or to attract Denver's lasting attention and involvement. In the end, everyone stands to gain by pulling together toward a common goal.

The impact of Mesa Verde on neighboring communities and tourism has permeated the park's history and promises to weigh heavily on its future. One issue of the past appears to have faded into insignificance, however—the specter of the Manitou Springs cliff dwellings. Superintendent Heyder observed in 1987 that the park only occasionally now receives letters about Manitou. Perhaps that regrettable heritage of McClurg's bitterness has, at last, been put to rest.

Mesa Verde National Park quietly passed its eightieth birthday in 1986. It has more than fulfilled the expectations of the women who fought so long and hard to preserve it. Compared to the amounts first allocated for the park, the 1986 budget of $2,337,400, plus supplementals, might seem like the mother lode of government funding, but in the 1980s the park is still plagued by the unwelcome specter of

fiscal problems caused by inadequate funding. It is a serious concern to the park administration. With pollution drifting in and visitation increasing, the fiscal squeeze threatens to shape the park's future in crucial ways. Making matters worse are the Mancos shale and the roads that cross it, which are, after all these years, still a primary source of anxiety for the Park Service at Mesa Verde. Over $3 million was spent in 1983 for stabilization of the entrance road through the slide area.[16] All the expense and effort of the past decade cannot guarantee that the slides will not run again.

Mesa Verde has managed to escape some of the major problems that threaten other national parks, including urban encroachment, development that threatens scenic resources, and contamination of freshwater sources. Mesa Verde has been able to retain much of its pristine environment through all the decades, largely because of its isolated location and the lack of surrounding urbanization.

The final page of Mesa Verde's archaeological chronicle has not been inscribed. The region is not a "sucked orange," as someone confidently affirmed some eighty years ago. So far the systematic search for sites has only been completed on Wetherill and Chapin mesas. Many unexcavated ruins remain, an archaeological mecca to draw future generations of archaeologists, who will arrive on the scene with advanced techniques for excavation and methods of analysis. Park Archaeologist Smith sees a changing role for Mesa Verde. He does not predict another Wetherill Mesa Project in the near future, or much park excavation.

I think the future of archaeology here is a very restricted one that will be focused mainly on preservation of archaeological ruins as they are. . . . The reason for this, is that there is such a rapid disappearance of the archaeological ruins outside the park. . . . I can foresee sometime in the future that there will be virtually nothing left outside the park boundaries for archaeologists to work on. So we see it as a kind of preserve to be sat upon, to be protected, to be kept intact, until there is a heck of a good reason to do the digging.[17]

The value of these ruins "is in the excavation and what they will tell us."

Public awareness and concern have slowed, but never ended, vandalism and looting outside the park; they have been stopped inside it, for the most part. The Ute Mountain Utes are determined to preserve the sites to the south that lie on their reservation. With that avenue of entry closed and the park itself largely isolated from dig-and-run vandals, the prospects for achieving that preservation for future generations seem promising.

The attempt to solve the mysteries of the Anasazi continues. The path that Jackson, the Wetherills, and Nordenskiold excitedly started down a century ago stretches on into the future. Although the full story may never be known, each bit and piece of evidence expands our appreciation of those fascinating people and their struggle to maintain life in the rugged Mesa Verde country. The narrative and the interpretation are ever expanding. Each return visit to the park will provide new insights and experiences. Only the most blasé twentieth-century tourists would find nothing new to excite their interest.

Mesa Verde is timeless, a cultural park that speaks to the past, the present, and the future. In her January 31, 1916, article in the *Denver Times*,

The official opening of the completed Wetherill Mesa Archaeological Project, June 13, 1987. Congressman Ben Nighthorse Campbell (second from right) challenged his listeners to remember the lessons and the legacy of Mesa Verde. Visitation in 1987 set a record: 728,569; of these visitors, 43,102 visited Wetherill Mesa.

Courtesy: Mesa Verde National Park

Willa Cather spoke for her age and tomorrow:

> Dr. Johnson declared that man is an historical animal. Certainly it is the human record, however slight, that stirs us most deeply, and a country without such a record is dumb, no matter how beautiful. The Mesa Verde is not, as many people think, an inconveniently situated museum. It is the story of an early race, of the social and religious life of a people indigenous to that soil and to its rocky splendors. It is the human expression of that land of sharp contours, brutal contrasts, glorious color and blinding light. The human consciousness, as we know it today, dwelt there, and a feeling for beauty and order was certainly not absent.

Jean Pinkley, fifty years later, in April, 1966, agreed with Cather and further concluded about the park she loved:

> Though Mesa Verde was set aside primarily to preserve and use wisely the prehistoric manifestations, the scenery is unique, and spectacular, the animal and plant life varied and interesting, and the geology presents a good example of certain phases of earth history. . . . This national park commemorates and reminds us of the debt we owe to those who have gone before. It gives pause to the brash citizen who proclaims that our good way of life is the invention and attainment of one particularly ingenious generation of Americans. It humbles our citizens into the realization that we owe so very much to all of the people of all lands and all times.[18]

The story of Mesa Verde National Park has been and will continue to be the struggle to preserve the Anasazi heritage and to interpret what happened here for future generations to enjoy and to learn from. May it never be said that Americans failed in their trust, their stewardship of this treasure.

≡ APPENDIX A ≡

SUPERINTENDENTS OF MESA VERDE NATIONAL PARK

William D. Leonard (Acting)	1906–07	C. Marshall Finnan	1931–33	W. Ward Yeager (Acting)	1946
Charles F. Werner (Acting)	1907	Ernest P. Leavitt	1933–35	Robert H. Rose	1946–52
Hans M. Randolph	1907–11	Paul R. Franke (Acting)	1935	Oscar W. Carlson	1952–58
Edward B. Linnen (Acting)	1911	Jesse L. Nusbaum	1936–39	Chester A. Thomas	1958–66
Richard Wright (Acting)	1911	Paul R. Franke	1939–40	Meredith M. Guillet	1966–72
Samuel E. Shoemaker	1911–13	John S. McLaughlin	1940–42	Ronald R. Switzer	1972–79
Thomas Rickner	1913–21	Jesse L. Nusbaum (Acting)	1942–46	Robert C. Heyder	1979–
Jesse L. Nusbaum	1921–31	John S. McLaughlin	1946		present

≡ APPENDIX B ≡

VISITOR TOTALS

Year	Total Visitors	Cumulative Total	Year	Total Visitors	Cumulative Total	Year	Total Visitors	Cumulative Total
1906	27	27	1922	4,251	20,573	1938	31,239	292,677
1907	73	100	1923	5,236	25,809	1939	32,843	325,520
1908	80	180	1924	7,109	32,918	1940	36,172	361,692
1909	165	345	1925	9,344	42,262	1941	42,406	404,098
1910	250	595	1926	11,600	53,862	1942	13,045	417,143
1911	206	801	1927	12,005	65,867	1943	4,621	421,764
1912	230	1,031	1928	16,872	82,739	1944	5,561	427,325
1913	280	1,311	1929	14,542	97,281	1945	12,994	440,319
1914	502	1,813	1930	16,741	114,022	1946	39,843	480,162
1915	663	2,476	1931	17,896	131,918	1947	52,975	533,137
1916	1,385	3,861	1932	15,885	147,803	1948	59,362	592,499
1917	2,223	6,084	1933	16,244	164,047	1949	78,024	670,523
1918	2,058	8,142	1934	21,859	185,906	1950	88,184	758,707
1919	2,287	10,429	1935	21,787	207,693	1951	99,309	858,016
1920	2,890	13,319	1936	25,580	233,273	1952	105,700	963,716
1921	3,003	16,322	1937	28,165	261,438	1953	136,123	1,099,839

Year	Total Visitors	Cumulative Total	Year	Total Visitors	Cumulative Total	Year	Total Visitors	Cumulative Total
1954	150,330	1,250,169	1965	378,278	3,974,553	1976	676,935	9,708,090
1955	161,303	1,411,472	1966	423,366	4,397,919	1977	664,894	10,372,984
1956	186,808	1,598,280	1967	534,983	4,932,902	1978	654,166	11,027,150
1957	193,927	1,792,207	1968	449,762	5,382,664	1979	474,477	11,501,627
1958	201,345	1,993,552	1969	513,771	5,896,435	1980	540,826	12,042,453
1959	217,357	2,210,909	1970	527,207	6,423,642	1981	588,897	12,631,350
1960	225,708	2,436,617	1971	518,462	6,942,104	1982	602,968	13,234,318
1961	227,658	2,664,275	1972	546,286	7,488,390	1983	604,115	13,838,433
1962	262,250	2,926,525	1973	482,851	7,971,241	1984	516,865	14,355,298
1963	325,306	3,251,831	1974	445,390	8,416,631	1985	656,271	15,011,569
1964	344,444	3,596,275	1975	614,524	9,031,155	1986	658,887	15,670,456

CHAPTER ONE

1. Charles C. Mason, "The Story of the Discovery and Early Exploration of the Cliff Houses at the Mesa Verde," typed copy, Colorado Historical Society, dated May 5, 1918. The story was published in the *Denver Post*, July 1, 1917, sec. 2, p. 6, with the notation that it had been checked over by the Wetherill brothers and "its facts vouched for."

2. The most likely date is December 8. The other date given was December 18. See Frederick H. Chapin, "The Cliff-Dwellings of the Mancos Canons," *American Antiquarian* (July, 1890), p. 195; and *Art Catalogue '92* (Minneapolis: Industrial Exposition, 1892). Richard Wetherill apparently was the source of the information. Mason said they were on a "cruise of exploration," with Wetherill looking for stray cattle. Richard Wetherill's story was told in the *Mancos Times*, Aug. 16, 1895.

3. Donald Cutter, "Prelude to a Pageant in the Wilderness," *Western Historical Quarterly* (Jan., 1977), pp. 8–9, 11; Don Cutter letter to author, Nov. 10, 1986.

4. Ted J. Warner (ed.), *The Dominguez-Escalante Journal*, trans. Fray Angelico Chavez (Provo, Utah: Brigham Young University, 1976), pp. 13–14.

5. *Missouri Intelligencer*, June 25, 1825; David Weber, *The Taos Trappers* (Norman: University of Oklahoma, 1971), p. 79. Weber concluded that Becknell's camp was perhaps in the area of the present-day park.

6. Jean Pinkley to Chief of Resource Studies, Sept. 24, 1964, Mesa Verde Correspondence, Mesa Verde National Park. For the Old Spanish Trail, see LeRoy and Ann Hafen, *Old Spanish Trail* (Glendale, Calif.: Arthur H. Clark, 1954), pp. 19, 157, 159; and John Kessell, "Sources for the History of a New Mexico Community: Abiquiu," *New Mexico Historical Review* (Oct., 1979), p. 267.

7. Hafen, *Old Spanish Trail*, pp. 341, 347.

8. Don Cutter letter to author, Nov. 10, 1986.

9. J. N. Macomb, *Report of the Exploring Expedition . . . in 1859* (Washington, D.C.: Government Printing Office, 1876), pp. 79–80, 83–84, 89, 95. J. S. Newberry, Notes, Mesa Verde National Park, Aug. 4, 6, and 8, 1859.

10. Pinkley to Chief of Resource Studies, Sept. 24, 1964, Mesa Verde Correspondence, Mesa Verde National Park. Attempts by Pinkley and others (and more recently by the author) to further identify Stangl proved fruitless. Pinkley believed Stangl belonged to some small independent trading party.

11. *New York Tribune*, Nov. 3, 1874; LeRoy Hafen (ed.), *The Diaries of William Henry Jackson* (Glendale, Calif.: Arthur H. Clark, 1959), pp. 296, 306–09; and W. H. Jackson, "First Official Visit to the Cliff Dwellings," *Colorado Magazine* (May, 1924), pp. 153–55.

12. W. H. Jackson, "Report," *Annual Report of the United States Geological and Geographical Survey* (Washington, D.C.: Government Printing Office, 1876), p. 370; William R. Birdsall, "The Cliff Dwellings of

the Canons of the Mesa Verde," *American Geographical Society Bulletin* (Dec. 31, 1891), pp. 610–11.

13. *New York Tribune*, Nov. 3, 1874; William Holmes, "Pottery of the Ancient Pueblos," *Fourth Annual Report of the Bureau of Ethnology* (Washington, D.C.: Government Printing Office, 1886), p. 284.

14. William Holmes, "Report," in Frederick V. Hayden's *Tenth Annual Report of the United States Geological and Geographical Survey* (Washington, D.C.: Government Printing Office, 1878), p. 408; *Rocky Mountain News* (weekly), Sept. 8, 1875, p. 1.

15. Clarence S. Jackson, *Picture Maker of the Old West, William H. Jackson* (New York: Charles Scribner's Sons, 1947), p. 234; *Rocky Mountain News*, March 5, 1876, p. 1, and March 28, 1876, p. 2; William H. Jackson, *Time Exposure* (New York: G. P. Putnam's, 1940), p. 243.

16. Detroit paper cited in *Durango Morning Herald*, Oct. 11, 1887. For Jackson's and Holmes's contributions, see E. Steve Cassells, *The Archaeology of Colorado* (Boulder, Colo.: Johnson, 1983), pp. 104–05; Chapin, "Cliff-Dwellings," p. 194; and Florence and Robert Lister,

Earl Morris and Southwestern Archaeology (Albuquerque: University of New Mexico, 1968), p. 1.

17. Alfred Morgan, "On the Cliff-Houses and Antiquities of South-Western Colorado and New Mexico," *Literary and Philosophical Society of Liverpool Proceedings* (66th Session), 1876–77, pp. 342–56.

18. Wm. Fellowes Morgan, "Description of a Cliff-House on the Mancos River of Colorado, with a Ground Plan," *American Association for the Advancement of Science Proceedings* (1879), pp. 300, 306. Howe's article appeared in the *Rocky Mountain News*, Nov. 25, 1877. (Howe's name may be Rowe.) *La Plata Miner* (Silverton, Colorado), July 17, 1880. The Aztec ruins are now part of Aztec Ruins National Monument in New Mexico.

19. Frank Fossett, *Colorado* (Denver: Daily Tribune, 1876), p. 437. See also Chapin, "Cliff-Dwellings," p. 194.

20. John Routt, *Message of Gov. Routt to the Second General Assembly of the State of Colorado* (Denver: Daily Times, 1879), p. 16.

21. There is a legend that a heliograph station was established on Point Lookout by troops from Fort Lewis. Post records

and Signal Corps reports do not confirm this, nor do studies on the military use of the heliograph in the 1880s. The fort was abandoned and became an Indian school in 1891.

22. Lister, *Earl Morris*, pp. 3–4, discusses relic collecting. *Durango Record*, April 23, Sept. 24, and Dec. 17, 1881; *Southwest*, Aug. 25, 1883; *The Idea*, May 16 and July 25, 1885, Feb. 20 and Sept. 25, 1886, and Aug. 13, 1888; and the *Durango Morning Herald*, Sept. 27, 1887, all have stories about visitors. Bernard J. Byrne, *A Frontier Army Surgeon* (New York: Exposition, 1962), p. 127, recounts his adventures in visiting a cliff dwelling.

23. Osborn registered at Durango's Grand Central Hotel on Nov. 25, 1882. See *Southwest*, same date. The discovery of Cliff Palace, of course, lit a fire under some old-timers, who suddenly remembered that they had been there in the 1880s. The Mesa Verde files contain some of these claims and records of the research attempting to prove or disprove them. The claims are irrelevant, because nobody did anything about promoting what he saw.

24. *Mancos Times*, Oct. 13, 1899; Gilbert and Virginia McClurg, "The Development

of the Mesa Verde National Park," *Travel* (July, 1916), p. 36. The Durango newspapers made no mention of her visits, and curiously, the Ute trouble she talked about seems to have occurred in 1881 or 1885.

25. *Weekly Tribune-Republican*, Dec. 16, 1886, p. 4. See also George Crofutt, *Crofutt's Grip-Sack Guide of Colorado* (Omaha: Overland Publishing, 1885).

26. *Durango Record*, Oct. 29, 1881; *The Idea*, Jan. 2, 1886; *Durango Morning Herald*, Sept. 27 and Nov. 12, 1887, Nov. 2 and Dec. 14, 1888. For the family history, see Frank McNitt, *Richard Wetherill Anasazi* (Albuquerque: University of New Mexico, 1966), pp. 9–11.

27. McNitt, *Anasazi*, p. 22. For the Wetherills of these years, see Mason, "Story," pp. 1–2; F. H. Newell, "Mesa Verde," *National Geographic* (Oct., 1898), p. 434; Jesse L. Nusbaum, *The 1926 Re-Excavation of Step House Cave* (Mesa Verde National Park: Mesa Verde Museum Assoc., 1981), p. 2.

28. The 1887–88 claim has caused some controversy, but Mason and the remaining Wetherills signed a statement to support Al; see Mason, "Story," p. 3, and John Wetherill to Mercy Dunbar, undated letter, Arizona State Museum Archives. The controversy of Al versus Richard was stirred up by two headstrong women who interpreted the facts in different ways; see Maurine S. Fletcher (ed.), *The Wetherills of the Mesa Verde: Autobiography of Benjamin Alfred Wetherill* (Rutherford, N.J.: Associated University Presses, 1977), pp. 108, 110, and appendix, and Jean Pinkley to Earl Jackson, Oct. 3, 1963, Letters Miscellaneous, Mesa Verde National Park.

29. Chapin, "Cliff-Dwellings," p. 196; *Biographical Sketches and Letters of T. Mitchell Prudden, M.D.* (New Haven: Yale University, 1927), p. 140; Palmer Henderson, "The Cliff Dwellers," *Literary Northwest* (May, 1893), p. 79; Nusbaum, *1926 Re-Excavation*, p. 9. The Chain account is found in Mason, "Story," p. 2; Chain's husband ran his store from 1873 to 1899 and, among other things, sold photographs of southwest Colorado.

CHAPTER TWO

1. John Wetherill to Mercy Dunbar, undated letter, Arizona State Museum Archives; Charles C. Mason, "The Story of the Discovery and Early Exploration of the Cliff Houses at the Mesa Verde," Colorado Historical Society, dated May 5, 1918, p. 3.

2. B. K. Wetherill to William H. Holmes, Feb. 11, 1890; see also Holmes to Wetherill, Jan. 31, 1890, and Wetherill to Holmes, March 3, 1890, Wetherill Collection, Smithsonian Institution. David Harrell, " 'We Contacted Smithsonian': The Wetherills at Mesa Verde," *New Mexico Historical Review* (July, 1987), p. 232.

3. *Durango Herald*, March 3, 7, 8, 27–29, and April 18, 1889; Mason, "Story," p. 3. The *Herald* carried a complete list of the relics in the March 27–29 issues.

4. LeRoy Hafen, "History of the State Historical Society of Colorado: The First Twenty-Five Years," *Colorado Magazine* (July, 1953), p. 176. "Letter," *El Palacio* (Oct., 1946), p. 268. The *Weekly Republican*, May 30, 1889, p. 4, said the owners were willing to sell for $2,800.

5. *The Archeologist*, Feb., 1894, quoted in Patricia C. Johnston, "Gustaf Nordenskiold and the Treasure of Mesa Verde," *American West* (July/Aug., 1979), p. 37; Mason, "Story," p. 4.

6. R. Wetherill to F. W. Putnam, April 7, 1890, quoted in Frank McNitt, *Richard*

Wetherill Anasazi (Albuquerque: University of New Mexico, 1966), p. 330.

7. T. Mitchell Prudden, "A Summer among Cliff Dwellings," *Harper's New Monthly Magazine* (Sept., 1896), p. 551.

8. Frederick H. Chapin, *The Land of the Cliff-Dwellers* (Boston: W. B. Clarke, 1892), pp. 101, 140, 144–45, 175–76, 178. Richard Wetherill recounted his troubles with the Utes in the *Mancos Times*, Aug. 16, 1895. Frederick H. Chapin, "The Cliff-Dwellings of the Mancos Canons," *The American Antiquarian* (July, 1890), pp. 201–03. See also pp. 204–06, 210.

9. Nordenskiold to parents, June 27, 1891, quoted in Olof W. Arrhenius, *Stones Speak and Waters Sing* (Mesa Verde National Park: Mesa Verde Museum Assoc., 1986), p. 6; Nordenskiold to father, July 11, 1891, translated copy, Gustaf Nordenskiold "File," Mesa Verde National Park.

10. Gustaf Nordenskiold, *The Cliff Dwellers of the Mesa Verde* (Glorieta, N.M.: Rio Grande Press, 1979 reprint), p. 24. For a list of sites visited and dug, see Arrhenius, *Stones*, pp. 19–35.

11. Nordenskiold, *Cliff Dwellers*, p. 13.

Roe Ethridge interview is found in the *Durango News*, March 31, 1950, p. 1.

12. Nordenskiold's story is found in the following: *Rocky Mountain News*, Sept. 19, 1891, p. 1, and Sept. 20, 1891, p. 12; *Weekly Republican*, Sept. 24, 1891, p. 4, Oct. 1, 1891, p. 4, and Oct. 8, 1891, p. 4; *Denver Republican*, Oct. 6, 1891, p. 1; *Pagosa Springs News*, Sept. 24, 1891; and *Ridgway Herald*, Oct. 15, 1891. The Silverton papers remaining for these months have no comments on Nordenskiold. Durango papers are nonexistent.

13. Arrhenius, *Stones*, pp. 31–33; Gustaf Nordenskiold "File," Mesa Verde National Park; Nordenskiold, *Cliff Dwellers*, p. 23. The District Court in Durango has no records of this case or of Nordenskiold.

14. Robert H. and Florence C. Lister, "The Legacy of Gustaf Nordenskiold," in Arrhenius, *Stones*, p. 73. For further information on Nordenskiold's contributions, see also David A. Breternitz and Jack E. Smith, "Mesa Verde," *National Parkways: Rocky Mountain and Mesa Verde* (Casper, Wyo.: World-Wide Research, 1972), p. 76. Ron Switzer's, Charlie Steen's, and Robert Lister's comments on Nordenskiold, *Cliff*

Dwellers, pp. 13, 18–19, 31–36; Jesse W. Fewkes, *Antiquities of the Mesa Verde National Park Spruce-Tree House* (Washington, D.C.: Government Printing Office, 1909), p. 3.

15. Richard Wetherill to Nordenskiold, Dec. 31, 1893, Wetherill Letters, Mesa Verde National Park.

16. Breternitz and Smith, "Mesa Verde," p. 76; Chapin, "Cliff-Dwellings," p. 197; McNitt, *Anasazi*, p. 33; *Biographical Sketches and Letters of T. Mitchell Prudden, M.D.* (New Haven: Yale University, 1927), pp. 140–41. Al's quote, Maurine S. Fletcher (ed.), *The Wetherills of the Mesa Verde: Autobiography of Benjamin Alfred Wetherill* (Rutherford, N.J.: Associated University Presses, 1977), p. 119; see also pp. 130–31. William R. Birdsall, "The Cliff Dwellings of the Canons of the Mesa Verde," *American Geographical Society Bulletin* (Dec. 31, 1891), p. 587.

17. For the preceding see Fletcher, *Wetherills*, p. 193 n. 3; material on the Alamo Ranch found in Miscellaneous File, Mesa Verde National Park; *Mancos Times*, April 28, May 5, June 2 and 16, 1893, Jan. 5, 1894, July 17 and 24, Aug. 7, 1896, and

Feb. 4, 1898; Mason/Wetherill agreement, July 4, 1895, Miscellaneous File, Mesa Verde National Park; McNitt, *Anasazi*, pp. 54–55; Prudden, "Summer," p. 550.

18. Walter Jakway to author, Jan., 1986. This, or something similar, may be the basis for the myth that the Wetherills used dynamite in excavating the ruins.

19. For the preceding comments by visitors, see Alice Palmer Henderson in "The Cliff-Dwellers," *Independent*, June 22, 1893, Virginia McClurg Collection, Pioneers' Museum, Colorado Springs; and *Mancos Times*, Aug. 16, 1895. The *Mancos Times*, 1894–98, has many references to tourists. Fletcher, *Wetherills*, p. 184.

20. *Catalogue of Cliff Dwellers' Exhibit* (Jackson Park, Ill.: H. Jay Smith Exploring Co., 1893), pp. 7–15; Mason, "Story," pp. 7–8; *Mancos Times*, May 26, Sept. 15, and Nov. 10, 1893.

21. *Art Catalogue '92* (Minneapolis: Industrial Exposition, 1892), p. 7; Palmer Henderson, "The Cliff Dwellers," *Literary Northwest* (May, 1893), p. 85.

22. Material for the Durango section is found in *Great Southwest*, April 13–14, 1893; *Durango Herald*, March 24,

1889; Chapin, *Cliff-Dwellers*, pp. 97–100; Richard McCloud, *Durango as It Is* (Durango: Durango Board of Trade, 1892), pp. 30–32. Interestingly, the revitalized Durango Board of Trade initially did not become excited about Mesa Verde; see 1892–93 minutes, Durango Public Library.

23. For Mancos, see *Mancos Times*, April 28, May 12, Aug. 18, Nov. 17 and 24, 1893, and June 14, 1899. Louise Switzgable to Don Watson, Jan., 1953(?), Mesa Verde National Park, Letters Miscellaneous.

24. *Montezuma Journal*, Aug. 4, 1899; see also issues June 2 and 9, and Aug. 18 and 25, 1899.

25. "Tourist Guide" (Denver: Carson-Harper, 1897), copy at Mesa Verde; *Mancos Times*, May 19, 1893, and Aug. 13, 1897, plus advertisements in Denver, Durango, and Mancos newspapers, 1890s. For the Wetherills and the D&RG, see Mesa Verde National Park, Miscellaneous File.

CHAPTER THREE

1. Wetherill to Holmes, March 3, 1890, Wetherill Collection, Smithsonian Insti-

tution. T. Mitchell Prudden, "A Summer among Cliff Dwellings," *Harper's New Monthly Magazine* (Sept., 1896), p. 552; F. H. Newell, "Mesa Verde," *National Geographic* (Oct., 1898), p. 434; Deric Nusbaum, *Deric in Mesa Verde* (New York: G. P. Putnam's Sons, 1926), p. 76; Florence and Robert Lister, *Earl Morris and Southwestern Archaeology* (Albuquerque: University of New Mexico, 1968), p. 5; and Don Watson, *Cliff Dwellings of the Mesa Verde* (Mesa Verde National Park: Mesa Verde Museum Association, 1954), p. 12.

2. Prudden, "Summer," p. 552; B. W. Ritter to Nordenskiold, March 10, 1894, quoted in Olof W. Arrhenius, *Stones Speak and Waters Sing* (Mesa Verde National Park: Mesa Verde Museum Assoc., 1986), p. 86; LeRoy Hafen, "History of the State Historical Society of Colorado: The First Twenty-Five Years," *Colorado Magazine* (July, 1953), p. 176; *Biographical Sketches and Letters of T. Mitchell Prudden, M.D.* (New Haven: Yale University, 1927), pp. 140–41; Frederick H. Chapin, "The Cliff-Dwellings of the Mancos Canons," *American Antiquarian* (July, 1890), p. 552. Frank Hall, *History of the State of Colorado* (Chi-

cago: Blakely, 1895), vol. 4, p. 231; *Great Southwest*, April 4, 1893; Newell, "Mesa Verde," p. 434; and John Ise, *Our National Park Policy* (Baltimore: Johns Hopkins Press, 1961), pp. 144–45, 147. *Mancos Times*, Oct. 13, 1896.

3. McClurg to Teller, April 4, 1898, McClurg to Wolcott, April 4, 1898, McClurg to McKinley, Feb. 17, 1899, and McClurg to Mrs. William McKinley, no date, Virginia McClurg Collection, Pioneers' Museum; *Weekly Republican*, Oct. 13, 1898, p. 1; *Colorado Springs Gazette*, April 15, 1900, p. 9; Virginia McClurg Collection, Pioneers' Museum.

4. *Mancos Times*, Oct. 13, 1899. *Denver Republican*, Oct. 13, 1898; *Rocky Mountain News*, Oct. 29, 1899, p. 11; and *Mancos Times*, Oct. 20, 1899.

5. *Rocky Mountain News*, Oct. 29, 1899, p. 11; and *Mancos Times*, Oct. 20, 1899.

6. *Mancos Times*, July 6, 1900; and John Hays Hammond, *The Autobiography of John Hays Hammond* (New York: Arno Press, 1974 reprint), p. 480. For the other women, see "Colorado Cliff Dwellings Association History," Mesa Verde National Park; Mrs. A. M. Camp, "Helen Allen-Webster-Stoiber-Rood-Ellis," *Pioneers of the San Juan Country* (Durango: Durango Printing, 1952), vol. 3, p. 145; Helen S. Daniels, "Lo, the Poor Indians!" *Pioneers of the San Juan Country*, vol. 3, pp. 130–32.

7. Nancy Woloch, *Women and the American Experience* (New York: Knopf, 1984), p. 292; see also pp. 287–90, 293. See also Karen J. Blair, *The Clubwoman as Feminist* (New York: Holmes & Meier, 1980), pp. 57–58, 63, 118-19.

8. Edmund Rogers, "Notes on the Establishment of Mesa Verde National Park," *Colorado Magazine* (Jan., 1952), pp. 14–15. Camp's story is found in Helen S. Daniels, *The Ute Indians of Southwestern Colorado* (Durango, Colo.: n.p., 1941), p. 40, and in an unidentified newspaper clipping, Mesa Verde National Park, Miscellaneous File. 1903 Report of Virginia McClurg, undated clipping, Mesa Verde Collection, Center of Southwest Studies, Fort Lewis College.

9. Jack E. Smith, "The Nusbaum Years," *Mesa Verde Occasional Papers* (vol. 1, no. 1, Oct., 1981), p. 10, and Nusbaum to Ronnie, April 12, 1950, Supt. File, Mesa Verde National Park.

10. Minutes Cliff Dwellings Association, Feb. 4, April 11, Aug. 7, 1901, and Oct. 15, 1902, "Colorado Cliff Dwellings Association History," Mesa Verde National Park; list of Mesa Verde bills and resolutions introduced in Congress. Archaeology Historic Records, Mesa Verde National Park; Patricia Hoben, "The Establishment of Mesa Verde as a National Park," M.A. thesis, University of Oklahoma, 1966, pp. 51–56.

11. *Mancos Times*, July 6, 1900, June 21 and 28, 1901; the *Colorado Telegraph*, Aug. 18, 1901, clipping and other material in the Colorado Cliff Dwellings Association material, Virginia McClurg Collection, Pioneers' Museum. McClurg to Madame, May 30, 1901, "Colorado Cliff Dwellings Association History," Mesa Verde National Park.

12. *Semi-Weekly Herald*, Sept. 9, 1901; *Mancos Times*, Sept. 6, 1901; *Durango Evening Herald*, Sept. 4, 1901; *Denver Republican*, Sept. 10, 1901, p. 1; *New York Herald*, Sept. 29, 1901, p. 7.

13. Frank McNitt, *Richard Wetherill Anasazi* (Albuquerque: University of New Mexico, 1966), pp. 179–80.

14. *Mancos Times*, June 22, July 6 and 20, Aug. 10, 17, and 24, 1900, for example.

15. Ralph W. Andrews, *Photographers of the Frontier West: Their Lives and Work* (Seattle: Superior Publishing, 1965), pp. 21, 24. Thomas M. McKee, "History of Mesa Verde Ruins," manuscript, Mesa Verde National Park.

16. Minnie Hickman Interview, June 18, 1982, Mesa Verde Oral History Project.

17. "Packing into Mesa Verde—1903 Style," *Four Corners Magazine* (Summer, 1972), pp. 61–62, 80.

18. *Rocky Mountain News*, July 14, 1903. *Durango Evening Herald*, Aug. 19, 1904, p. 1. Hoben, "Establishment," pp. 55–56.

19. *Denver Times*, June 12, 1904, p. 5. *Circular Relating to Historic and Prehistoric Ruins of the Southwest and Their Preservation* (Washington, D.C.: Government Printing Office, 1904), pp. 3–4, 7. Other names suggested included Cliff Dwelling Park and Mesa Verde.

CHAPTER FOUR

1. For the preceding, see Shafroth to McClurg, May 4, 1900, Virginia McClurg Collection, Pioneers' Museum; Margaret Keating, "Knowledge of Ages Is Buried in Mesa Verde," *Modern World* (Oct., 1907), p. 155; and Patricia Hoben, "The Establishment of Mesa Verde as a National Park," M.A. thesis, University of Oklahoma, 1966, p. 57.

2. For the homestead entries, see Historic Sites File, Mesa Verde National Park.

3. *Rocky Mountain News*, Jan. 22, 1905, p. 10.

4. "Mesa Verde National Park," *Senate Report No. 1428*, 59th Cong., 1st sess., 1905-06, I, pp. 1–3. "Mesa Verde National Park," *Report No. 4944 House of Representatives*, 59th Cong., 1st sess., 1905-06, III, pp. 1–8.

5. Robert Shankland, *Steve Mather of the National Parks* (New York: Knopf, 1951), p. 50; Robert C. Euler, "A Dedication to the Memory of Edgar Lee Hewett 1865–1946," *Arizona and the West* (Fall, 1963), pp. 287–88. Alfred Runte, *National Parks: The American Experience* (Lincoln: University of Nebraska, 1979), pp. 71–73, 98. John Ise, *Our National Park Policy* (Baltimore: Johns Hopkins, 1961), pp. 149–53.

6. *Pueblo Chieftain*, Nov. 9, 1905, clipping at Mesa Verde.

7. *Rocky Mountain News*, Feb. 13, 1906, p. 3, and March 11, 1906, p. 10; *Denver Times*, Feb. 25, 1906, sec. 3, p. 5.

8. *Denver Times*, Feb. 25, 1906, sec. 3, p. 5; *Pueblo Chieftain*, Feb. 13, 1906, no page, Virginia McClurg Collection, Pioneers' Museum; *Denver Post*, Feb. 23, 1906, clipping at Mesa Verde National Park. *Rocky Mountain News*, March 11, 1906, pp. 9–10; see also issue of Feb. 13, 1906, p. 3.

9. Hewett to William Holmes, chief of the Bureau of American Ethnology, June 12, 1906, Archaeology Historic Records, Mesa Verde National Park. *Mancos Times-Tribune*, April 13, 1906. Peabody praised Hewett for his "invaluable service."

10. *Congressional Record*, 59th Cong., 1st Sess., 1906, XL, Part 9, p. 8818.

11. Ise, *Our National Park Policy*, pp. 136, 142.

12. *Mancos Times-Tribune*, May 18 and 25, and June 15 and 19, 1906. Unidentified clipping, Mesa Verde National Park.

13. *Denver Times*, Aug. 11, 1907, and unidentified clipping, Mesa Verde National Park. Keating, "Knowledge," p. 149; see also p. 155. James Peabody, during his 1903–05 administration, was ardently anti-

union and dragged Colorado through a sordid two years of strike breaking.

14. Helen S. Daniels, "Lo, the Poor Indians!" *Pioneers of the San Juan Country* (Durango, Colo.: Durango Printing, 1952), vol. 3, pp. 130–31; *Denver Times*, undated, quoted in Gilbert and Virginia McClurg, "The Development of the Mesa Verde National Park," *Travel* (July, 1916), p. 36; and Edmund Rogers, "Notes on the Establishment of Mesa Verde National Park," *Colorado Magazine* (Jan., 1952), pp. 12–13.

15. For the impact of Mesa Verde, see Robert and Florence Lister, *Those Who Came Before* (Tucson: University of Arizona, 1983), pp. 81, 86, 109, 140. Mrs. W. S. Peabody, "The Mesa Verde National Park," *Modern World* (Oct., 1907), p. 159. Raymond Thompson, "Cliff Dwellings and the Park Service," summary of paper presented, World Conference on Cultural Parks, Sept. 16–24, 1984, Mesa Verde Archives. Lida Frowe, "The Mesa Verde National Park," *Modern World* (Nov., 1906), pp. 7, 8, 10.

16. Lister and Lister, *Those Who Came Before*, pp. 8, 131.

17. Eugene Parsons, "The Mesa Verde National Park," *American Antiquarian* (1906), p. 266.

CHAPTER FIVE

1. Wm. Leonard to Sec. of the Interior, Oct. 13, 1906, Mesa Verde Correspondence, National Archives; Superintendent's File, Mesa Verde National Park. The *Mancos Times-Tribune*, Aug. 23, 1907, stated that J. S. Spear was temporarily supervising the park; Spear was at the Fort Lewis Indian School, but the park has no record of his appointment. Some of the early records of Mesa Verde were lost in a fire in the 1930s, leaving gaps in the administrative history.

2. *Denver Times*, Aug. 11, 1907 (?), clipping Mesa Verde National Park. Lucy Peabody, Folder, Mesa Verde National Park. For a positive slant on the park's creation, see unidentified newspaper clipping, Aug. 24, 1906, Miscellaneous File, Mesa Verde National Park.

3. *Rocky Mountain News*, Oct. 25 and 27, and Nov. 16, 1906. Manitou Cliff Dwellings File, Mesa Verde National Park.

Mancos Times-Tribune, Aug. 23, 1907. Unidentified clipping (Manitou Springs), Oct. 27, 1906, Miscellaneous File, Mesa Verde National Park. The Durango Historical and Archaeological Society brought the issue to a head in late October; see the *Rocky Mountain News*, Nov. 16, 1906.

4. Virginia McClurg Collection, Pioneers' Museum; Gilbert and Virginia McClurg, "The Development of the Mesa Verde National Park," *Travel* (July, 1916), pp. 36–37; and Nusbaum memo, Feb. 5, 1946, Lucy Peabody, Folder, Mesa Verde National Park. The Balcony House project was finished in 1911.

5. Archaeology Historic Records, Mesa Verde National Park.

6. *Mancos Times-Tribune*, July 26, Aug. 2, and Sept. 6 and 13, 1907, and *Denver Times*, Aug. 11, 1907.

7. Randolph to Thomas Ryan, Oct. 7, 1907, and Ryan to Randolph, Oct. 25, 1907, Letters Miscellaneous, Mesa Verde National Park. Hans Randolph, *Report of the Superintendent of the Mesa Verde National Park 1908* (Washington, D.C.: Government Printing Office, 1908), p. 6.

8. Florence and Robert Lister, *Earl*

Morris and Southwestern Archaeology (Albuquerque: University of New Mexico, 1968), pp. 11–12. Edgar Hewett, "Report on the Ruins of Mesa Verde, Colorado," undated, but prior to 1908, copy Archaeology Historic Records, Mesa Verde National Park. Margaret Keating, "Knowledge of Ages Is Buried at Mesa Verde," *Modern World* (Oct., 1907), p. 151. 1st Assist. Sec. of the Interior to Fewkes, March 19, 1908, Miscellaneous File, Mesa Verde National Park. Jesse W. Fewkes, *Antiquities of the Mesa Verde National Park: Cliff Palace* (Washington, D.C.: Government Printing Office, 1911), pp. 9, 78. J. Walter Fewkes, *Report Excavation and Repair of Ruins* (Washington, D.C.: Government Printing Office, 1909), p. 16.

9. See, for example, Lister and Lister, *Earl Morris*, pp. 11–12; Robert and Florence Lister, *Those Who Came Before* (Tucson: University of Arizona, 1983), p. 134; and David A. Breternitz and Jack E. Smith, "Mesa Verde," *National Parkways: Rocky Mountain and Mesa Verde* (Casper, Wyo.: World-Wide Research, 1972), p. 76. For the contemporary view of Fewkes, see *Mancos Times-Tribune*, May 8 and 15, and

June 5, 1908, and Aug. 8, 1919.

10. *Mancos Times-Tribune*, May 8 and Aug. 7, 1908; Fewkes, *Report*, pp. 10–11. Jean Bader Interview, July 29, 1986; Randolph to Interior Secretary James R. Garfield, Sept. 9 and 19, 1907, Letters Miscellaneous, Mesa Verde National Park. Kelly material, Superintendent's File, Mesa Verde National Park.

11. Hans Randolph, *Report of the Superintendent of Mesa Verde National Park, 1909* (Washington, D.C.: Government Printing Office, 1909), p. 6. See also *Smithsonian Annual Report 1909*, pp. 46–47.

12. For water, see Robert H. Rose, *Water Supply History of Mesa Verde National Park* (Mesa Verde National Park: Mesa Verde National Park, 1952), pp. 17, 18, 22–23. Randolph, *Report . . . 1910*, pp. 6–7. *Mancos Times-Tribune*, 1907–09.

13. Eva Mills Anderson, "A Tenderfoot at the Cliff Dwellings of the Mesa Verde," *Chautauquan* (July, 1908), pp. 194, 201, 202–04, 206.

14. Nusbaum's comments are found in a July 26, 1946, memo, Archaeology Historic Records, Mesa Verde National Park. *Mancos Times-Tribune*, June–Dec., 1910,

contains only one unexplained comment referring to Randolph: The Nov. 11 issue stated that Mrs. H. M. Randolph had left for Denver, prior to leaving for California to "make her future home." She was back the next spring.

15. For the Randolph situation, see *Mancos Times-Tribune*, April 21 and May 19, 1911, and *Semi-Weekly Herald* (Durango), April 27 and May 11, 1911. R. A. Ballinger to Andrew Kennedy, Nov. 28, 1910, and Kennedy to the Secretary, Dec. 21, 1910, Mesa Verde National Archives, Records of the National Park Service, Record Group 79.

16. Department of Interior to Wright, June 16, 1911, Correspondence 1911, Mesa Verde National Park. Kelly actually had been given a salary increase, based on the premise that he would devote full time to his ranger duties.

CHAPTER SIX

1. The inventory is found in Richard Wright, Acting Supt., to Sec. of Interior, Sept. 28, 1911. Activities of 1911, Dept.

of Interior to Wright, May 23, June 26, and Aug. 11, 1911, Dept. of Interior to Shoemaker, Oct. 5, 1911. The beavers, Supt., Yellowstone, to Supt., Mesa Verde, Dec. 11, 1911, Correspondence 1911, Mesa Verde National Park.

2. *Proceedings of the National Park Conference . . . September 11 and 12, 1911* (Washington, D.C.: Government Printing Office, 1912), pp. 115–16. Alfred Runte, *National Parks: The American Experience* (Lincoln: University of Nebraska, 1979), pp. 95–96, elaborates on Marshall's views.

3. Wright's comment is found in *Proceedings*, p. 174. *Mancos Times-Tribune*, May 19, 1911. John Spear, Supt. Ute Mountain Reservation, Navaho Springs, to Dept. of Interior, Sept. 7, 1912, Correspondence 1912, Mesa Verde National Park. See also Rickner reports of the Superintendent of Mesa Verde, 1911–15. Ricardo Torres-Reyes, *Mesa Verde National Park* (Washington, D.C.: Dept. of the Interior, 1970), pp. 9–13, carefully traces the boundary adjustments.

4. Tawa (John Clark) Testimony in Utes, "Minutes May 5, 1911, Council," Mesa Verde National Park.

5. Chief Jack House Interview, Sept. 11, 1967.

6. Rickner to Taylor, no date, 1914, Ansel Hall, Records, William Winkler, Cortez, Colorado.

7. Horace M. Albright, *The Birth of the National Park Service* (Salt Lake City: Howe Brothers, 1983), p. 64.

8. Samuel Shoemaker, for example, recommended moving the headquarters: "Report of the Superintendent," *Reports of the Department of the Interior . . . 1912* (Washington, D.C.: Government Printing Office, 1913), pp. 712, 714–17; Dept. of Interior to Supt., Dec. 11, 1913, Correspondence 1913, Mesa Verde National Park; *Mesa Verde National Park, Season of 1915* (Washington, D.C.: Government Printing Office, 1915), pp. 25–28. *Mesa Verde . . . 1918*, pp. 47–48.

9. *Durango Weekly Democrat*, June 19, 1914; Taylor to Secretary of the Interior, April 30, 1914, and Secretary of the Interior to Taylor, May 5, 1914, Mesa Verde Correspondence, National Archives; Densil H. Cummins, "Social and Economic History of Southwestern Colorado, 1860–1914," Ph.D. dissertation, University of Texas,

1951, pp. 497–505; Marion C. Wiley, *The High Road* (Denver: State Department of Highways, 1976), pp. 9, 15; Ehrhart was quoted in Mae Lacy Baggs, *Colorado: The Queen Jewel of the Rockies* (Boston: Page, 1926 edition), pp. 324–25.

10. Superintendent's Monthly Report, Oct., 1919, Mesa Verde National Park.

11. *Durango Herald*, July 12, 1913; *Durango Weekly Herald*, July 24, 1913; *Mancos Times-Tribune*, Aug. 24, 1917, Aug. 9 and 16, 1918.

12. *Mesa Verde . . . 1915*, pp. 5–6. Rickner to Sec. of the Interior, Feb. 13, 1914, Correspondence 1914, Mesa Verde National Park.

13. *Durango Weekly Democrat*, June 19, 1914; Thomas Rickner, "Report of the Superintendent," *Reports of the Department of the Interior . . . 1914* (Washington, D.C.: Government Printing Office, 1915), pp. 803–04.

14. *Mancos Times-Tribune*, Sept. 7, 1917. Sweeney to Rickner, Jan. 11, 1915, Miscellaneous File, Mesa Verde National Park. Rickner, "Report of the Superintendent," *Reports of the Department of the Interior, 1917* (Washington, D.C.: Govern-

ment Printing Office, 1918), pp. 817, 858; "Report of the Superintendent," 1918, p. 167.

15. Rickner, "Report of the Superintendent," 1915, p. 981; National Park Service, *Annual Report of the National Park Service for 1919* (Washington, D.C.: Government Printing Office, 1920), pp. 15–16.

16. Stephen Mather to Rickner, Oct. 20, 1915, Miscellaneous File, Mesa Verde National Park; Rickner, "Report of the Superintendent," 1918, p. 169; National Park Service, *Report of the Director of the National Park Service 1918* (Washington, D.C.: Government Printing Office, 1918), p. 73; Jeep file, Ansel Hall, Records, Winkler; *Mesa Verde 1915*, p. 5; Rickner to Director, May 27, June 15, 28, and 30, 1918, Correspondence 1918, Mesa Verde National Park; Nusbaum memo, undated, Superintendents' File, Mesa Verde National Park.

17. Albright, *Birth*, p. 32; and John Ise, *Our National Park Policy* (Baltimore: Johns Hopkins Press, 1961), pp. 185–92.

18. *Mancos Times-Tribune*, Sept. 14, 1917; Hill to Albright, Sept., 1917, Correspondence 1917, Mesa Verde National Park; Albright to Jeep, May 24, 1918, Correspondence 1918, Mesa Verde National Park; copy of report, Ansel Hall, Records, Winkler.

19. Ise, *Our National Park Policy*, pp. 32–34, 80–83, 209–10. Richard A. Bartlett, *Yellowstone: A Wilderness Besieged* (Tucson: University of Arizona, 1985), pp. 122–23, 128, 154–55, 202.

20. Ise, *Our National Park Policy*, p. 170; Rickner, "Report," 1914, pp. 788, 796; Department of Interior to Wright, July 27, 1911, and Wright to Sec. of the Interior, Aug. 2, 1911, Correspondence 1911, Mesa Verde National Park; Shoemaker, "Report," 1912, pp. 709, 716–17; Shoemaker to Secretary, June 14, 1912, Correspondence 1912, Mesa Verde National Park; Grazing Hearing Records, Mesa Verde National Park; Albright, *Birth*, pp. 73–74; Rickner to Director, Jan. 31, 1919, Correspondence 1919, Mesa Verde National Park.

21. Todd to Shoemaker, Jan. 9 and March 6, 1912, Correspondence 1912, Mesa Verde National Park; *Mancos Times-Tribune*, Oct. 7, 1907; Wright to Sec. of the Interior, June 29, 1911, Hogg to Shoemaker, Dec. 28, 1911, Dept. of Interior to Shoemaker, Oct. 25, 1911, Todd to Shoemaker, Nov. 4, 1911, Correspondence 1911, Mesa Verde National Park; Shoemaker to Secretary, June 14 and July 8, 1913, Correspondence 1913, Mesa Verde National Park; Shoemaker, "Report," 1912–13; Rickner, "Reports," 1914–16; Ise, *Our National Park Policy*, pp. 165–66; Meredith Guillet Interview, Oct. 8, 1986; Torres-Reyes, *Mesa Verde*, pp. 14–16. The Jordan Mine was the other lease, but in the 1913 boundary adjustment it was found to be out of the park.

22. *Marfa New Era*, July 7, 1916; D&RG to Wright, May 30, 1911, Correspondence 1911, Mesa Verde National Park; National Park Service, *Annual Report of the National Park Service 1917*, 1918. *Denver Post*, Oct. 28, 1917, and *Denver Times*, Sept. 14, 1917, clippings, Miscellaneous File, Mesa Verde National Park. Runte, *National Parks*, chapter 5, discusses the "See America First" campaign.

23. D&RG to Rickner, Oct. 29, 1915, Correspondence 1915, Mesa Verde National Park; Dept. of Interior to Wright, June 28 and 30, 1911, Correspondence 1911, Mesa Verde National Park; Hill's comment is

found in *Proceedings of the National Park Conference . . . September 11 and 12, 1911.*

24. Willa Sibert Cather, "Mesa Verde Wonderland," *Denver Times*, Jan. 31, 1916, p. 7. See also Edith Lewis, *Willa Cather Living* (New York: Knopf, 1953), pp. 94–99.

25. Curtis W. Buchholtz, *Rocky Mountain National Park: A History* (Boulder: Colorado Associated University Press, 1983), pp. 126–36. Enos A. Mills, *The Rocky Mountain National Park* (New York: Doubleday, 1924), pp. 85–91. Mills estimated that about fifty thousand people visited the region.

26. Mills to Rickner, Sept. 20, 1915, Correspondence 1915, Mesa Verde National Park.

27. *Rocky Mountain News*, Jan. 1, 1918, clipping, Miscellaneous File, Mesa Verde National Park. Rickner's 1918 report, p. 157, has the breakdown on traffic.

28. Dept. of Interior to Rickner, Dec. 10, 1915, Correspondence 1915, Mesa Verde National Park.

29. *Mancos Times-Tribune*, Aug. 24 and 31, and Sept. 7, 1917; *Denver Times*, Sept. 10, 1917, p. 3; McClurg and McClurg, "Development," p. 34.

CHAPTER SEVEN

1. For Nusbaum, see Jack E. Smith, "The Nusbaum Years," *Mesa Verde Occasional Papers* (vol. 1, no. 1, Oct., 1981), p. 11; E. Steve Cassells, *The Archaeology of Colorado* (Boulder, Colo.: Johnson, 1983), p. 109; A. V. Kidder, "Reminiscences in Southwest Archaeology," *Kiva* (April, 1960), pp. 22, 24, 26; *Mancos Times-Tribune*, Aug. 7, 1908.

2. Nusbaum, "Speech to Westerners," C. Marshall Finnan File, Mesa Verde National Park; Nusbaum to Mather, June 9, 1921, Correspondence 1921, Mesa Verde National Park; Nusbaum to Acting Director, April 25, 1922, Nusbaum, Correspondence, Mesa Verde National Park; Nusbaum memo, Superintendent's File, Mesa Verde National Park. Ricardo Torres-Reyes, *Mesa Verde National Park* (Washington, D.C.: Department of the Interior, 1970), pp. 119–21, describes visitors' complaints. Rosemary Nusbaum, *Tierra Dulce: Reminiscences from the Jesse Nusbaum Papers* (Santa Fe, N.M.: Sun Stone, 1980), pp. 74–76.

3. Nusbaum to Arno Cammerer, June

5, 1922, Correspondence 1922, Mesa Verde National Park.

4. Nusbaum, *Tierra Dulce*, pp. 72–73.

5. Ibid., p. 76; Jesse L. Nusbaum, "Report of the Superintendent," *Report of the Director 1921* (Washington, D.C.: Government Printing Office, 1921).

6. Nusbaum, "Report," 1921, p. 234, and Nusbaum, "Monthly Report," Aug. 4, 1921, Jan. 5, Feb. 3, and April 6, 1922, Mesa Verde National Park; Dept. of Interior to Nusbaum, Aug. 23, 1921, and Nusbaum to F. W. Hodge, Dec. 10, 1921, Correspondence 1921, Mesa Verde National Park.

7. Stephen Mather to Nusbaum, Jan. 31, 1925, Correspondence 1925, Mesa Verde National Park.

8. Grazing Hearing Records, Mesa Verde National Park; Nusbaum, "Monthly Report," April 5, 1922, Mesa Verde National Park; Nusbaum to Cammerer, June 5, 1922, Nusbaum to George Stephan, Dec. 1, 1922, and Nusbaum to Director, April 11 and 20, 1927, Nusbaum, Correspondence, Mesa Verde National Park. Nusbaum, *Tierra Dulce*, pp. 77–78.

9. Nusbaum, "Report," 1921, p. 234;

Nusbaum to Director, Aug. 1, 1942, Grazing Hearing Records, Mesa Verde National Park; and John Ise, *Our National Park Policy* (Baltimore: Johns Hopkins Press, 1961), pp. 303, 435–37, 474–76.

10. Robert H. Rose, *Water Supply History of Mesa Verde National Park* (Mesa Verde National Park: Mesa Verde National Park, 1952), pp. 19, 27, 29; Secretary of the Interior, *Annual Report of the Secretary of the Interior* (Washington, D.C.: Government Printing Office, 1928), p. 179.

11. *Mesa Verde National Park* (Washington, D.C.: Government Printing Office, 1927), pp. 6, 13–14, 51–53, 55; Nusbaum, *Tierra Dulce*, pp. 74–75.

12. Earl Pomeroy, *In Search of the Golden West* (New York: Knopf, 1957), pp. 199, 200, 204. Curtis W. Buchholtz, *Rocky Mountain National Park: A History* (Boulder: Colorado Associated University Press, 1983), pp. 167, 177. Yellowstone had over 260,000 visitors in 1929: Richard A. Bartlett, *Yellowstone: A Wilderness Besieged* (Tucson: University of Arizona, 1985), p. 99.

13. Book of Impressions, Mesa Verde Archives.

14. Director to Nusbaum, Jan. 31, 1927, Nusbaum to Director, May 15, 1926, Feb. 7, 1927, Nusbaum, Correspondence, Mesa Verde National Park; Nusbaum, "Report," Jan. 5, 1922, and Jan. 20, 1927; U.S. Dept. of Agriculture to Nusbaum, Nov. 28, 1921, Nusbaum to Director, May 24, 1924, and March 18, 1925, Nusbaum to 4th Assistant Postmaster General, Jan. 27 and April 27, 1925, and June 18, 1926, Nusbaum, Correspondence, Mesa Verde National Park; Nusbaum, "Report," 1921, p. 233; National Park Service, *Report of the Director of the National Park Service 1921* (Washington, D.C.: Government Printing Office, 1918), p. 71, and *1929*, p. 100.

15. Nusbaum to Warren E. Boyer, Aug. 11, 1922, Nusbaum to Director, Feb. 7, 1927, Nusbaum to Lee, March 15, 1950, Nusbaum, Correspondence, Mesa Verde National Park; "Superintendent Reports, 1925, 1929–30," Mesa Verde National Park. Horace M. Albright and Frank J. Taylor commented on the Navajo culture in *"Oh, Ranger!" A Book about the National Parks* (Stanford, Calif.: Stanford University, 1929), pp. 85–86.

16. Nusbaum to Hugh Comming, Surgeon General, March 12, 1925, Nusbaum, Correspondence, Mesa Verde National Park; *Denver Post*, Feb. 11, 1926, p. 11; and National Park Service, *Report of the Director of the National Park Service 1926*, p. 45.

17. Alden C. Hayes, "The Wetherill Mesa Project," *Naturalist* (vol. 20, no. 2, 1969), p. 21; Switzer, "Foreword," Gustaf Nordenskiold, *The Cliff Dwellers of the Mesa Verde* (Glorieta, N.M.: Rio Grande Press, 1979 reprint), pp. 13–14. Nusbaum did work with A. E. Douglas to use tree rings to date some of the ruins.

18. For Nusbaum's activities as a fund raiser and his eventual relationship with the Rockefellers, see Nusbaum to Albright, March 24, 1925, Superintendents' File, Mesa Verde National Park.

19. Nusbaum memo, undated, Superintendents' File, Mesa Verde National Park. Smith, "Nusbaum Years," pp. 9–11, 23. Helen Wells Frahm Interview, Feb. 9, 1981. Albright, *Birth*, pp. 158–59, has a somewhat different version of the Rockefeller visit. He said the Rockefellers traveled under the name Davison to Yellowstone, Glacier, and Mesa Verde national parks.

20. Nusbaum to Duke de Kiddo, April 25, 1926, Miscellaneous File, Mesa Verde National Park; and *Mancos Times-Tribune*, July 23, 1926. Amy Thompson, "Mesa Verde Experiences," letter to author, Dec. 6, 1985.

21. Concessions program, 1920s, Ansel Hall, Records, Winkler material; National Park Service, *Report of the Director of the National Park Service 1923* (Washington, D.C.: Government Printing Office, 1923), p. 71; *Mesa Verde 1927*, pp. 60–61.

22. The Jeep/Nusbaum controversy may be followed in the *Mancos Times-Tribune*, March 12, 1920; Nusbaum, "Monthly Report," Sept. 15, 1926, Mesa Verde National Park; Nusbaum to Oddie Jeep, July 22, 1927; Oddie Jeep to Chas. Hall, Feb. 19, 1924; Chas. Hall to Jesse Nusbaum, Feb. 20, 1924, Nusbaum, Correspondence, Mesa Verde National Park. In 1924 Oddie had indicated that she might be willing to sell the concessions, but her price seemed too high and a potential purchaser shied away.

23. National Park Service, *Report of the Director 1923*, p. 73; *Mesa Verde 1927*, pp. 6–7; Nusbaum, "Monthly Report," Feb., 1926, Mesa Verde National Park;

Morris to Clarkson, Aug. 13, Clarkson to Nusbaum, Aug. 23, Nusbaum to Clarkson, Aug. 23, 1927, Nusbaum, Correspondence, Mesa Verde National Park. Pomeroy, *In Search of the Golden West*, pp. 40, 58, 59. Robert Beers, Interview, March 26, 1987. Nusbaum to Judge J. J. Downey, Jan. 29, 1928, Roads Outside the Park File, Mesa Verde National Park.

24. Marion C. Wiley, *The High Road* (Denver: State Dept. of Highways, 1976), pp. 19 and 24; *Year Book of the State of Colorado 1924* (Denver: Brook-Heffner, 1924), p. 39; National Park Service, *Report of the Director of the National Park Service 1923*, p. 72. Nusbaum, *Tierra Dulce*, pp. 78–79.

25. *Mancos Times-Tribune*, July 9, 1926; Nusbaum to Duke de Kiddo, April 25, 1926, Miscellaneous File, Mesa Verde National Park; Eugene Parsons, "Jesse Nusbaum and His Work," *The Trail* (Feb., 1924), pp. 12, 15; Laura Gilpin, "The Dream Pictures of My People," *Art and Archaeology* (Aug., 1926), pp. 12–13.

26. Nusbaum to Director, Feb. 7, 1927, Miscellaneous File, Mesa Verde National Park.

27. Deric Nusbaum, *Deric in Mesa Verde*

(New York: G. P. Putnam's Sons, 1926), p. 76. See also Nusbaum to Duke de Kiddo, April 25, 1926, Miscellaneous File, Mesa Verde National Park.

28. Manitou pamphlet, Manitou Cliff Dwelling File, Mesa Verde National Park. Nusbaum to Director, March 21, 1924, and Chief Inspector to Director, April 26, 1924, Nusbaum, Correspondence, Mesa Verde National Park.

29. Nusbaum, *Tierra Dulce*, pp. 76–77, 84. The Klan was strong in southwestern Colorado in the 1925–27 era, as it was in the entire state.

30. Robert Shankland, *Steve Mather of the National Parks* (New York: Knopf, 1951), p. 250; Ise, *Our National Park Policy*, pp. 301–02; Bartlett, *Yellowstone*, pp. 98–99; *Colorado Yearbook*, 1928–29, p. 7; Ansel Hall, *Guide to Mesa Verde* (San Francisco: Mesa Verde Co., n.d.), p. 23. *National Park Service Annual Report 1922* (Washington, D.C.: Government Printing Office, 1922), pp. 49–50.

31. Edward Taylor, "Speech," *Congressional Journal*, 1924, copy in Durango Public Library.

CHAPTER EIGHT

1. *Mesa Verde Notes*, Sept., 1935.

2. Horace M. Albright, *The Birth of the National Park Service* (Salt Lake City: Howe Brothers, 1983), p. 159; Robert Heyder Interview, Feb. 18, 1987.

3. C. Coyne Thompson Interview, Feb. 10, 1986; C. Marshall Finnan, *Annual Report for Mesa Verde National Park* (Mesa Verde National Park: Mesa Verde National Park, 1932), pp. 1, 6.

4. Alvene and Fury Dalla Interview, July 9, 1986. Jackson Clark Interview, Feb. 16, 1987; Phyllis Jones Interview, Dec. 8, 1985.

5. Albright to Nusbaum, Oct. 24, 1930, Grazing Hearing Records, Mesa Verde National Park. See also Finnan, "Annual Report, 1932." For visitor information, see *Mesa Verde Notes*, Dec., 1934, and Dec., 1939. The disparity in annual appropriations was not so great; Rocky Mountain doubled Mesa Verde by the late 1930s.

6. For the preceding, see Robert H. Rose, *Water Supply History of Mesa Verde National Park* (Mesa Verde National Park: Mesa Verde National Park, 1952), pp. 30–32; Memo, Feb. 26, 1936, and Chas. Gould Report 1936, Management File, Mesa Verde National Park; C. Marshall Finnan to Horace Albright, Aug. 31, 1931, and H. C. Bryant to Director, March 4, 1933, Miscellaneous File, Mesa Verde National Park; *Year Book of the State of Colorado 1935–36* (Denver: n.p., 1935–36), p. 388; National Park Service, *Report of the Director of the National Park Service 1932* (Washington, D.C.: Government Printing Office, 1932), p. 51; *Mesa Verde Notes*, Sept., 1935, Sept., 1938, and Dec., 1939.

7. *Mesa Verde National Park* (Washington, D.C.: Government Printing Office, 1941).

8. Florence Lister and Robert Lister, *Earl Morris and Southwestern Archaeology* (Albuquerque: University of New Mexico, 1968), pp. 101–02; Switzer, "Foreword," Gustaf Nordenskiold, *The Cliff Dwellers of the Mesa Verde* (Glorieta, N.M.: Rio Grande Press, 1979 reprint), pp. 13–14. Morris to Director, Dec. 28, 1934, and Leavitt to Director, Nov. 13, 1934, Letters Miscellaneous, Mesa Verde National Park.

9. Vandalism File, Mesa Verde National Park; Franke to Hoover, Aug. 31, 1938, Policing File, Mesa Verde National Park.

10. Finnan to Director, Aug. 28, 1933, Letters Miscellaneous, Mesa Verde National Park; "Superintendent's Monthly Report," Dec. 7, 1935, May 3, 1938, and Sept. 5, 1939, Mesa Verde National Park; and Charles Richney to Leavitt, April 9, 1934, and Frank to Fred Trotter, Oct. 4, 1937, Miscellaneous File, Mesa Verde National Park. *Mesa Verde Notes*, May 20, 1936.

11. Staff Conference Minutes, June–Aug. 24, 1936.

12. Charles Quaintance to George Wright, March 4, 1935, Wildlife Surveys and Reports, Mesa Verde National Park.

13. Taylor to Nusbaum, March 6, 1939. See also Camp to Taylor, Feb. 27, 1939, Nusbaum to Director, March 7, 1939, *Cortez Sentinel*, Feb. 23, 1939, and *Denver Post*, March 8, 1939, clipping, Archaeology Historic Records, Mesa Verde National Park.

14. Kenny Ross Interview, July 29, 1986.

15. Robert Coates, "The C.C.C.," *Mesa Verde Notes*, Sept., 1933; Judy Crook, "A History of the Civilian Conservation Corps at Mesa Verde National Park," 1984 paper, Center of Southwest Studies, Fort Lewis College; Park Development Outline, Oct. 1, 1932, Civilian Conservation Corps

Records, Mesa Verde National Park. See also Conrad L. Wirth, *Parks, Politics and the People* (Norman: University of Oklahoma, 1980), chapters 5 and 6. Civilian Conservation Corps Records, Mesa Verde National Park. The peak total of C.C.C. camps was in June, 1935, with 2,916.

16. Secretary of the Interior, *Annual Report of the Secretary of the Interior 1935* (Washington, D.C.: Government Printing Office, 1935), pp. 199, 227, 229; Meredith Guillet Interview, Oct. 8, 1986.

17. John McNamara and C. Coyne Thompson Interview, Feb. 10, 1986.

18. Civilian Conservation Corps Records, Mesa Verde National Park; *Mesa Verde Notes*, Sept. 1933. Robert Beers Interview, March 26, 1987.

19. Keith Paisley analysis, April 15, 1942, Miscellaneous File, Mesa Verde National Park. Jackson Clark Interview, Feb. 16, 1987.

20. John McNamara and C. Coyne Thompson Interview, Feb. 10, 1986. Richard A. Bartlett, *Yellowstone: A Wilderness Besieged* (Tucson: University of Arizona, 1985), pp. 296–302.

21. Curtis W. Buchholtz, *Rocky Mountain National Park: A History* (Boulder: Colorado Associated University Press, 1983), pp. 183–87. John Ise, *Our National Park Policy* (Baltimore: Johns Hopkins Press, 1961), pp. 355–57, 360–63.

22. 1937 correspondence Gallup and Cortez Chambers of Commerce, and minutes, Nov. 12–13, 1935, meeting, Roads Outside the Park File, Mesa Verde National Park.

23. R. E. Hauser to Leavitt, July 29, 1934, H. W. Balsley to Leavitt, Aug. 9, 1935, A. E. Palen to Finnan, Jan. 13, 1932, Roads Outside the Park File, Mesa Verde National Park.

24. National Park Service, *Report of the Director of the National Park Service 1930* (Washington, D.C.: Government Printing Office, 1930), p. 121; Concessions Agreement, 1930–49, copy Mesa Verde National Park; Gilbert Wenger, *The Story of Mesa Verde National Park* (Denver: Mesa Verde Museum Association, 1980), p. 76. Abbie Jane Wagner Interview, Jan. 21, 1983. Bartlett, *Yellowstone*, pp. 99–100. Ansel Hall, Records, Winkler material.

25. June Hall Interview, Sept. 16, 1985, Dale Anderson interviewer.

26. Ansel Hall, Records, Winkler material; Robert Shankland, *Steve Mather of the National Parks* (New York: Knopf, 1951), pp. 259–62.

27. *Mesa Verde Notes*, Sept., 1938.

28. "Monthly Report," June 10 and Aug. 10, 1942, Mesa Verde National Park; Angelo D. Brewer Interview, July 7, 1981, Mesa Verde Oral History Project.

29. Superintendent's "Monthly Report," 1942–45, Mesa Verde National Park, especially see Oct. 12, 1945; Prairie Dog Survey report, Aug. 9, 1943, Mesa Verde National Park.

30. Kenny Ross Interview, July 29, 1986; Robin Hall Turner Interview, Dec. 9, 1985.

31. See Grazing Hearing Records, Mesa Verde National Park.

CHAPTER NINE

1. A. Levine to H. Tolson, Jan. 16, 1945, Nusbaum Memo, Feb. 5, 1946, Lucy Peabody, Folder, Mesa Verde National Park. For the television request, see the Superintendents' Monthly Reports, Sept. 13, 1945,

Mesa Verde National Park. McClurg died in 1931, Peabody in 1934.

2. Superintendents' Monthly Reports, Sept. 13, 1945, Mesa Verde National Park.

3. See minutes of June 24–July 22, 1946, Staff Meetings Reports, Mesa Verde National Park. Robert H. Rose, *Water Supply History of Mesa Verde National Park* (Mesa Verde National Park: Mesa Verde National Park, 1952), pp. 33–37, 47–48, and 51–52.

4. Mountain Lion File, in the Wildlife Surveys and Reports, and various superintendents' reports, 1946–59, Mesa Verde National Park. John Ise, *Our National Park Policy* (Baltimore: Johns Hopkins Press, 1961), chapter 27.

5. Staff Meetings Reports, July 15 and Aug. 19, 1946, Nov. 29, 1948, and Dec. 8, 1959, Mesa Verde National Park; *Year Book of the State of Colorado 1956–58* (Denver: n.p., 1956–58), p. 798.

6. Letters, newspaper clippings, memos, Roads Outside the Park File, Mesa Verde National Park.

7. Marion C. Wiley, *The High Road* (Denver: State Dept. of Highways, 1976), pp. 29, 31. Art Gomez, "The Fabulous Four Corners," Ph.D. dissertation, Albuquerque, University of New Mexico, 1987, pp. 98, 103–11, 117, 122.

8. Yeager Report, 1946, Archaeology Historic Records, Mesa Verde National Park; Staff Meetings Reports, Oct. 8, 1947, and Aug. 30, 1948, Mesa Verde National Park; *Year Book of the State of Colorado 1956–58*, p. 589; *Denver Post*, Sept. 16, 1957, clipping Miscellaneous File, Mesa Verde National Park.

9. Ise, *Our National Park Policy*, pp. 534–37, 540, 546. *State of the Parks— 1980 Report to the Congress* (Washington, D.C.: National Park Service, 1980), p. 1. *Reader's Digest* quoted in Conrad L. Wirth, *Parks, Politics and the People* (Norman: University of Oklahoma, 1980), pp. 237, 258.

10. *Denver Post*, Aug. 20 and Sept. 16, 1957; clippings and Mission 66 1957 report, Management File, Mesa Verde National Park. Bill and Merrie Winkler Interview, Dec. 16, 1986. Staff Meetings Reports, Dec. 15, 1959, Mesa Verde National Park.

11. O'Bryan, see David A. Breternitz and Jack E. Smith, "Mesa Verde," in *National Parkways: Rocky Mountain and Mesa Verde* (Casper, Wyo.: World-Wide Research, 1972), p. 76. Robert Lister to author, March 17, 1987.

12. Alden C. Hayes, "The Wetherill Mesa Project," *Naturalist* (vol. 20, no. 2, 1969), p. 21; Alden C. Hayes, *The Archeological Survey of Wetherill Mesa* (Washington, D.C.: National Park Service, 1964), pp. 1–2.

13. Robert H. Lister, "Archeology for Layman and Scientist at Mesa Verde," *Science* (May 3, 1968), pp. 492–93. Douglas Osborne, "Solving the Riddles of Wetherill Mesa," *National Geographic Magazine* (Feb., 1964), p. 155. Hayes, "Wetherill," pp. 21–22. Hayes, *Archeological Survey*, pp. 2–3. Carroll A. Burroughs, "Searching for Cliff Dwellers' Secrets," *National Geographic Magazine* (Nov., 1959), pp. 619, 625.

14. Mesa Verde Company Records, 1940s, 1950s, William Winkler; Jan. 16, 1959, report, Miscellaneous File, Mesa Verde National Park. Bill and Merrie Winkler Interview, Dec. 16, 1986. June Hall Interview, Sept. 16, 1985, Dale Anderson, interviewer. Travel Summary Annual Reports 1945, 1948, and 1952 list where

visitors came from, Mesa Verde National Park.

15. See, for example, Staff Meetings Reports, July 17, 1951, Mesa Verde National Park.

16. Pinkley letter, Aug. 3, 1958, Miscellaneous File, Mesa Verde National Park. Jack Rudy to author, Sept. 29, 1986.

17. 1951 Vandalism, Vandalism File, Mesa Verde National Park; Staff Conference Minutes, July 26, 1949, and Nov. 28, 1951, Mesa Verde National Park.

18. Bill and Merrie Winkler Interviews, Dec. 16, 1986, and Sept. 23, 1987. Jeannie Lee Jim Interview, April 16, 1981, Mesa Verde Oral History Project.

19. Bill and Merrie Winkler Interview, Dec. 16, 1986; Kenny Ross Interview, July 29, 1986.

CHAPTER TEN

1. Al Lancaster Interview, Feb. 22, 1986. Robert Lister to author, March 17, 1987.

2. Robert H. Lister, "Archeology for Layman and Scientist at Mesa Verde," *Science* (May 3, 1968), pp. 492–94; Alden C.

Hayes, "The Wetherill Mesa Project," *Naturalist* (vol. 20, no. 2, 1969), pp. 21–23; Douglas Osborne, "Solving the Riddles of Wetherill Mesa," *National Geographic Magazine* (Feb., 1964), p. 155; Gilbert Wenger to author, Aug. 4, 1986.

3. Hayes, "Wetherill," p. 23. The project produced over three dozen articles and monographs as well.

4. For the University of Colorado, see Robert H. Lister, *Emergency Archaeology in Mesa Verde National Park, Colorado, 1948–1966* (Boulder: University of Colorado, 1968), p. 1. "Big Boom at Mesa Verde," *Empire Magazine* (*Denver Post*), Nov. 17, 1963, p. 13. Robert Lister to author, March 17, 1987. Superintendent's Monthly Report, July, 1965, Mesa Verde National Park.

5. Superintendent's Monthly Report, Aug., 1965, Mesa Verde National Park.

6. John Ise, *Our National Park Policy* (Baltimore: Johns Hopkins Press, 1961), pp. 608–09.

7. Bill and Merrie Winkler Interview, Dec. 16, 1986.

8. Curtis W. Buchholtz, *Rocky Mountain National Park: A History* (Boulder: Colorado Associated University Press,

1983), pp. 202-05. There were even stronger objections to some of the Mission 66 programs in that park. Gilbert Wenger to author, Aug. 4, 1986.

9. Superintendent's Monthly Report, June 1965, Mesa Verde National Park; Pinkley to Ansel Hall, Jan. 9, 1962, and Pinkley to Arrhenius, Sept. 27, 1964, Miscellaneous File, Mesa Verde National Park. Pinkley retired in 1966.

10. Pinkley to Rocky Mountain AAA, Sept. 30, 1964, Miscellaneous File, Mesa Verde National Park. She could also have gotten upset with the *Year Book of the State of Colorado 1962–64*, (Denver: n.p., 1962–64), p. 924, which apparently copied the same source as the AAA.

11. *Yearbook of the State of Colorado 1962–64*, pp. 818–19, 822–23; Art Gomez, "The Fabulous Four Corners," Ph.D. dissertation, University of New Mexico, 1987, pp. 131–33; "Master Plan for Mesa Verde National Park, Aug., 1964," pp. 5–7; Camp, quoted in Staff Meetings Reports, Dec. 8, 1959, Mesa Verde National Park.

12. Chester A. Thomas, "Grass Roots Public Relations," Superintendents' File, Mesa Verde National Park.

13. Staff Meetings Reports, April 5, 1965,

and Superintendent's Monthly Report, June, 1965, both Mesa Verde National Park.

14. Staff Meetings Reports, Sept. 17, 1963, Mesa Verde National Park; Superintendent's Monthly Report, March, 1967, Mesa Verde National Park; Staff Meetings Reports, July 2, 1968, Mesa Verde National Park; Gilbert Wenger to author, Aug. 4, 1986. Acting Supt. to Director, Dec. 23, 1966, Floods and Storms File, Mesa Verde National Park.

15. Superintendent's Monthly Reports, Aug., 1965, and Aug., 1967, Mesa Verde National Park.

16. 1961 file, Vandalism File, Mesa Verde National Park.

17. Superintendent's Monthly Report, June, 1965, April, 1966, Mesa Verde National Park; Wildlife Surveys and Reports, 1966, Mesa Verde National Park; Atchison to Lechleitner, June 13, 1968, and Lechleitner to Loe, June 27, 1969, Wildlife Surveys and Reports, Mesa Verde National Park.

18. Meredith Guillet Interview, Oct. 8, 1986. Bill and Merrie Winkler Interview, Dec. 16, 1986. One of the problems, according to Gil Wenger, was the confiscation of House's rifle for shooting deer in the park, Wenger to author, Oct. 10, 1986.

19. Staff Meetings Reports, March 15, 1960, and Superintendent's Monthly Report, Dec., 1965, both Mesa Verde National Park. *Montezuma Valley Journal*, Jan. 6, 1968.

CHAPTER ELEVEN

1. George Hartzog, Jr., "Management Considerations," *Second World Conference on National Parks* (Morges, Switzerland: International Union for Conservation of Nature, 1974), pp. 160–61. See also, Curtis W. Buchholtz, *Rocky Mountain National Park: A History* (Boulder: Colorado Associated University Press, 1983), pp. 206–07.

2. 1973 Press Release, Press Release File, Mesa Verde National Park; Gilbert Wenger to author, Aug. 4, 1986; *Mesa Verde: General Management Plan May, 1979* (N.p.: Department of the Interior, 1979), p. 3; *Mesa Verde National Park, Colorado* (Washington, D.C.: Government Printing Office, 1976), p. 55; Superintendent's 1979 Report, p. 2, Mesa Verde National Park; Robert Heyder Interview, Feb. 18, 1987.

3. Ronald R. Switzer to author, Aug. 22, 1987.

4. Superintendent's 1979 Report, p. 2, Mesa Verde National Park.

5. *Mesa Verde: . . . 1976*, pp. 4–8; see also Hartzog, "Management Considerations," p. 161, and *Mesa Verde: . . . 1976*, p. 2.

6. *Los Angeles Times*, Sept., 1973, clipping, Center of Southwest Studies, Fort Lewis College. Ronald R. Switzer to author, Aug. 22, 1987. Bill and Merrie Winkler Interview, Dec. 16, 1986. Beverly Cunningham Interview, Feb. 25, 1987. Heyder thought it unfair that Switzer was blamed for the 1979 road problems.

7. Press Releases 1974–75, Press Release File, Mesa Verde National Park.

8. Bill and Merrie Winkler Interviews, Dec. 16, 1986, and Sept. 8, 1987; Gilbert Wenger to author, Oct. 31, 1986. Long-time ranger Gil Wenger hated to see the Mesa Verde Company leave; he said the park staff had "absolutely great relationships" with Bill.

9. Bill and Merrie Winkler Interview, Dec. 16, 1986; and Superintendent's Annual

Reports, 1976 and 1977, Mesa Verde National Park.

10. 1977–79 Complaint File, Mesa Verde National Park.

11. Jackson Clark Interview, Feb. 16, 1987; Hartzog, "Management Considerations," p. 161.

12. Historic Sites File, Mesa Verde National Park; Staff Meetings Reports, July 31, 1973, Mesa Verde National Park; Jackson Clark Interview, Feb. 16, 1987. Superintendent's Annual Reports, 1976 and 1979, Mesa Verde National Park.

13. Watson, quoted in *Mesa Verde: General Management Plan*, p. 3.

14. Superintendent's Annual Report 1976, Mesa Verde National Park; Gilbert Wenger to author, Oct. 31 and Nov. 15, 1986.

15. Staff Meeting Reports, June 28, 1973, Mesa Verde National Park.

16. Superintendent's Report 1979, Mesa Verde National Park; *Durango Herald*, April 30, 1979, p. 1, and the *Montezuma Valley Journal*, May 2–June 1, 1979, tell the story of the slide.

17. "Mesa Verde National Park Master Plan, Sept. 1975 Draft," pp. 50–51, photocopy, Mesa Verde National Park. "Fire Danger," 1974 Press Release, Press Release File, and "Fires," Management File, both Mesa Verde National Park.

18. See Staff Meeting Reports, Feb. 24, 1970, and Superintendent's Report 1979, both Mesa Verde National Park.

EPILOGUE

1. For the visitor survey, see Superintendent's Report, 1980, Mesa Verde National Park; Press Release, Press Release File, Sept. 17, 1980, Mesa Verde National Park; and Robert Heyder Interview, Feb. 18, 1987. Richard A. Bartlett, in his *Yellowstone: A Wilderness Besieged* (Tucson: University of Arizona, 1985), also wrestled with where history ends and current events begin, pp. 365, 383.

2. *Air Pollution Effects on Parks and Wilderness Areas* (Mesa Verde National Park: n.p., 1984), pp. 51, 57.

3. Superintendent's Annual Reports, 1983–86, Mesa Verde National Park; Robert Heyder Interview, Feb. 18, 1987; Jackson Clark Interview, Feb. 16, 1987; Bill and Merrie Winkler Interview, Dec. 16, 1986; Beverly Cunningham Interview, Feb. 18, 1987; Bartlett, *Yellowstone*, p. 372.

4. *Durango Herald*, Nov. 7, 1986. See also Superintendent's Annual Reports, 1983–86, Mesa Verde National Park, and July 19, 1984, Press Release, Press Release File, Mesa Verde National Park; Bill and Merrie Winkler Interview, Dec. 16, 1986. Jack Smith Interview, March 3, 1987.

5. Jack Smith Interview, March 3, 1987.

6. Robert Heyder Interview and Superintendent's Annual Reports, 1982, 1983, Mesa Verde National Park. "Mesa Verde National Park," *Report No. 4944 House of Representatives* (Washington, D.C.: Government Printing Office, 1906), p. 5. Superintendent's Annual Report, 1985, Mesa Verde National Park.

7. Superintendent's Annual Reports, 1982 and 1985, Mesa Verde National Park; Oct. 5, 1981, Press Release, Press Release File, Mesa Verde National Park; "Are Our National Parks in Danger?" *U.S. News and World Report*, July 7, 1986, p. 68; Robert Heyder Interview, Feb. 18, 1987.

8. *New York Times*, Aug. 10, 1987, p. A12.

9. Information for the preceding paragraphs was found in Superintendent's Annual Reports, 1980–86, Mesa Verde National Park; Staff Meeting Reports, Feb.

3, April 23, and June 19, 1984, Mesa Verde National Park; June 13, 1984, and May 28, 1985, Press Releases, Press Release File, Mesa Verde National Park; *Mesa Verde National Park* (Washington, D.C.: National Park Service, 1984).

10. Gilbert Wenger to author, Nov. 15, 1986; "Program for Ceremonies Commemorating the 75th Anniversary of Mesa Verde National Park"; Superintendent's Annual Reports, 1982, 1983, Mesa Verde National Park; Staff Meeting Reports, Aug.–Sept., 1984, Mesa Verde National Park. Interestingly, neither the *Denver Post* nor the *New York Times* carried any reports from the conference. The *Durango Herald*, Sept. 18–23, 1984, reported on conference sessions. Alfred Runte, *National Parks: The American Experience* (Lincoln: University of Nebraska, 1979), pp. 181–84, discusses the World Conference on National Parks.

11. Mesa Verde Indian Art Festival, Management File, Superintendent's Annual Report 1983, Staff Meetings Reports July 10, 1984, July 18, 1985, Press Release, Press Release File, all Mesa Verde National Park.

12. Jackson Clark Interview, Feb. 16, 1987.

13. Bill and Merrie Winkler Interview, Dec. 16, 1986; Ken Brengle Interview, March 25, 1987; Mike Dexter Interview, March 25, 1987. *Southwest Colorado Vacation Guide* (Cortez: Montezuma Valley Journal, 1986).

14. Robert Heyder Interview, Feb. 18, 1987.

15. *Denver Post*, 1979–85 index. Robert Heyder Interview, Feb. 18, 1987.

16. Superintendent's Annual Report, 1983, Mesa Verde National Park; see also Superintendent's Annual Report, 1980, Mesa Verde National Park; Robert Heyder Interview, Feb. 18, 1987, and *State of the Parks—1980* (Washington, D.C.: National Park Service, 1980), pp. viii, 52, 55.

17. E. Steve Cassells, *The Archaeology of Colorado* (Boulder, Colo.: Johnson, 1983), p. 110; and Robert H. Lister, "Archeology for Layman and Scientist at Mesa Verde," *Science* (May 3, 1968), pp. 495–96. Jack Smith Interview, March 3, 1987.

18. Jean Pinkley, Interpretive Prospectus, Archaeologists File, Mesa Verde National Park.

≡ BIBLIOGRAPHY ≡

INTERVIEWS AND CORRESPONDENCE

Bader, Jean. Interview, July 29, 1986.

Bauer, Esma Rickner. Interview, April 23, 1982, Mesa Verde Oral History Project.

Beers, Robert. Interview, March 26, 1987.

Brengle, Ken. Interview, March 25, 1987.

Brewer, Angelo D. Interview, July 7, 1981, Mesa Verde Oral History Project.

Clark, Jackson. Interview, Feb. 16, 1987.

Cook, Georgia. Interview, April 4, 1986.

Cunningham, Beverly. Interview, Feb. 25, 1987.

Cutter, Don. Correspondence, Nov. 10, 1986.

Dalla, Alvene and Fury. Interview, July 9, 1986.

Dexter, Mike. Interview, March 25, 1987.

Emerson, Myrtle Morefield. Interview, March 7, 1979, Mesa Verde Oral History Project.

Frahm, Helen Wells. Interview, Feb. 9, 1981, Mesa Verde Oral History Project.

Goff, Walter. Interview, April 7, 1982, Mesa Verde Oral History Project.

Guillet, Meredith. Interview, Oct. 8, 1986.

Hall, June. Interview, Sept. 16, 1985, by Dale Anderson.

Harrison, Michael. Interview, Oct. 15, 1986.

Heyder, Robert. Interview, Feb. 18, 1987.

Hickman, Minnie. Interview, June 18, 1982, Mesa Verde Oral History Project.

House, Chief Jack. Interviews, Aug. 29 and Sept. 11, 1967, University of Utah.

Jakway, Walter. Correspondence, Jan., 1986.

Jim, Jeannie Lee. Interview, April 16, 1981, Mesa Verde Oral History Project.

Jones, Phyllis. Interview, Dec. 8, 1985.

Lancaster, Al. Interview, Feb. 22, 1986.

Lister, Robert. Correspondence, March 17, 1987.

McNamara, John. Interview, Feb. 10, 1986.

Micheals, Wilfred. Interview, April 30, 1976, Mesa Verde Oral History Project.

Ross, Kenny. Interview, July 29, 1986.

Rudy, Jack. Correspondence, Sept. 29, 1986.

Smith, Jack. Interview, March 3, 1987.

Swenk, Grace Thomas. Interview, April 29, 1981, Mesa Verde Oral History Project.

Switzer, Ronald R. Correspondence, Dec. 12, 1985; Jan. 8 and Aug. 22, 1987.

Thompson, Amy. Correspondence, Dec. 6, 1985.

Thompson, C. Coyne. Interview, Feb. 10, 1986.

Turner, Robin Hall. Interview, Dec. 9, 1985.

Wagner, Abbie Jane. Interview, Jan. 21, 1983, Mesa Verde Oral History Project.

Wenger, Gilbert. Correspondence, Aug. 4 and Oct. 31, 1986; March 8, 1987.

Winkler, Bill and Merrie. Interviews, Dec. 16, 1986; Sept. 8 and 23, 1987.

Wyatt, Art. Interview, March 20, 1986.

NEWSPAPERS

Billings Gazette (Billings, Montana).
  March 23, 1947.
The Cliff Dweller (Mesa Verde). 1935–38.
Denver Post. 1917, 1926, 1957, 1979–86.
Denver Republican. Oct. 6, 1891; Sept. 10,
  1901.
Denver Times. June 12, 1904; Feb. 25,
  1906; Aug. 11, 1907; 1917.
Durango Evening Herald. 1901, 1904.
Durango Herald. 1888–89, 1913, 1979–86.
Durango Herald-News. Aug. 31, 1952.
Durango Morning Herald. 1887–88.
Durango News. 1950.
Durango Record. 1881.
Durango Weekly Democrat. 1914.
Durango Weekly Herald. 1889, 1913.
Great Southwest (Durango, Colorado).
  1893.
The Idea (Durango, Colorado). 1885, 1886,
  1888.
Kansas City Times. June 22, 1956.
Kiva Krier (Mesa Verde). 1933, 1935.
La Plata Miner (Silverton, Colorado).
  1879–83.
Mancos Times. 1893–1902.
Mancos Times-Tribune. 1906–11,
  1917–20, 1926, 1928, 1934–35, 1937.

Marfa New Era (Marfa, Texas). July, 1916.
Mesa Verde Notes (Mesa Verde National
  Park). 1930–39.
The Mesa Verdian. Nov. 6, 1935.
Missouri Intelligencer (Franklin, Missouri).
  June 25, 1825.
Montezuma Journal (Cortez, Colorado).
  1897, 1899, 1901, 1903, 1906, 1913.
Montezuma Valley Journal (Cortez,
  Colorado). 1968, 1979, 1981.
News Bulletin (Mesa Verde). 1984–85.
New York Herald. Sept. 29, 1901.
New York Times. 1876, 1889–90. 1893,
  1897–99, 1905–10, 1960–63, 1980–87.
New York Tribune. Nov. 3, 1874.
Pagosa Springs News (Pagosa Springs,
  Colorado). 1891.
Ridgway Herald (Ridgway, Colorado).
  Oct. 15, 1891.
Rocky Mountain News (Denver,
  Colorado). 1874–77, 1882, 1891, 1899,
  1903, 1905, 1906, 1918.
Semi-Weekly Herald (Durango, Colorado).
  1901, 1911.
The Southwest (Durango, Colorado). 1883.
Weekly Republican (Denver, Colorado).
  1889, 1891, 1893, 1898, 1906.
Weekly Tribune-Republican (Denver,
  Colorado). 1882, 1886.

ARCHIVES & PRIVATE
COLLECTIONS

Albright, Robert. Diary, 1935. Mesa Verde
  National Park.
"Colorado Cliff Dwellings Association
  History," Mesa Verde National Park.
Crook, Judy. "A History of the Civilian
  Conservation Corps at Mesa Verde
  National Park." Unpublished paper,
  Aug., 1984, Center of Southwest Studies,
  Fort Lewis College, Durango, Colorado.
Durango Board of Trade Minutes, 1892–
  96. Durango, Colorado, Public Library.
First World Conference on Cultural Parks
  Records. Mesa Verde National Park.
Hall, Ansel. Records. William Winkler,
  Cortez, Colorado.
Hewett, Edgar. Field Notes, 1906–09.
  Mesa Verde National Park.
———. "Report of the Ruins of Mesa
  Verde, Colorado." Mesa Verde National
  Park.
McClurg, Gilbert. Gilbert McClurg
  Collection. Colorado College, Colorado
  Springs.
McClurg, Virginia. Virginia McClurg
  Collection. Pioneers' Museum, Colorado
  Springs.

McKee, Thomas M. "History of Mesa Verde Ruins." Mesa Verde National Park.
———. Manuscript. Mesa Verde National Park.
Mason, Charles C. "The Story of the Discovery and Early Exploration of the Cliff Houses at Mesa Verde." Colorado Historical Society, Denver.
"Master Plan of Mesa Verde National Park, Aug., 1964." Mesa Verde National Park.
Mesa Verde. National Archives. Records of the National Park Service, Record Group 79.
Mesa Verde Collection. Colorado College, Colorado Springs.
Mesa Verde Collection. Fort Lewis College, Durango, Colorado.
Mesa Verde Collection. Pioneers' Museum, Colorado Springs.
Mesa Verde Company Records. William Winkler, Cortez, Colorado.
Mesa Verde Correspondence. National Archives, Washington, D.C.
Mesa Verde File. *Durango Herald*, Durango, Colorado.
Mesa Verde File. Federal Records Center, Denver.

Mesa Verde Mss. Colorado Historical Society, Denver.
Mesa Verde National Park:
  Archaeologist Monthly Reports.
  Archaeologists File.
  Archaeology Historic Records.
  Book of Impressions.
  Civilian Conservation Corps Records.
  Complaint File.
  Correspondence, 1911–23.
  Crime Prevention Plan.
  Finnan, C. Marshall, File.
  Floods and Storms File.
  Grazing Hearing Records.
  Heliograph Station File.
  Historic Sites File.
  Hospital File.
  Letters Miscellaneous.
  Management File.
  Manitou Cliff Dwellings File.
  Miscellaneous File.
  Park Naturalist Reports, 1937–50.
  Policing File.
  Prairie Dog Survey Report.
  Press Release File, 1973–75, 1981–84.
  Roads Outside the Park File.
  Schedules, 1968–76.
  Staff Conference Minutes, 1935–51, 1959–63.

  Staff Meetings Reports, 1964–70, 1973–75, 1984.
  Superintendent's Annual Report, 1976, 1979–80, 1982–83, 1985.
  Superintendents' File.
  Superintendents' Log of Events, 1978.
  Superintendents' Memorandums to Employees and Residents, 1936–40.
  Superintendents' Monthly Reports, 1920s–1960s.
  Travel Summary Annual Report.
  Two Story Cliff House File.
  Vandalism File.
  Wildlife Surveys and Reports, 1929–46.
Mesa Verde Pamphlet File. Durango Public Library, Durango, Colorado.
Newberry, J. S. Notes. Mesa Verde National Park.
Nordenskiold, Gustaf. File. Mesa Verde National Park.
Nusbaum, Jesse. Correspondence. Mesa Verde National Park.
Peabody, Lucy. Folder. Mesa Verde National Park.
Utes. Minutes May 5, 1911, Council. Mesa Verde National Park.
Wetherill, John. Letter. Arizona State Museum Archives, Tucson.
Wetherill Collection. Smithsonian

Institution, Washington, D.C.
Wetherill Letters. Mesa Verde National Park.

UNPUBLISHED MATERIALS

Cummins, Densil H. "Social and Economic History of Southwestern Colorado, 1860–1948," Ph.D. dissertation, University of Texas, 1951.

Gomez, Art. "The Fabulous Four Corners," Ph.D. dissertation, University of New Mexico, 1987.

Hoben, Patricia. "The Establishment of Mesa Verde as a National Park," M.A. thesis, University of Oklahoma, 1966.

Lavender, David, "Mesa Verde National Park," copy in author's files.

PUBLISHED MATERIALS

Air Pollution Effects on Parks and Wilderness Areas. Mesa Verde National Park: N.p., 1984.

Albright, Horace M. *The Birth of the National Park Service: The Founding Years, 1913–33.* Salt Lake City: Howe Brothers, 1983.

Albright, Horace M., and Taylor, Frank J. *"Oh, Ranger!" A Book about the National Parks.* Stanford, Calif.: Stanford University, 1929.

Alter, J. Cecil. *Through the Heart of the Scenic West.* Salt Lake City: Shepard, 1927.

Anderson, Eva Mills. "A Tenderfoot at the Cliff Dwellings of the Mesa Verde." *The Chautauquan* (July, 1908), 194–206.

Andrews, Ralph W. *Photographers of the Frontier West: Their Lives and Works.* Seattle: Superior Publishing, 1965.

"Are Our National Parks in Danger?" *U.S. News and World Report* (July 7, 1986), 68.

Arrhenius, Olof W. *Stones Speak and Waters Sing.* Mesa Verde National Park: Mesa Verde Museum Association, 1986.

Art Catalogue '92. Minneapolis: Industrial Exposition, 1892.

Baggs, Mae Lacy. *Colorado: The Queen Jewel of the Rockies.* Boston: Page Co., 1926 ed.

Barber, Edwin. "The Ancient Pueblos." *American Naturalist* (Sept., 1878), 606–14.

Bartlett, Richard A. *Yellowstone: A Wilderness Besieged.* Tucson: University of Arizona, 1985.

Beam, George L. *The Prehistoric Cliff Dwellings of Mesa Verde.* Denver: George L. Beam, 1916(?).

"Big Boom at Mesa Verde." *Empire Magazine* (*Denver Post*) (Nov. 17, 1963), 13–15.

Biographical Sketches and Letters of T. Mitchell Prudden, M.D. New Haven: Yale University, 1927.

Birdsall, William Randall. "The Cliff Dwellings of the Canons of the Mesa Verde." *American Geographical Society Bulletin* (Dec. 31, 1891), 584–620.

Birney, Hoffman. *Roads to Roam.* Philadelphia: Penn Publishing, 1930.

Blair, Karen J. *The Clubwoman as Feminist: True Womanhood Redefined, 1860–1914.* New York: Holmes & Meier, 1980.

Breternitz, David A. "Mesa Verde National Park: A History of Its Archaeology." *Essays and Monographs in Colorado History* (1983, no. 2), 221–34.

Breternitz, David A., and Smith, Jack E. "Mesa Verde," in *National Parkways: Rocky Mountain and Mesa Verde.*

Casper, Wyo.: World-Wide Research, 1972.

Buchholtz, Curtis W. *Rocky Mountain National Park: A History*. Boulder: Colorado Associated University Press, 1983.

Burroughs, Carroll A. "Searching for Cliff Dwellers' Secrets." *National Geographic Magazine* (Nov., 1959), 619–25.

Byrne, Bernard J. *A Frontier Army Surgeon*. New York: Exposition, 1962.

Camp, Mrs. A. M. "Helen Allen-Webster-Stoiber-Rood-Ellis." *Pioneers of the San Juan Country*, vol. 3. Durango, Colo.: Durango Printing, 1952.

Cassells, E. Steve. *The Archaeology of Colorado*. Boulder, Colo.: Johnson, 1983.

Catalogue of Cliff Dwellers' Exhibit. Jackson Park, Ill.: H. J. Smith Exploring Co., 1893.

Cather, Willa. "Mesa Verde Wonderland." *Denver Times* (Jan. 31, 1916), 7.

Chapin, Frederick H. "Cliff-Dwellings of the Mancos Canons." *The American Antiquarian* (July, 1890), 192–210.

———. *The Land of the Cliff-Dwellers.* Boston: W. B. Clarke, 1892.

Circular Relating to Historic and Prehistoric Ruins of the Southwest and Their Preservation. Washington, D.C.: Government Printing Office, 1904.

The Cliff Dwellers. Chicago: H. Jay Smith, 1893.

Coates, Robert. "The C. C. C." *Mesa Verde Notes* (Sept., 1933), 1–3.

Colorado Cliff-Dwellings Association. *A Bill Creating the Colorado Cliff Dwellings National Park*. N.p.: Colorado Cliff-Dwellings Assoc., n.d.

Come into Western Colorado: Mesa Verde Nat'l Park Circle Trip. Durango: Western Colorado Chamber of Commerce, c. 1924.

Crofutt, George. *Crofutt's Grip-Sack Guide of Colorado*. Omaha: Overland Publishing, 1885.

Cutter, Donald C. "Prelude to a Pageant in the Wilderness." *The Western Historical Quarterly* (Jan., 1977), 5–14.

Daniels, Helen S. "Lo, the Poor Indians!" *Pioneers of the San Juan Country*, vol. 3. Durango, Colo.: Durango Printing, 1952.

———. *The Ute Indians of Southwestern Colorado*. Durango, Colo.: n.p., 1941.

Ellis, Fern D. *Come Back to My Valley: Historical Remembrances of Mancos, Colorado*. Cortez, Colo.: Cortez Printers, 1976.

Endlich, Frederic M. "Report." *9th Annual Report USGS*. Washington, D.C.: Government Printing Office, 1877.

Euler, Robert C. "A Dedication to the Memory of Edgar Lee Hewett 1865–1946." *Arizona and the West* (Fall, 1963), 287–90.

] F. E. S. "Aztec Remains in La Plata County, Colo." *Kansas City Review of Science* (vol. 6, no. 7, 1882), 442.

Fewkes, Jesse W. *Antiquities of the Mesa Verde National Park Cliff Palace*. Washington, D.C.: Government Printing Office, 1911.

———. *Antiquities of the Mesa Verde National Park Spruce-Tree House*. Washington, D.C.: Government Printing Office, 1909.

———. "The First Pueblo Ruin in Colorado Mentioned in Spanish Documents." *Science* (Sept. 14, 1917), 255–56.

———. *Report Excavation and Repair of Ruins*. Washington, D.C.: Government Printing Office, 1909.

———. *Reports of the Mesa Verde National Park*. . . . Washington, D.C.: Government Printing Office, 1908.

Finnan, C. Marshall. *Annual Report for Mesa Verde National Park*. Mesa Verde National Park: Mesa Verde, 1932.

Fletcher, Maurine S. (ed.). *The Wetherills of the Mesa Verde: Autobiography of Benjamin Alfred Wetherill*. Rutherford, N.J.: Associated University Presses, 1977.

Fossett, Frank. *Colorado*. Denver: Daily Tribune, 1876. New York: C. G. Crawford, 1879.

Freeman, Ira S. *A History of Montezuma County*. Boulder, Colo.: Johnson, 1958.

Frowe, Lida Gertrude. "The Mesa Verde National Park." *The Modern World* (Nov. 1906, vol. 2), 7–11.

Gannett, Henry. "Prehistoric Ruins in Southern Colorado." *Popular Science Review* (1880), 666–73.

Gilpin, Laura. "The Dream Pictures of My People." *Art and Archaeology* (Aug., 1926), 12–19.

Hafen, LeRoy R. "Armijo's Journal of 1829–30. . . ." *Colorado Magazine* (April, 1950), 120–31.

———. "History of State Historical Society of Colorado, The First Twenty-Five Years." *Colorado Magazine* (July, 1953), 161–85.

Hafen, LeRoy R. (ed.). *The Diaries of William Henry Jackson*. Glendale, Calif.: Arthur H. Clark, 1959.

Hafen, LeRoy R., and Hafen, Ann W. *Old Spanish Trail*. Glendale, Calif.: Arthur H. Clark, 1954.

Hall, Ansel. *Guide to Mesa Verde*. San Francisco: Mesa Verde Co., n.d.

———. *Mesa Verde: A Brief Guide*. N.p., 1938.

Hall, Frank. *History of the State of Colorado*. Chicago: Blakely, 1895.

Hammond, John Hays. *The Autobiography of John Hays Hammond*. New York: Arno Press, 1974 ed.

Hardacre, Emma C. "The Cliff-Dwellers." *Scribner's Monthly* (Dec., 1878), 266–76.

Harrell, David. " 'We Contacted Smithsonian': The Wetherills at Mesa Verde." *New Mexico Historical Review* (July, 1987), 229–48.

Hartzog, George, Jr. "Management Considerations." *Second World Conference on National Parks*. Morges, Switzerland: International Union for Conservation of Nature, 1974.

Hayden, Frederick V. *Tenth Annual Report of the United States Geological and Geographical Survey*. Washington, D.C.: Government Printing Office, 1878.

Hayes, Alden C. *The Archeological Survey of Wetherill Mesa*. Washington, D.C.: National Park Service, 1964.

———. "The Wetherill Mesa Project." *Naturalist* (vol. 20, no. 2, 1969), 18–25.

Henderson, Palmer. "The Cliff Dwellers." *The Literary Northwest* (May, 1893), 79–86.

Holmes, William. "Pottery of the Ancient Pueblos." *Fourth Annual Report of the Bureau of Ethnology*. Washington, D.C.: Government Printing Office, 1886.

Ingersoll, Ernest. *The Crest of the Continent*. Chicago: R. R. Donnelley, 1887.

Ise, John. *Our National Park Policy: A Critical History*. Baltimore: Johns Hopkins Press, 1961.

Jackson, Clarence. *Picture Maker of the Old West: William H. Jackson*. New York: Charles Scribner's, 1947.

Jackson, William H. "Ancient Ruins in Southwestern Colorado." *The American Naturalist* (1876), 31–37.

———. "First Official Visit to the Cliff Dwellings." *Colorado Magazine* (May, 1924), 151–59.

———. "Report." *Annual Report of the United States Geological and Geographical Survey.* Washington, D.C.: Government Printing Office, 1876.

———. *Time Exposure.* New York: G. P. Putnam's, 1940.

Johnston, Patricia Condon. "Gustaf Nordenskiold and the Treasure of Mesa Verde." *American West* (July/Aug., 1979), 34–43.

Keating, Margaret. "Knowledge of Ages Is Buried in Mesa Verde." *The Modern World* (Oct., 1907), 149–55.

Kessell, John. "Sources for the History of a New Mexico Community: Abiquiu." *New Mexico Historical Review* (Oct., 1979), 249–85.

Kidder, A. V. "Reminiscences in Southwest Archaeology: 1." *The Kiva* (April, 1960), 1–32.

King, Thomas Gordon. "An Exploration of the Region Occupied by the Cliff Dwellers." *The Archaeologist* (June, 1893), 101–05.

Lavender, David. *David Lavender's Colorado.* New York: Doubleday & Co., 1976.

Laws and Regulations Relating to the Mesa Verde National Park, Colorado.

Washington, D.C.: Government Printing Office, 1908.

Leavitt, Ernest P. *Annual Report Mesa Verde National Park.* Mesa Verde National Park: Mesa Verde National Park, 1933.

"Letter." *El Palacio* (Oct., 1946), 268.

Lewis, Edith. *Willa Cather Living.* New York: Knopf, 1951.

Lister, Florence C., and Lister, Robert H. *Earl Morris and Southwestern Archaeology.* Albuquerque: University of New Mexico, 1968.

Lister, Robert H. "Archeology for Layman and Scientist at Mesa Verde." *Science* (May 3, 1968), 489–96.

———. *Emergency Archaeology in Mesa Verde National Park, Colorado, 1948–1966.* Boulder: University of Colorado Press, 1968.

Lister, Robert H., and Lister, Florence C. *Those Who Came Before.* Tucson: University of Arizona, 1983.

McCloud, Richard. *Durango as It Is.* Durango, Colo.: Durango Board of Trade, 1892.

McClurg, Gilbert, and McClurg, Virginia. "The Development of the Mesa Verde National Park." *Travel* (July, 1916),

34–37, 54.

McClurg, Virginia. "The Making of Mesa Verde into a National Park." *Colorado Magazine* (Nov., 1930), 216–19.

McNitt, Frank. *Richard Wetherill Anasazi.* Albuquerque: University of New Mexico, 1966.

Macomb, J. N. *Report of the Exploring Expedition . . . in 1859.* Washington, D.C.: Government Printing Office, 1876.

Mesa Verde. Washington, D.C.: National Park Service, 1984.

Mesa Verde: General Management Plan May, 1979. N.p.: U.S. Department of the Interior, 1979.

Mesa Verde Historical Administrative District: An Architectural and Historical Study. Denver: U.S. Department of the Interior, 1974.

Mesa Verde National Park. Washington, D.C.: Government Printing Office, various dates, 1915–86.

"Mesa Verde National Park." *Report No. 4944 House of Representatives,* 59th Congress, 1st session, 1905–06. Washington, D.C.: Government Printing Office, 1906.

"Mesa Verde National Park." *Senate Report No. 1428,* 59th Congress, 1st session, 1905–06.

Mesa Verde National Park, Colorado. Washington, D.C.: Government Printing Office, 1976.

Mesa Verde National Park Master Plan September, 1975, Draft. Washington, D.C.: U.S. Department of the Interior, 1975.

Mesa Verde National Park Resources Management Plan, Cultural Resources Descriptive Component. Mesa Verde National Park: U.S. Department of the Interior, 1984.

Mindeleff, Cosmos. "A Cliff-Dwelling Park in Colorado." *Scientific American* (May 11, 1901), 297–98.

Morgan, Alfred. "On the Cliff-Houses and Antiquities of South-Western Colorado and New Mexico." *The Literary and Philosophical Society of Liverpool Proceedings* (66th Session 1876–77), 342–56.

Morgan, Wm. Fellowes. "Description of a Cliff-House on the Mancos River of Colorado, with a Ground Plan." *American Association for the Advancement of Science Proceedings* (1879, vol. 27), 300–06.

National Park Service. *Annual Report of the National Park Service* (1916–33). Washington, D.C.: Government Printing Office, 1916–33.

———. *Report of the Director of the National Park Service* (various dates, 1918–58). Washington, D.C.: Government Printing Office, 1918–58.

Newell, F. H. "Mesa Verde." *National Geographic* (Oct., 1898), 431–34.

Nordenskiold, Gustaf. *The Cliff Dwellers of the Mesa Verde.* Stockholm: P. A. Norstedt, 1893.

———. *The Cliff Dwellers of the Mesa Verde.* Glorieta, N.M.: Rio Grande Press, 1979 reprint.

Nusbaum, Deric. *Deric in Mesa Verde.* New York: G. P. Putnam's Sons, 1926.

Nusbaum, Jesse L. *The 1926 Re-Excavation of Step House Cave.* Mesa Verde National Park: Mesa Verde Museum Association, 1981.

———. "Report of the Superintendent." *Report of the Director of the National Park Service,* 1921, 1922, 1927, 1929. Washington, D.C.: Government Printing Office, 1921, 1922, 1927, 1929.

Nusbaum, Rosemary. *Tierra Dulce:*

Reminiscences from the Jesse Nusbaum Papers. Santa Fe, N.M.: Sun Stone Press, 1980.

Osborne, Douglas. "Solving the Riddles of Wetherill Mesa." *National Geographic Magazine* (Feb., 1964), 155–95.

"Packing into Mesa Verde—1903 Style." *Four Corners Magazine* (Summer, 1972), 56–62, 80.

Parsons, Eugene. "Jesse Nusbaum and His Work." *The Trail* (Feb., 1924), 12–18.

———. "The Mesa Verde National Park." *The American Antiquarian* (1906), 265–66.

Peabody, Mrs. W. S. "The Mesa Verde National Park." *The Modern World Magazine* (Oct., 1907), 159–62.

Peet, Stephen D. "The Cliff-Dwellers and Their Works." *American Antiquarian* (1890), 85–104.

Pomeroy, Earl. *In Search of the Golden West: The Tourist in Western America.* New York: Knopf, 1957.

Proceedings of the National Park Conference . . . September 11 and 12, 1911. Washington, D.C.: Government Printing Office, 1912.

Prudden, T. Mitchell. "A Summer among

Cliff Dwellings." *Harper's New Monthly Magazine* (Sept., 1896), 545–61.

Randolph, Hans. *Report of the Superintendent of the Mesa Verde National Park, 1908–10.* Washington, D.C.: Government Printing Office, 1908–10.

Rickner, Thomas. "Report of the Superintendent of the Mesa Verde National Park." *Reports of the Department of the Interior . . . 1914–20.* Washington, D.C.: Government Printing Office, 1915–21.

Rogers, Edmund. "Notes on the Establishment of Mesa Verde National Park." *Colorado Magazine* (Jan., 1952), 10–17.

Rose, Robert H. *Water Supply History of Mesa Verde National Park.* Mesa Verde National Park: Mesa Verde National Park, 1952.

Routt, John. *Message of Gov. Routt to the Second General Assembly of the State of Colorado.* Denver: Daily Times, 1879.

Rules and Regulations, Mesa Verde National Park. Washington, D.C.: Government Printing Office, 1927.

Runte, Alfred. *National Parks: The American Experience.* Lincoln: University of Nebraska, 1979.

Salmond, John A. *The Civilian Conservation Corps, 1933–42.* Durham, N.C.: Duke University, 1967.

Secretary of the Interior. *Annual Report of the Secretary of the Interior* (1928–46). Washington, D.C.: Government Printing Office, 1928–46.

Shankland, Robert. *Steve Mather of the National Parks.* New York: Knopf, 1951.

Shoemaker, Samuel E. "Report of the Superintendent of the Mesa Verde National Park." *Reports of the Department of the Interior . . . 1912–1913.* Washington, D.C.: Government Printing Office, 1913, 1914.

Smith, Jack E. *Mesas, Cliffs, and Canyons: The University of Colorado Survey of Mesa Verde National Park, 1971–77.* Mesa Verde National Park: Mesa Verde Museum Association, 1987.

———. "The Nusbaum Years." *Mesa Verde Occasional Papers* (vol. 1, no. 1, Oct., 1981), 9–23.

Smithsonian Institution. *Annual Report of the Board of Regents of the Smithsonian Institution* (various years 1877–1926).

Washington, D.C.: Government Printing Office, 1877–1927.

Southwest Colorado Vacation Guide. Cortez, Colo.: Montezuma Valley Journal, 1986.

State of the Parks—1980, A Report to the Congress. Washington, D.C.: National Park Service, 1980.

Taylor, Edward T. "Speech." *Congressional Journal* (1924).

Thompson, Raymond H. *Cliff Dwellings and Park Service: Archeological Tourism in the Southwest.* Mesa Verde National Park: n.p., n.d.

Torres-Reyes, Ricardo. *Mesa Verde National Park: An Administrative History, 1906–70.* Washington, D.C.: Department of the Interior, 1970.

Warner, Ted J. (ed.). *The Dominguez-Escalante Journal.* Provo, Utah: Brigham Young University, 1976.

Watson, Don. *Cliff Dwellings of the Mesa Verde.* Mesa Verde National Park: Mesa Verde Museum Association, 1954.

———. *Indians of the Mesa Verde.* Mesa Verde National Park: Mesa Verde Museum Association, 1955.

Weber, David J. *The Taos Trappers.*

Norman: University of Oklahoma Press, 1971.

Wenger, Gilbert R. *The Story of Mesa Verde National Park*. Denver: Mesa Verde Museum Association, 1980.

West, George. "A Visit to Mesa Verde." *Year Book of the Public Museum of the City of Milwaukee, 1930*. Milwaukee: Cannon Printing, 1932.

Wetherill, Al. "As I Remember." *The Desert Magazine* (May, 1945), 4–6.

Wiley, Marion C. *The High Road*. Denver: State Department of Highways, 1976.

Wirth, Conrad L. *Parks, Politics and the People*. Norman: University of Oklahoma, 1980.

Woloch, Nancy. *Women and the American Experience*. New York: Knopf, 1984.

Wright, Richard. *Report of the Acting Superintendent of the Mesa Verde National Park*. Washington, D.C.: Government Printing Office, 1911.

Year Book of the State of Colorado 1918–64. Denver: various publishers, 1918–64.

"Your Society's Expedition to Mesa Verde." *National Geographic Magazine* (Jan., 1959), 154–56.

ARCHIE
1941

STORY BY
**BRIAN AUGUSTYN &
MARK WAID**

LINE ART BY
PETER KRAUSE

COLORING BY
KELLY FITZPATRICK

LETTERING BY
JACK MORELLI

EDITORS
**MIKE PELLERITO &
VICTOR GORELICK**

WITH
**STEPHEN OSWALD
JAMIE LEE ROTANTE
VINCENT LOVALLO**

EDITOR-IN-CHIEF
VICTOR GORELICK

PUBLISHER
JON GOLDWATER

INTRODUCTION

Archie, Jughead, Betty, and Veronica are some of the strongest, most dynamic characters in comics. No matter what challenges these characters encounter, no matter the style of storytelling, the core of these characters is solid and, as we continue to discover, remarkably able to handle everything we throw at them. For most of Archie's career (since 1941, actually) he and his pals 'n' gals have been the center of entertaining stories of high school hijinks. However, in the past few years, we've been testing just how much Archie can handle (you may have noticed the headlines). There's been Archie marrying Veronica and Archie marrying Betty in *Life with Archie*, Archie's died (also in *Life with Archie*), he fought the zombie apocalypse in *Afterlife with Archie*, been a superhero, a super spy, a time traveler, leader of a rock band, fought werewolves, teamed up with many celebrities, got a fresh new reboot with modern stories and, of course, stars in the major hit TV series *Riverdale*.

So what's next? What hasn't been done? We needed to do something new, something different. In all the years of Archie, we always had him reflect the times, usually the best of times. But let's face it—we created Archie in 1941, the world was at war, America was about to be attacked at Pearl Harbor and enter World War II. The kids who were reading those funny books back then needed an escape, because they or their loved ones were about to enter the toughest situation the world had ever seen. If Archie was actually a real teenager in 1941, what would happen? What would be next? What would he do?

That's exactly what this series tackled. Instead of Archie reflecting the escape, this time he's put smack dab in the middle of the real world in 1941. And we plan on doing even more of these "New Beginning" stories that play with historical fiction. Next, we'll see Archie set against the birth of Rock 'n' Roll in the '50s, the cultural upheaval of the '60s, and beyond.

However, let's start at the beginning... 1941.

··· CHAPTER ONE ···

CHAPTER ONE: The LAST SUMMER

CHAPTER THREE

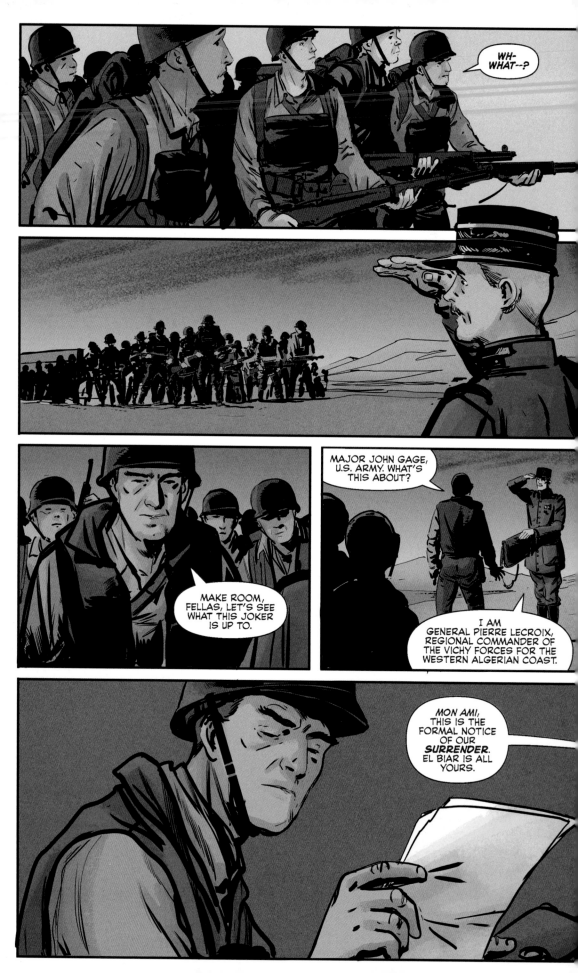

CHAPTER FIVE

RIVERDALE.

"I'M LEAVING."

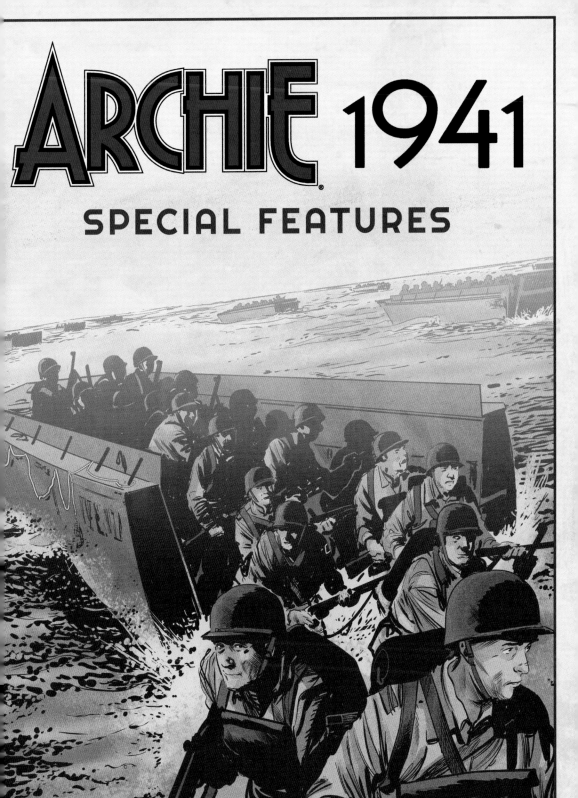

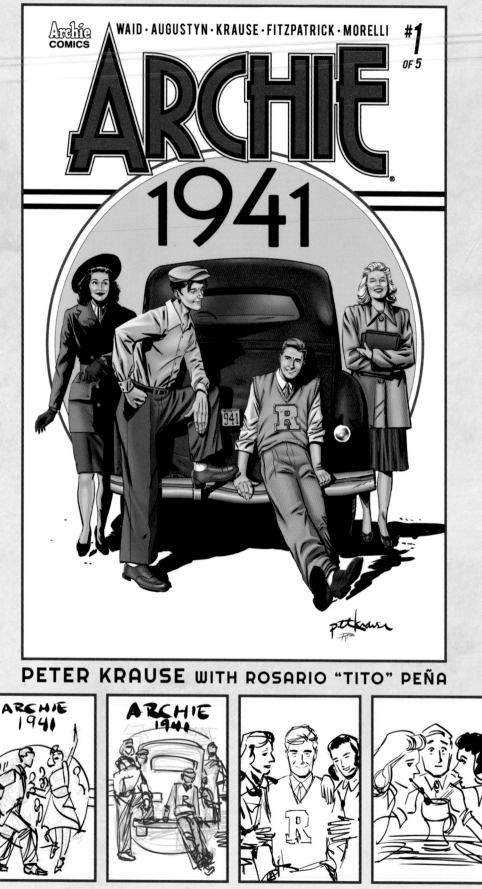

PETER KRAUSE WITH ROSARIO "TITO" PEÑA

CONCEPT SKETCHES BY PETER KRAUSE

PETER KRAUSE

CONCEPT SKETCHES BY PETER KRAUSE

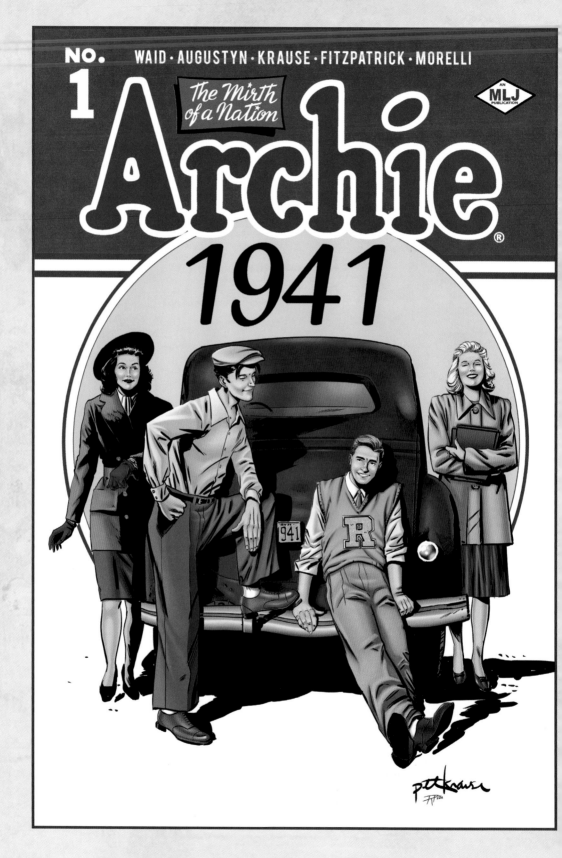

PETER KRAUSE WITH ROSARIO "TITO" PEÑA

SANYA ANWAR

FRANCESCO FRANCAVILLA

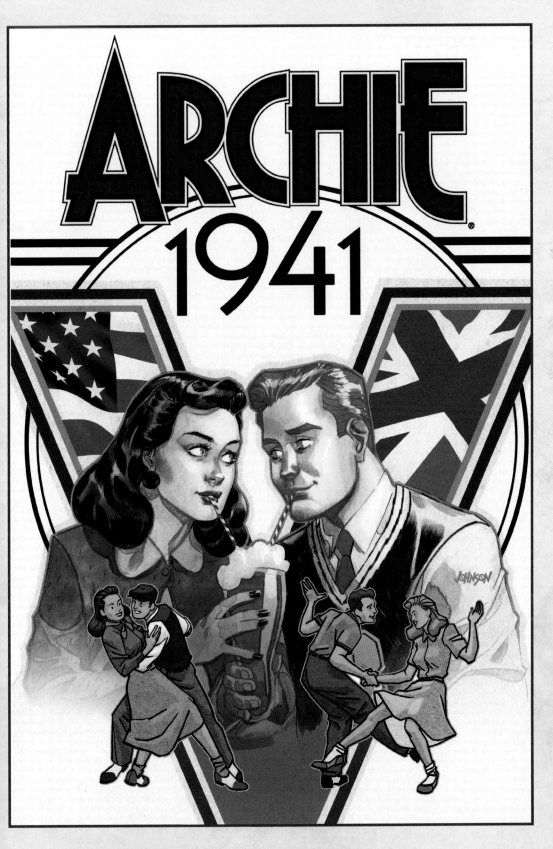

DAVE JOHNSON

AARON LOPRESTI

DAN PARENT

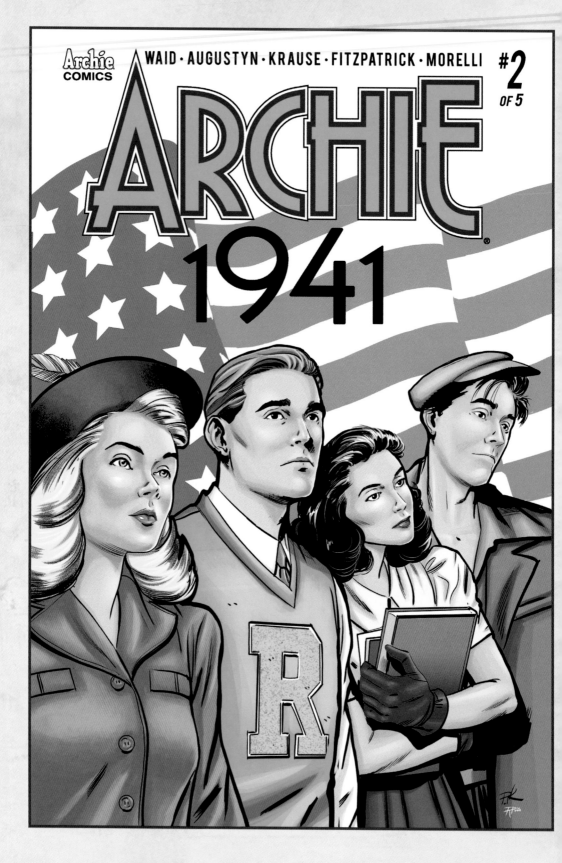

PETER KRAUSE WITH ROSARIO "TITO" PEÑA

PETER KRAUSE

AUDREY MOK

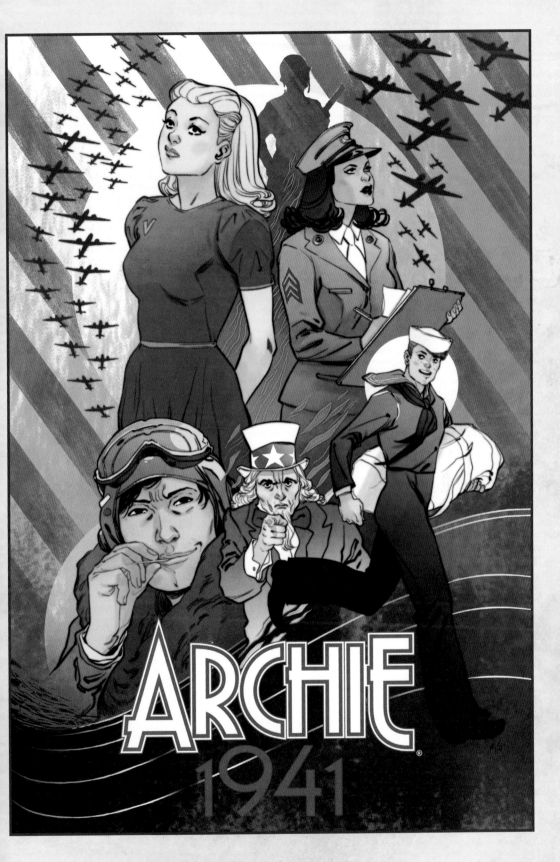

MARGUERITE SAUVAGE

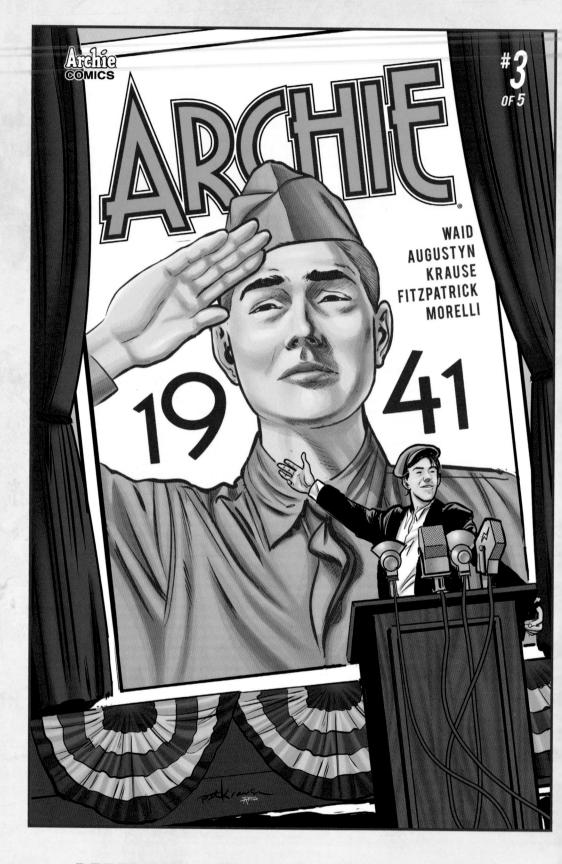

PETER KRAUSE WITH ROSARIO "TITO" PEÑA

PETER KRAUSE

DEREK CHARM

RAY ANTHONY HEIGHT WITH ROSARIO "TITO" PEÑA

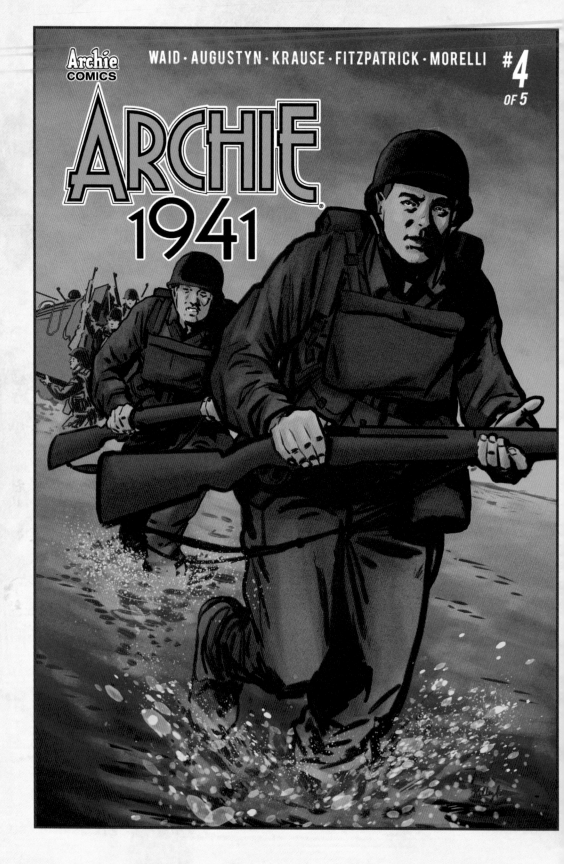

PETER KRAUSE WITH **KELLY FITZPATRICK**

PETER KRAUSE

JON LAM

CORY SMITH WITH ROSARIO "TITO" PEÑA

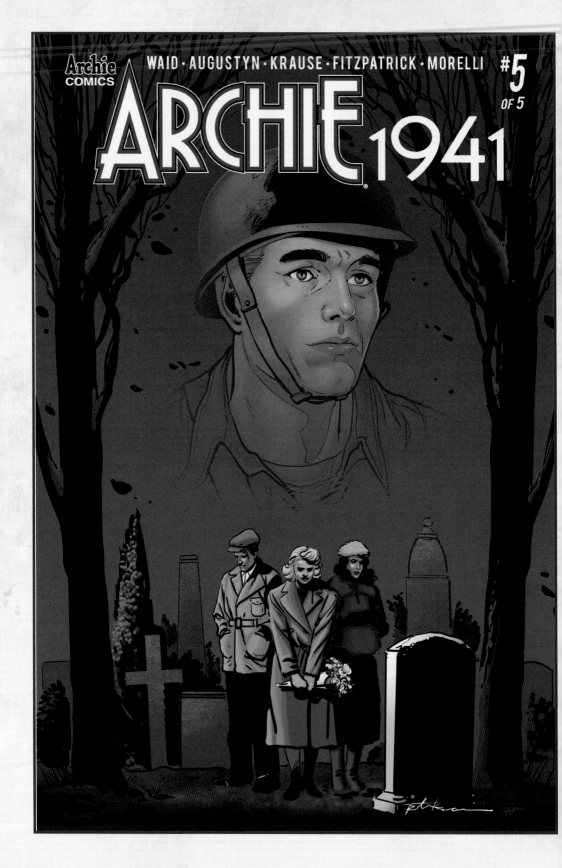

PETER KRAUSE WITH ROSARIO "TITO" PEÑA

PETER KRAUSE

TULA LOTAY

JERRY ORDWAY WITH GLENN WHITMORE

PETER KRAUSE

Betty

Ronnie

Kumi

Hermione Lodge

Alice Cooper

PETER KRAUSE

Fred Andrews

Hiram Lodge

Pop Tate

Geraldine Grundy

3·7·18

PETER KRAUSE

TITLE: **Archie 1941**   ISSUE/MONTH: **#1**   **cover**

LAYOUT ARTIST: **Krause**

JACK MORELLI

ARCHIE: 1941 CREATIVE TEAM INTERVIEW

Archie Comics have always been a fun, timeless reflection of teenage years. Since their first appearance in *Pep Comics*, back in 1941, the characters have showcased the joys of being a teen. With each following new decade the comics were consistently working to stay up-to-date with modern trends, fashions and fads in an entertaining way. But when you think about it, most people's teenage years are usually some of the most dramatic and chaotic times of their lives. And when looked at against the backdrop of an ever-changing world, it's made for some of the best stories in fiction. Thus the idea came about: what would these fun-loving kids from Riverdale, who came to be in 1941, be like in real life?

That's where *Archie: 1941* started.

Series editor Mike Pellerito sat down for a Q&A with the team:
MIKE: This is really an all-star creative team. What about this project and taking Archie and the gang back 1941 and that specific time period appealed to you?

MARK: First off, as a comics historian, the gimmick was intriguing to me—to revisit the year that Archie was "born." But you can't write a series around a cute gimmick; it's not nearly a big enough motor to drive the thing. I liked how it forced me to dig deeper, to take an objective look at what the world of 1941 really was as America's involvement in the Second World War was imminent.

BRIAN: The option of finding the drama in the foaming nod war and life-changing choices appealed tremendously. Using America's best known teens to tell the dramatic story through them made it personal and upped the stakes. Plus any chance to work with my friend Mark Waid is always a great treat.

PETE: It was a bucket list checkoff getting to draw Archie and the Riverdale crew. Drawing them in my own style and set in 1941 just seemed so natural once we all settled in—like, why hadn't this been done before?

KELLY: I've always been really interested in different takes on different characters in the Archie universe. I'm also a bit obsessed with history and historical fiction. This gave me an opportunity to flex my gritty war-time coloring muscles too.

MIKE: Mark, you just finished a landmark reimagining of *Archie*, which focused on a more realistic, modern take on the character. In this project you took Archie and put him in a more realistic 1941, the year Archie first came to be. Archie is always Archie, but 1941 and the reboot are very unique. How did your approach differ between the two books?

MARK: The difference was strictly in the way we approached the humor. In the modern-day books, to my mind, I was always writing a comedy with heart rather than a drama. I always said that, to me, it doesn't feel like an *Archie* story unless he gets his head stuck in a bucket of paint (figuratively speaking) at some point. But with *Archie: 1941*, given the gravity of the era and of the war, I shifted the balance towards drama with a bit of comedy—and yet, still, heart.

MIKE: Projects like this require a lot of knowledge. How much knowledge did you already have about this time period?

MARK: For all my other failings, I'm a pretty smart guy, but when it comes to matters of history and geography, I'm crashingly stupid. All those teachers you hear about who get their students interested in history by making it "come alive" for them? I never had one of those teachers, and thus most of the actual history I know revolves around Superman and Elvis. That's why I knew I needed to ally with my old friend Brian Augustyn. Not only do we make a good writing team, but Brian's much more learned about that era than I'll ever be, thank God.

BRIAN: I've always been a history buff—especially because my parents grew up in this era, and my grandparents lived through it. My parents were pre-teens and my grandparents a bit too old; they both worked in war-factories, making weapons and munitions. The stories I've absorbed over the years helped immensely.

PETE: My parents were both alive during the 1940s, although younger than high school in 1941. I was steeped in big bands growing up, and my dad had a natural fascination with WW2. It didn't seem to be too far in the past to me when I was a child.

KELLY: Quite a bit of knowledge! I had a holocaust course in college and have always been interested in the human id. It's the same reason I find *Lord of the Flies* and the TV show *Survivor* fascinating. I've always read a lot of books on the subject and would recommend books by Edwin Black to read up on more.

MIKE: *Archie: 1941* had a massive amount of research to it; which even meant a major change was made to the story. Can you tell us about what happened there? Did anything else change about the story as you learned more about the time period?

MARK: The biggest thing that changed was this: in the original outline, a great deal of the early drama was built on the dread of the townspeople, once America entered the war, as to whether or not the draft would take all their beloved young men away. Entire subplots were built around when and how Archie and Jughead and Moose and the rest would be drafted, because, hey, after all, what was the draft age in 1941, anyway? Eighteen, right? BZZZZT. It was 21, come to find out—and that meant re-thinking just exactly how each of our boys would get involved with the military.

BRIAN: Frankly, a good number of the war-time story was changed by research. Common misconceptions had us looking in the wrong directions at first. Fortunately, research saved us from the wrong plot points, but showed us even better ways to go. For instance, while researching, I found the true story of the small North African city that surrendered at the beach on the first allies' invasion. It gives us a lighter take on Archie entering the war and gives contrast to Kassarine Pass battle at the end of that same issue (#4).

More of those discoveries kept us true to history.

MIKE: A lot of time characters can "lead the way" for a storyteller. Did the development of any of the characters surprise you?

MARK: Brian did some great stuff with Veronica by basing her on Gloria Grahame as Violet in *It's a Wonderful Life*—the "party girl" whose flightiness is gradually tempered with age but who remains largely innocent nonetheless. There are about a million ways you can recast the Betty/Veronica relationship in any given context, and Brian found the perfect one here.

BRIAN: Well, Mark is the master, so his comments mean a whole lot. We found, as we always do, that we work well together and it's a blast to do so. We keep each other honest. I discovered a few surprising facts about some of the characters; Veronica, ever the perennial party-girl, discovers and confesses her loneliness, and tells Betty, bonding the two. Reggie, always played as a bully and a thoughtless jerk becomes a better friend to Archie than ever, and ultimately a hero. Two of the more petty characters grow up in the course of this story. Also, as it should ever be, Betty and Archie are a couple forever, which to my mind is perfect.

PETE: Writers talk of characters seemingly writing themselves or dictating the story. As I got more into the drawing, I had something similar happen as each of the Riverdale characters seemed to dictate their body language and their interaction to others. I attribute that to a great story by Mark and Brian.

KELLY: Reggie surprised me.

MIKE: There's a lot of heavy emotion in this story. How did you decide how each character would handle these situations? Jughead and Betty in particular had the most intense reactions. How did that come about?

MARK: In my original outline, it was Pop Tate whose rage permeated most of the series. We stayed with his motivation—that Pop lost his son in a previous military conflict—but Brian wisely did something I'd have never thought to do: make Jughead the angry one, livid at the loss of the people around him and a perceived betrayal at Archie's hands. "My" modern-day Jughead tends to be a lot more of an aloof, roll-with-any-punch guy, but Brian's instincts were right for the story and, in reflection, right for the character.

As I recall, it wasn't until we got to writing the last issue that we'd decided Betty would leave Riverdale, and her beats in chapter five were some of my favorite parts of the entire series. They're a testament to the storytelling ability of Pete Krause; in the script, I'd written a long, involved monologue from Betty as a "voice-over" covering her journey to the train station, but when Pete turned in his pages, all the emotion was right there in the silence.

BRIAN: At the heart of any character-centered story is the differing emotions of different characters facing the same actions. It shows how some are surprisingly allied, or at odds with each other. That drives the story as it plays out. Also, the war was too big a thing to take lightly. Some of the emotion we discover is the humor our characters find in life. In wartime, the reactions flip the expected; i.e. Jughead finds it nearly impossible to joke at first. And the emotions give the cast more a real—or realistic—humanity.

MIKE: Pete is one of the best artists around and it's impossible to imagine this book in another artist's hands. What was amazing was how your illustrations made Riverdale look like it was based on an actual town; it was so realistic from the very first panel of Riverdale High School all the way to the scenes on the battlefield. Every location from Pop's to the battlefield was a completely realized environment. How did you approach the art to get this real world feel?

ETE: A bit of research, of course. Catalog reprints of the time were a big help, and I leaned eavily on the book *Long Time Coming: A Photographic Portrait of America, 1935-1943* by lichael Lesy. I used my high school building which was built in the 1920s—Minneapolis oosevelt—as a model for Riverdale's high school. And the internet was a help—a nod to the es Moines, IA public library system for having high school yearbooks of the time available nline. Those yearbooks were invaluable for getting hairstyles correct.

MIKE: Pete, you've got such an amazing style, the way you handled characters' "acting" was erfect. Do you try to base the characters' physical reactions on their personality types or is it ust something of the moment?

ETE: Again, each of the Archie crew seemed to let me know what was "right" for hem—hard to describe it differently. Betty and Jughead, especially. And I have a soft spot or Pop—Mark and Brian did a wonderful job with his story.

MIKE: So much of *1941*'s look was influenced by the gorgeous color work of Kelly, one of the est in the business. Were you able to find much color reference of the time?

ELLY: I must be on a government watch list by how much weird war time stuff I'm googling. m lucky I'm internet savvy and have worked on several war books. It's also nice when ollaborators send me reference too.

MIKE: Kelly, what I love about your work is that in each project you take on you employ a very nique approach in style and palette. How did you formulate your plan on colors for *1941* as pposed to the *Archie* reboot?

ELLY: I wanted *Archie: 1941* to feel like a period piece. It's why I made it grainy and eferenced clothing and building interior colors and patterns that fit with the time frame. I lways go into each project thinking about how colors will serve the story and the art.

MIKE: Did you have any tricks to get in the mindset and keep the mood of *Archie: 1941*? ld songs or movies for instance?

MARK: My movie touchstone, and one Brian and I talked about often, was the Oscar-winning Villiam Wyler film *The Best Years of Our Lives*, chronicling the lives of ex-soldiers as they eturned to civilian life.

RIAN: I listened to a lot of music from the early 1940s; including love songs, big band hits, nd particularly War-based songs, such as "I'll be Seeing You," and so on.

ETE: For me it was all visual. I did find an old war recruiting film online *Service With The olors* that I watched several times.

ACK: Every time new pages came over the transom to letter, I would have to play Glenn liller's version of "Perfidia." The perfect theme song to this book for me. And when I needed great big smile, I'd switch to the YouTube video of the Andrews Sisters (no relation to our eckle-faced fave) singing "I'm Gettin' Corns For My Country." Patty Andrews is just a monster alent! Last but not least, anything by Bing Crosby. Especially because comic artist Joe Sinnott, e living embodiment of what Tom Brokaw dubbed "the Greatest Generation," and HUGE rosby fan, would hit me with a pizza at the next lunch if I ever left out Der Bingle. And Joe as on that awful meat-grinder called Okinawa, so I'm no match! Thanks for saving the world or punks like us, Joe!

MIKE: Speaking of movies, if you had to dream cast for *Archie: 1941* with actors from that time period, whom would you pick?

MARK: For Betty, maybe Judy Garland if she'd been capable of not stealing the show (doubtful). For Veronica, Gloria Grahame. Jackie Cooper or Robert Blake would have been an interesting Reggie. And by elimination and a careful scour of the IMDB "Child Stars of the 1930s" section, we're kinda stuck with Mickey Rooney as Archie, aren't we?

BRIAN: It's easier to cast the adults, for me. Fred would be Hal Perry, the *Great Gildersleeve*, star who was the world's greatest at spit takes and growl and sputter moments. Claudette Colbert as Mary. Hiram Lodge might be a part for Charles Bickford. I see a young Bill Holden as Archie, giving the story the leading man it deserves—young star, Deanna Durbin. Is it too on the nose to cast Carl "Alfalfa" Switzer as Jughead? Finally, how about Charles Coburn as Pop Tate?

PETE: Doris Day—she was born in 1922 so that puts her right in the sweet spot for Betty. That's a no-brainer.

JACK: Fun! If the movie was being made in 1941/42, the young actors would have to have been born in the early to mid 1920s and working by '41 to count? So with that as our metric, I think teen star Gale Storm would be an excellent Betts, and newbie Ava Gardner a great Ronnie. I like Huntz Hall for Juggie, with fellow Dead End kid Gabe Dell as Reggie. Charlie Ruggles always reminds me of Hiram Lodge, alongside Victor Moore for Pop Tate. See them both in the wonderful *It Happened on Fifth Avenue*. Finally, for me the slam-dunk choice for Archie is the young Donald O'Connor. If you don't know him, check out any clips from *Mr. Big*, or *What's Cookin'* from the early 1940s. During that time he always played a wise-cracking, klutzy but well-meaning and lovable High School Lothario. In *Private Buckaroo* he even lies about his age to join the Army!

MIKE: Do any of you have a favorite scene or moment of the story? What about it hit you?

MARK: My favorite scene is when Archie, overseas, can't figure out how to express to a thousands-of-miles-away-Betty just how he feels about her until he stumbles across a young nurse who could be her twin. That moment still gets to me.

BRIAN: I love the scene where a tipsy Fred Andrews and Betty's dad try to enlist in the Army, only to be turned down gently by the recruiter. As amusing as the situation is, it also has an underlying sweetness; we realize that Fred, through his slightly alcoholic haze, believes that if he were to war, then Archie might be spared. After playing Fred as a hard ass pushing Archie to be more of a man, this was also a tipping point for Fred... and for other story elements as well.

PETE: Pops wishing for no war for the kids. Betty waiting for the train to take her away. And the last hug between Jughead and Archie. All very emotional, very relatable.

JACK: I was moved to see that it was Reggie who gave his life to save Archie. The two rivals had a long, not very amicable shared history. But when it mattered most, with such pettiness so far away, either man would instinctively risk paying the ultimate price for the other. Another great moment was when Moose stepped in to help Chuck fight off the racist thugs who were attacking him. Moose had been desperate to make a stand for the sake of both his country and his world in the battle overseas, and was deeply distraught at his inability to do so. And yet, at home in that dark alley alongside his friend, he was doing exactly that.

MIKE: Last Question is for Victor Gorelick: Victor, you've been at Archie for over 60 years. You've regularly given this book high praise. It was a lot of fun to work with you on it. But what was your favorite moment of the series?

VC: First, I would like to say this series was, in my opinion, the best produced by this company since I've been at Archie. In 1941 an uneasy atmosphere in the country was contagious. The writers' and artists' meticulous attention to detail and most importantly, what it was like for parents, children and especially teenagers during that time in history. The moment of the series that stood out for me was Betty waiting at the train station with her one suitcase and ticket out of Riverdale. This scene reminded me of a train station in New London, Connecticut. In circa 1945 my mother (who was born and raised in New London) and I watched from the window, as my uncle, dressed in his army uniform, waved to us with a big smile on his face. During the four years he spent fighting over in France (invasion of Normandy) and Germany, his parents and sisters thought he would never come home again.

ABOUT THE CREATIVE TEAM:

For over three decades, Mark Waid has written hundreds of comic book characters, but perhaps one of the most relatable and real out of the bunch is Archie! Waid's history with Archie spans across titles such as the fun and frantic superhero series *The Fox*, the dramatic 2015 *Archie* series and of course *Archie: 1941*. Waid's latest Archie project is set to rock the world as Archie's music career takes off in *Archie: 1955*!

Brian Augustyn is a comic book writer and editor from Chicago whose works include *Gotham by Gaslight*, *Flash*, *Out There*, *Crimson* and many more.

Peter Krause has over 25 years of experience as a comic book illustrator. He has drawn for Marvel, DC and many other comic publishers. Krause's past credits include *Star Trek: The Next Generation*, *Power Of Shazam!*, *Metropolis: Special Crimes Unit*, and *Daredevil: Road Warrior* which was nominated for an Eisner Award. His work with writer Mark Waid on BOOM! Studios *Irredeemable* garnered multiple Eisner nominations, and he co-created *Insufferable* with Waid for Thrillbent digital comics.

Kelly Fitzpatrick is a Hugo nominated comic book colorist and illustrator currently living in Portland, OR. Her work has appeared in Archie, Dark Horse, DC, Image, Oni Press, and Young Animal amongst various other publications. She spends all of her free time doting on her dog, Archie, as well as training dogs.

Jack Morelli is a comic book letterer and author who, in addition to Archie, has worked for DC and Marvel. Jack always puts beyond 100% into his work. His love, care and understanding for the process always shines through making him one of the brightest members of the Archie team.

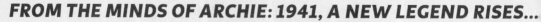

FROM THE MINDS OF ARCHIE: 1941, A NEW LEGEND RISES...

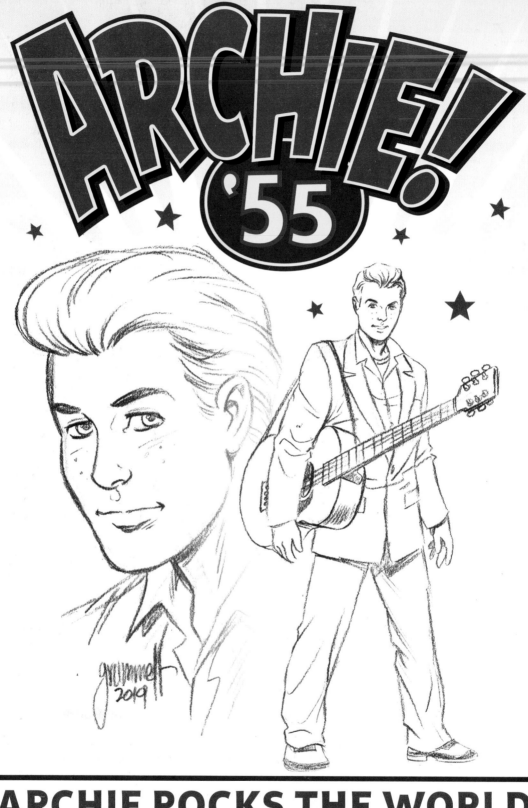

ARCHIE!! '55

ARCHIE ROCKS THE WORLD
WAID • AUGUSTYN • GRUMMETT
SMITH • WHITMORE • MORELLI
DOORS OPEN SEPTEMBER 2019